Geographies (

The John Hope Franklin Series in African American History and Culture

Waldo E. Martin Jr. and Patricia Sullivan, editors

Geographies of Liberation

THE MAKING OF AN
Afro-Arab Political Imaginary

Alex Lubin

The University of North Carolina Press / Chapel Hill

This book was published with the assistance of the
John Hope Franklin Fund of the University of North Carolina Press.

© 2014 The University of North Carolina Press
All rights reserved
Set in Utopia and Aller types by codeMantra
Manufactured in the United States of America

Complete cataloging information for this title is
available from the Library of Congress.
ISBN 978-1-4696-1288-1 (pbk.: alk. paper)
ISBN 978-1-4696-1289-8 (ebook)
18 17 16 15 14   5 4 3 2 1

Dedicated to Barbara Lubin

Contents

Illustrations

Acknowledgments

This project has been profoundly shaped by the multiple geographies in which it has traveled. At the University of New Mexico (UNM) I have been surrounded by colleagues focused on the critical study of the colonial present as well as Albuquerque, a city in which the colonial present is ever visible. The Department of American Studies at UNM has been a productive location for my scholarship, not only because of the terrific intellectual work of the faculty and graduate students there, but also because of the friendships that sustain an academic life. Thanks to Alyosha Goldstein, Rebecca Schreiber, David Correia, and Michael Trujillo for co-teaching, plotting together, and discussing ideas that entered this book. I am also grateful to a long list of graduate assistants who helped with this project over many years. Thanks to Sandy Rodrigue for holding it all together. Colleagues at UNM outside the Department of American Studies were also important friends and interlocutors to this project. I am especially grateful to Les Field, who read a very rough draft of this entire project and gave encouragement as needed.

Major parts of this project were shaped by Beirut, Lebanon, at the American University of Beirut (AUB), and in the Center for American Studies and Research (CASAR). Taking my scholarship to Beirut and placing it in global circulation not only has made this project stronger but also has enabled certain insights about transnational scholarship. I am grateful to colleagues at AUB who have encouraged my work and suffered through its early stages. I am especially thankful to Patrick McGreevy, Nancy Batakji Sanyoura, Waleed Hazbun, Sirene Harb, and Adam Waterman. CASAR is a center that hosts scholars who, like me, are in global circulation. During my years in Beirut I have benefited from late-night conversations over smoky Arak and spicy potatoes with Marwan Kraidy, Jasbir Puar, Elena Glasberg, Robert Reid Pharr, Lisa Hajjar, and Vijay Prashad.

Over the course of working on this project I have benefited tremendously from the feedback that came after I presented parts of the study at the American Studies Association Annual Conference, the University of California at Santa Barbara Center for New Racial Studies, the Geography Department at the University of California at Berkeley, the English Department at the University of Florida, the American Studies Department at the

University of Notre Dame, the Charles Warren Center at Harvard University, the American Studies Center at Hassan II University in Casablanca, and CASAR at the American University of Beirut.

A traveling career brings a scholar into contact with numerous fellow-traveling intellectuals who offer feedback over the course of a project. I have been fortunate to have had impromptu conversations, and sometimes intellectual exchanges, with Vijay Prashad, Alyosha Goldstein, Patrick Wolfe, Cynthia Young, J. Kehaulani Kauanui, Bill Mullen, Malini Schueller, Amy Kaplan, Melani McAlister, Moustafa Bayoumi, Brian Edwards, Mounira Soliman, Jake Dorman, Jake Kosek, Ruth Wilson Gilmore, Marwan Kraidy, David Roediger, Keith Feldman, Jordana Rosenberg, Gaye Johnson, Cedric Robinson, Ilan Pappé, Sami Shalom Chetrit, Tikva Honig Parnass, Ziad Abbas, Sari Hanafi, Hilton Obenziner, Rabab Abelhadi, and Reuven Abergil.

The University of North Carolina Press has been nothing less than superb. Thanks go to Sian Hunter, who saw something in the project and was a supportive acquiring editor. And special appreciation goes to Mark Simpson-Vos, who seamlessly ushered this project to completion. The anonymous readers of this manuscript provided much needed constructive criticism and encouragement.

If scholarship is informed by geographic contexts as it travels to completion, it is also informed by the location of its departure. I am Barbara Lubin's son, as I am often introduced. Like many American Jews, my mother grew up in a Zionist household where support for Israel was unquestioned. But after being taken to Israel/Palestine around 1986 by a group of Palestinian students from San Francisco State University, my mother had a moment of dissonance when she recognized that the trees her family had helped to plant in Israel were now growing atop destroyed Palestinian villages. What makes my mother unique is that she translated her disgust of the colonial project into a political movement by forming the Middle East Children's Alliance (www.mecaforpeace.org), which has become one of the most important consciousness-raising and humanitarian relief organizations supporting Palestinian issues in the United States. She and her partner, Howard Levine, have done this work at great personal cost and despite receiving death threats, government harassment, and social ostracization.

My mother does what she does because, as she always told me, "it's the right thing to do." I was raised in a generation different from that of my mother, when unquestioned support for Israel was not formative. Moreover, I was fortunate to be the child of Barbara Lubin, who in addition to her work on Palestine, fought to mainstream special education in Berke-ley's public schools, helped pass the nation's first commercial rent control laws, served as a delegate for Jesse Jackson during his first run for presi-dent, and founded Jews for Jesse Jackson *after* Jackson's unfortunate racial slur about Jews and New York. I came to political consciousness while lick-ing the sour adhesive strip on the backs of the many envelops my mother used for political campaigns. *Geographies of Liberation* is possible only because my mother has always shown me that another world is possible.

My entire family helped sustain my momentum in this project. My brother Charlie—courtesy clerk, union member, softball catcher, and gentleman—sustains my enduring belief in life beyond the normative. What makes travel and traveling scholarship bearable is the knowledge that home is also a traveling architecture built out of affect and love. Solo-mon Lubin, Eyob Lubin, and Kelly Gallagher—my traveling companions—make it all worthwhile.

Geographies of Liberation

Geographies of Liberation

[Tiberius's] people are best examined at a distance.
They are particularly uncomely Jews, Arabs, and negroes.
—Mark Twain, The Innocents Abroad

I'm a Christian, but my father came from a Kenyan family that includes
generations of Muslims. As a boy, I spent several years in Indonesia and heard
the call of the azaan at the break of dawn and at the fall of dusk. As a young man,
I worked in Chicago communities where many found dignity and peace in
their Muslim faith. —Barack Obama, "Remarks by the President
on a New Beginning," June 4, 2009

In his June 4, 2009, address at Cairo University, President Barack Obama occupied a contradictory space. As the president of the United States he was the leader of one of the last remaining great powers, an empire that was, at the time, providing financial and military support to Hosni Mubarak, the authoritarian leader of Egypt whose rule would come to an end within three years at the hands of Egypt's popular rebellion and the Arab uprisings. Obama's administration, like U.S. administrations prior to it, had given political, financial, and military support to the Mubarak regime believing that the security Arab authoritarian leaders like Mubarak provided to regional U.S. allies like Israel took precedence over meeting the Egyptian people's democratic aspirations.[1] President Obama believed that his address would reset the fraught history of U.S. engagement with the Arab world, an engagement that since 1948 has privileged Israeli security and U.S. economic and military interests. He advocated the creation of a Palestinian state and the full recognition on the part of Palestinians of Israel as a Jewish state; he did not call for a fundamental recalibration of U.S. geopolitical power and policy, instead advocating reforms to Muslim/Arab attitudes and to civil society in the Arab world.[2]

1

In his attempt to repair the history of bad faith between the United States and the Arab world and to chart a "new beginning," Obama hoped that he could represent the United States through the lens of the black freedom movement, a lens that he believed illustrated the promise of liberalism in guaranteeing full national inclusion and the promise of nonviolent social movements. In making this case, Obama presented social change as the providence of nonviolent protest followed by slow transformation in state policies. As an example, he drew on a version of civil rights historiography that highlighted the efficacy of nonviolent protest and ignored the presence within that movement of armed self-defense and survival.[3] "Resistance through violence and killing is wrong and it does not succeed. For centuries, black people in America suffered the lash of the whip as slaves and the humiliation of segregation. But it was not violence that won full and equal rights. It was a peaceful and determined insistence upon the ideals at the center of America's founding. The same story can be told by people from South Africa to South Asia; from Eastern Europe to Indonesia."[4] In this formulation, one that presents the United States as an exceptional state to be emulated globally, racial discrimination and slavery in the United States are understood as moments of divergence from the values of the U.S. liberal state—dilemmas that can be overcome, rather than problems that are foundational to it—and the arc of U.S. history is seen to be constantly moving toward the ideals of a "more perfect union."[5]

It is, perhaps, ironic that in a speech about the exceptional nature of U.S. liberal democracy, Obama invoked the history of groups for whom the full promise of liberal statehood has failed. The speech linked black civil rights, Jewish diasporic politics, and Palestinian statelessness as having analogous histories that united Arabs, African Americans, and Jews in a shared past of racial exclusion and exile. For example, while making an argument for his government's "special relationship" with Israel, Obama referenced Jewish exile in the modern world and the Holocaust: "Around the world, the Jewish people were persecuted for centuries, and anti-Semitism in Europe culminated in an unprecedented Holocaust."[6] Moreover, he offered rhetorical support for and recognition of Palestinians' aspirations for a homeland when he spoke of the Palestinians' displacement in the formation of the Israeli state: "It is also undeniable that the Palestinian people—Muslims and Christians—have suffered in pursuit of a homeland. For more than 60 years they've endured the pain of dislocation. Many wait in refugee camps in the West Bank, Gaza, and neighboring lands for a life of peace and security that they have never been able to lead. They endure the daily humiliations—large and small—that come with occupation."[7]

Hence, in attempting some rhetorical balance between Jewish European and non-Jewish Palestinian exile, Obama identified the overlapping histories of groups who have been involuntarily and violently forced beyond the pale of liberal statehood, and in this way he demonstrated the *limits* of the ideals he was attempting to valorize. The Jew fleeing European modernity in the nineteen and twentieth centuries, the black American fleeing racial violence in the U.S. throughout the long civil rights era, and the Palestinian fleeing Israeli occupation and seeking return to Palestine all exemplify the *limits* of citizenship and the violent belongings and exclusions that constitute the modern nation-state. These groups illustrate how the domains of citizenship and of civil society can be animated by violent exclusions and expulsions that are not merely the consequence of bad faith and national dilemmas but are, rather, constitutive of the state itself.

Obama's address to the Muslim world required amnesia about the violence of nation-states, including the one he leads. He ignored his own state's imperial forays into the Middle East throughout most of the twentieth century and its imbalanced economic and military support to Israel.[8] He overlooked Israel's post-1967 occupation of the West Bank and expanding Israeli settler communities.[9] Moreover, he avoided discussing the ways that his own administration's prosecution of the war on terror within the U.S. has diminished the currency of citizenship for Arab and Muslim Americans, whose civil liberties have been systematically violated during a moment the U.S. state has deemed "exceptional."[10]

Yet Obama wasn't merely an imperial president lecturing to an audience who had suffered decades of U.S. foreign policy, although he was certainly that. He was the first African American president of the United States, and one who had, as a child, lived in an Islamic society, and his address in Cairo unearthed memories of past African American engagement with Cairo, a city that sits at the strategic meeting point between the Arab Middle East and the African continent. In July 1964, Malcolm X delivered his famous address to the meeting of the Organization of African Unity in Cairo on behalf of the Organization of Afro-American Unity in which he signaled his break from the Nation of Islam and his embrace of Afro-Arab politics. Cairo was then a city led by Gamel Abdel Nasser, who more than any other political leader sought to make Cairo the crossroads of Arab and black nationalisms.[11]

Obama's speech was therefore contradictory in the following way: In making the case to the Muslim world for the promise of peaceful liberal inclusion into the nation-state, in making a comparison between the U.S. civil rights movement and the plight of Jewish and Palestinian exiles,

Obama unwittingly invoked a taboo memory of the exile and the exile's political and violent exclusion from modernity's promise.[12] For the exile, liberation has not come from the politics of national inclusion but only from forging cosmopolitan and mobile attachments within and between various geopolitical entities and imaginaries. Exiles dwell beyond national belonging envisioned by Obama, in a sort of modernity that Edward Said—drawing on the insight of the German Jewish refugee Theodor Adorno—famously called "contrapuntal." Contrapuntal identities are produced in the collision of the exile's competing national attachments, between home and homelessness; Said recognized that the contradictions of the exile's belongings produce a different sort of consciousness, a "second sight."[13] Contrapuntalism names the consciousness of being between national inclusion and exile.

Geographies of Liberation is a study of the political imaginaries that reside beyond modernist racial ideologies and modernity's most powerful political imaginary, the nation-state. I am interested in excavating the exiled and often hidden political consciousness that gets forged beyond—but as a result of—the development of modern nation-states, particularly in the modern Middle East. In this project I uncover the making of a political imaginary across and beyond the nation-state that has united questions of Jewish diasporic politics, black internationalism, and Palestinian exile. I am interested in uncovering an Afro-Arab political imaginary—produced by exiles—that has been articulated under changing geopolitical contexts leading from the polycultural imperial world of the Ottomans to the rapid ascendency of the modern nation-state.[14] This project is about uncovering a political imaginary that has been forged by black and Arab intellectuals, of which many were also Jewish, throughout the post–U.S. Civil War/post-Ottoman era. I will show how transformations in governance initiated by expanding colonial and imperial rule in the United States and in the Middle East, as well as nationalist awakenings on the part of minorities, inspired corresponding transformations in Afro-Arab political imaginaries. In this way, drawing on the work of Walter Mignolo and Anibal Quijano, I will map the dialectic between formations of modern nationalism as a process of coloniality and the political imaginaries, or decolonial imaginaries, created by Afro-Arab intellectuals.

Although the Obama campaign and presidency provides a rich introductory setting for this project, the idea for this book actually began outside the United States in a very different political context and from another epistemology. In the summer of 2004 I delivered a lecture at Birzeit University outside Ramallah, Palestine, on the history of antimiscegenation laws in the United States. Israel had recently passed a new citizenship law that precluded Palestinians from obtaining Israeli citizenship through marriage to Palestinian citizens of Israel, and in my talk I sought to draw some cursory comparisons between the United States in 1848 and modern Israel.[15] Following my lecture linking U.S. antimiscegenation laws in the mid-nineteenth century to Israel's twenty-first-century citizenship act, the Palestinian students in the audience asked me why, given my comparison, were African Americans largely supportive of Israeli policies, especially since they felt these policies so often replicated the history of U.S. settler colonialism and white supremacy. Why did most U.S. civil rights leaders view Israel with sympathy and identification while ignoring, or even participating in, racial stereotyping of Palestinians? The students' questions triggered a memory that many of the most radical and internationalist African American intellectual leaders had indeed been supporters of the creation of the State of Israel, and even strong supporters of Israeli expansion during the 1967 war. My quick but insufficient answer to the students' questions was that in 1948 most of the U.S. political left supported Israel's creation and that African American support for Israel endured through the 1967 Six-Day War because of the strong bond within the U.S. civil rights movement uniting African Americans and Jews. My response bracketed the history of African American/Jewish relations to a domestic saga of interethnic solidarity and rivalry, completely ignoring the diasporic and internationalist dimensions of the topic. Yet even as I offered this response, I knew that a more complex story was required. Why, during the twentieth century when black internationalists embraced the global politics of anti-imperialism, did not the African American left identify with peoples' struggles in the Arab world?

As I will demonstrate in the following chapters, African American luminaries like Ralph Bunche, Paul Robeson, and W. E. B. Du Bois and civil rights leaders like Martin Luther King Jr., Bayard Rustin, and John L. Lewis all expressed, at times, unwavering support for Israeli policies in the years between 1948 and 1967, and even beyond that time. The black internationalist W. E. B. Du Bois frequently supported Israel's creation and often reproduced the Zionist mythology of Palestine as an uninhabited desert made to bloom under European Zionist tutelage.[16] Paul Robeson famously said that he would fight alongside Zionists just as he had fought alongside the Spanish loyalists during the Spanish civil war.[17] During a political moment when black power organizations began to criticize Israeli policies, especially in the post-1967 era, the civil rights leaders A. Philip Randolph and Bayard Rustin formed a political organization called the Black Americans in Support of Israel Committee (BASIC).[18] Dr. Martin Luther King Jr. publicly defended Israel and warned black power supporters not to equate Zionism with racism.[19] In the contemporary moment, it is often the Congressional Black Caucus (CBC) that constitutes the most vociferous support for Israeli policies, despite a more complicated CBC history of challenging Israeli policies in the West Bank and Gaza.[20] Yet black American identification with Israel cannot be explained only by appeals to leftist Jewish support for the U.S. civil rights movement; indeed, in this book I argue that the internationalist ideals of Zionism as well as the seeming restorative justice of the modern nation-state also explain this complex bond.

Of course, there are well-known African American critics of Israeli policies as they pertain to Palestinians, and they should be read without assuming criticism of Israel is anti-Semitic. Malcolm X was critical of Israeli colonialism, as have been many black nationalists and anticolonialists ranging from members of the Nation of Islam to the Black Panther Party to Shirley Graham Du Bois and her son David Graham Du Bois.[21] This dissent has often been interpreted through the prism of black/Jewish relations in the United States. Seen through this lens, black American support for or dissent against Israel is used to measure black anti-Semitism or the relative strength of the U.S. Jewish/African American left coalition. Cornel West and Michael Lerner, as well as Richard Kazarian and Robert Weisbord, have understood black criticism of Israel in terms of tensions between black and Jewish communities in the United States.[22] In this book, criticism of Israel on the part of black Americans is not read merely as an example of U.S. black/Jewish relations, but as an example of black internationalism that requires historical explanation.

What began in the occupied West Bank as a talk about antimiscegenation laws in the United States and citizenship laws in Israel opened up more fundamental questions about comparative diasporic politics, homelands, and the politics of nationalism. Understanding U.S. black attitudes about Israel requires a scholarly approach that moves beyond domestic histories of black/Jewish relations in the United States and that looks to ways that both groups have engaged liberation politics globally and in relation to the organizing logic of the nation-state. Through researching early pan-Africanist attempts to imagine futures outside Western nation-states, I have encountered the ways that some black radicals drew material and imaginative connections to Palestine and the question of the Jewish diasporic politics. By tracing the migration of former Ottoman subjects to the new imperial metropole of London in the wake of World War I, I discovered that pan-African politics intersected with pan-Arab politics. Reading through Ralph Bunche's biography as he worked on the United Nations Special Committee on Palestine (UNSCOP) revealed a submerged history of the binational movement in Palestine that, for Bunche, resonated with the 1930s Popular Front politics shaping urban black politics in the United States. Examining the Black Panther Party's newspaper uncovered early Palestinian writing on the June 1967 war and the internationalist politics of both groups. Listening to contemporary hip hop has revealed Afro-Arab soundscapes that develop a political imaginary within the context of neoliberal transformations and related securitization within Israel, Palestine, and the United States.

Jewish diasporic thinkers, black Americans, and Palestinians have, throughout history and especially in the twentieth century, had special insight into the violent exclusions that seem inherent to the project of modernity. For these groups, the Enlightenment projects of colonialism and nation-state formation have often meant being cast beyond the pale of the national community and being relegated to "the other." Each of these groups has carried the scar of racial violence, exclusion, and expulsion that seem to animate the practices of modern nation-states. Jean Paul Sartre, Hannah Arendt, Richard Wright, Paul Gilroy, Edward Said, and many more have, in various contexts, identified anti-Semitism, orientalism, and anti-black racism as central to the project of modernity, although each wrote about different geographic contexts and historical moments. While each group's histories are particular to each group, in this study I am interested in exploring their shared and sometimes overlapping politics of exclusion, statelessness, and exile in order to excavate how a variety of subalterns throughout the late nineteenth and twentieth centuries reconstituted the geographies of modernity into what I am calling a geography of liberation.

The geographies of liberation are dialectal spaces produced in the collision between nationalism and colonialism, on one hand, and subaltern decolonial and liberation politics, on the other. This collision produces a transgressive geography within which Afro-Arab intellectuals have articulated political imaginaries beyond nationalism and colonialism. The geographies of liberation are thus spaces of dissonance produced when the exile compares the world as it is with a restructured world he or she would like to create. More specifically, geographies of liberation are constituted by moments when black intellectuals—in the U.S., in the Caribbean, in Egypt, in Palestine, in Israel, and *of* multiple places and juridical formations—developed radical political understandings of liberation that emerged through a comparative and spatial politics between the United States and Palestine and, later, Israel. Here I am focusing on the creative acts of imagination and political consciousness that led late-nineteenth- and early-twentieth-century Caribbean intellectuals to see in the history of Palestine an analog for black liberation in the Americas, or that led black Americans in the 1950s to view the Egyptian nationalist movement as a useful model of politics in the U.S., or that led Arab, Mizrahi Jews in Israel in the 1970s to see possibilities for decolonial politics in the U.S. Black Panther Party.

What connects black radical politics globally, I argue, is not merely the recognition of shared histories of racial violence and exclusion; rather, it is the recognition across continents, across national borders, and across religious beliefs of contending with shared conditions of colonial violence, even while local and regional differences in language and power ultimately make the comparisons appear arbitrary. Indeed, the recognition that Israel and the United States can be compared, or that black politics in the U.S. are similar to black politics in the Maghreb, is made possible not because the United States, Israel/Palestine, and North Africa are indeed the same, or because they compare easily; it is because comparative histories of colonialism produce an analytic that exposes something important and productive about the colonial world as well as the desire of the oppressed to undertake its refashioning. What the comparison of colonial sites of antiblack violence reveals are the global borderlands where modern decolonial histories are constituted by a transnational assemblage of local, regional, and sometimes indigenous epistemologies and worldviews.

The complex subject positions produced under colonialism and nationalism, subject positions that have made certain people simultaneously at home and homeless, require a scholarship that places historical subjects within conjunctural, overlapping, and global histories. In *Geographies of Liberation*, I analyze political imaginaries forged in multiple geopolitical spaces, including within national homelands, colonized spaces, and decolonial social movements.[23] "Geographies of liberation" is a term I employ to trace a global and comparative history; it is a concept with an academic genealogy in the so-called transnational turn in American studies as well as in the emergence within critical ethnic studies of studies of border thinking and decolonization.[24]

In this book I understand power in terms of coloniality, or "colonial modernity."[25] Although the nation-state is the hegemonic political imaginary of the twentieth century, Walter Mignolo and Anibal Quijano have argued that nations themselves are products of a previous colonial formation, what they each term the process of "coloniality."[26] Coloniality names the development of a modern world system divided by race and geopolitical power from which modern nation-states emerged.[27] Coloniality, or colonial modernity, produced a Eurocentric world order that achieved global hegemony through its ability to govern social relations, produce racial difference, and rationalize difference through its control of the production of knowledge. The colonial difference was ultimately organized through a system of nation-states that transformed older colonial distinctions into national distinctions. Racial and national difference, for Mignolo and Quijano, are traces of colonialism.[28]

Geographies of Liberation draws on the insights of Mignolo, who argues that a "decolonial imaginary" exists in the uneven spaces—produced by race, economy, and geopolitics—formed by colonial borders. The colonial world for Mignolo is constituted not only by racial domination and subjugation but also by the presence of colonial borderlands that are themselves loci of enunciation where colonized subjects articulate what he calls "border thinking."[29] Within the contradictory and fractured spaces of colonial difference, emergent cultural formations articulate the subaltern's attempt to reconfigure and reconstruct the geographies of modernity in ways that often articulate "communities of shared fate" beyond and across geopolitical and biopolitical boundaries.[30]

Geographies of Liberation traces the emergence of an Afro-Arab political imaginary within the context of changing geopolitical configurations and ascendant national awakenings. I argue that an Afro-Arab political imaginary emerged in response to global geopolitical transformations that enshrined new political communities and structures, and especially within the modern Middle East. During the period of this study the Middle East was fundamentally transformed by the decline of the Ottoman Empire in the late nineteenth and early twentieth centuries, the formation of European mandate governments under the aegis of the League of Nations, the mid-twentieth-century creation of independent Middle Eastern states and the United Nations (UN) partition of Palestine, the 1967 Israeli expansion into the occupied Palestinian territories and Gaza, and the neoliberalization of international governance that enshrined the so-called Oslo Peace Process and the termination, within the United States, of "welfare as we know it." Each of these transformations enshrined new legal and affective bonds of belonging and inspired different sorts of transnational political imaginaries linking African Americans to Arab concerns and, sometimes, vice versa. For example, within the context of a declining Ottoman Empire, African Americans engaged the Arab world through the lens of Ottoman polyculturalism and the Western logic of diaspora. In the context of the League of Nations mandate system, African American pan-Africanists engaged pan-Arabists who articulated a global vision of the rights of national minorities. In 1946–48, during debates about the partition of Palestine, the politics of binationalism within the context of the United Nations became the organizing logic of a limited Afro-Arab solidarity movement. After the 1967 Israeli colonial occupation of the West Bank and Gaza, the Black Panther Party's politics of intercommunalism became the organizing logic of solidarity between the Palestine Liberation Organization (PLO), the U.S. black power movement, and a small group of Mizrahi Jews in Israel. In the contemporary period it is the ascendance of neoliberal politics in Israel, Palestine, and the United States, in conjunction with wars on gangs, drugs, and terror, that makes hip hop and poetry a legible Afro-Arab political imaginary.

Because *Geographies of Liberation* is a transnational project, I analyze geopolitical transformations in Palestine and the Arab world in relation to similar transformations shaping the black freedom movement in the United States. In this way, the book is organized by overlapping and intersecting histories. Hence, in addition to foregrounding geopolitical transformations globally and in the Middle East in particular, I also focus on historical changes within the U.S. black freedom movement when I examine the politics of U.S.-based African colonization movements and early pan-Africanism, the transition from internationalist black politics to post–World War II nation-bound civil rights movements, the reemergence of internationalist and anti-imperialist movements in the post-1968 era, and the containment of black internationalist projects through the deployment of post-1980s neoliberal policies aimed at privatizing social safety net programs directed to urban black communities in conjunction with the alarming rates of black incarceration.

Although I am interested in processes of comparative racialization of blacks in the United States and Arabs in Israel and Palestine, I am not arguing for a symmetrical comparison. I recognize that the demands of African American U.S. citizens are different from the demands of Palestinian stateless refugees. Moreover, I agree with Brent Edwards, who has persuasively argued that black internationalist politics are always articulated via uneven social relations and mistranslations.[31] Hence black Americans, even as they rejected and criticized the imperial politics of the United States, nevertheless entered the terrain of internationalist politics as relatively more privileged than their Palestinian peers. Similarly, Arab Israelis, even as they may be racialized black within Israel, enjoy certain material and psychological rights and benefits that are regularly denied Palestinian Israelis, as well as Palestinians in the West Bank and Gaza. The point of comparative work, it seems to me, is not to assert that two disparate local conditions are *the same*; rather, it is to ask why African Americans, Palestinians, and Jews have found comparisons to be meaningful and useful in the forging of a liberationist project. What are the conditions of possibility under which transnational political imaginaries have been forged? What are the possibilities and limits of these imaginaries?

In this project I use the terms "Afro" and "Arab" somewhat loosely, with full recognition that these categories can describe the same body and are, in themselves, highly problematic. Moreover, I treat the category "Jew" as qualitatively different from the categories "Afro" and "Arab." I do so in order to avoid treating a religious identity as consonant with race or ethnicity, although I recognize that Jews *have been* racialized in certain Western contexts and have, at times, embraced self-definitions rooted in nationalistic and racial discourse. It would be incorrect, for example, to speak of Islam as a racial category, given the presence of multiple racial groups that practice Islam and call themselves Muslim. The Islamic Ummah is a multiracial category, even though there are ongoing efforts within the contemporary United States to racialize Arab Muslims.[32] Similarly, I recognize that Jewishness has been racialized, particularly in the context of modern European nationalisms, even though Judaism has always been a multiracial faith, practiced by diverse peoples across the globe. In a sense the refusal to consider Jews as a racial group and the choice to view Jewishness as a religious faith is to stake an antiracist position that refuses to collapse a diasporic Jewish identity into a European or white racial experience. At the same time, I am interested in how and where Jews *have been* racialized or view themselves as a race in order to understand how race and nation became the primary currency of recognition and inclusion at particular historical conjunctures. In this book I sometimes include Jews in the categories "Afro" and "Arab," recognizing, for example, that many Israeli Jews are, in fact, from Arab, Mizrahi, or Sephardic background and that Jews in Ottoman Palestine identified as, and were, Arab. Yet in making this case I will necessarily offend those for whom "the Jewish people" is a category of racial belonging, distinct from Arab and black racial identities, and not merely a faith community.[33] The conflict between competing understandings of Jewish belonging is one of the subjects of this book and the historical debates animating Chapter 3, in particular. I obviously write from a political position—that Jewish nationalism is a historical product of modernity and not an essence or historical inevitability.

In the wake of the transformations brought by the 1948 Arab-Israeli war and the 1967 Six-Day War, it has become difficult, if not impossible, to understand the diasporic imaginaries that shaped African American, Jewish, and Muslim and Arab identities at the turn of the twentieth century and throughout the tumultuous years leading to the UN's partition of Palestine. Even more difficult is breaking free of the modernist racial categories "Arab," "black," and "Jew" that can all too easily define geopolitical conflicts in misleading and simplistic terms. In the opening of this introduction, I quote Mark Twain's revealing description of the Palestinian city of Tiberius in his 1869 novel, *The Innocents Abroad*. At the time of Twain's travels through Palestine, Tiberius was a diverse city located within the Ottoman Empire. Twain describes Tiberius's population using Western and orientalist categories of description: "They are particularly uncomely Jews, Arabs, and negroes."[34] Yet these categories had little local currency or meaning in mid-nineteenth-century Tiberius. Indeed, the very same body could easily fit all of Twain's categories, as would be the case of North African Jews in Palestine. The normative geographies of modernity, as Mark Twain illustrates, constitute blackness as non-Islamic and Judaism as non-Arab. Blackness and Islam are paradoxical for Americans, not least because Islamic Africa is often erased from our imagination of the African continent and public discussions of an "Arab/Israeli conflict" all too often overlook and erase the fact that a majority of Israel's Jewish populations are non-Ashkenazi and often inhabit identities constituted by Arab *and* Jewish cultures.[35]

Although this project begins in the late nineteenth century, with black travel writing about Palestine, 1948 is a pivotal year in this story that deserves to be marked as a fundamental turning point in Afro-Arab political imaginaries. For Israelis, 1948 is the moment of national liberation, the moment when their European exile came to an end, while for Palestinians it is the year of the *nakba*, or catastrophe, the moment in which they were, as Edward Said once wrote, "exiled by exiles."[36] It was also the year that saw the ascendance of the United Nations and the framework of "national liberation" that would inform decolonization movements throughout Africa and Asia. The formation of the United Nations led to the creation of the State of Israel, the dispossession of the Palestinian people, and recognition of the international declaration of human rights; but the UN also profoundly redrew lines of political affiliations, communities, and belongings. Arab Jews from places like Morocco, Iraq, Lebanon, Yemen, and Iran began to affiliate as Jews with a "birthright" to Israel. Palestinians dispossessed from their ancestral homes engaged in a national liberation movement for Palestinian statehood. In post–World War II America, African Americans increasingly turned their political activities away from the pan-Africanist projects of black internationalism to nation-bound move-ments for civil rights within the framework of the liberal state.[37] Each of these groups turned to a framework of nation-state, the very framework that instigated their exile, which brought with it different lines of belong-ing and even new memories. My interest here is in the belongings that got transformed by the formation of new national belongings. These displaced belongings, what Howard Zinn once called "the pasts' fugitive moments of compassion," most interest me here.[38]

The aesthetic politics I locate in *Geographies of Liberation* have shaped Edward Said's understanding of an exilic consciousness in his writing about the plight of the stateless Palestinian refugees, a group that has been largely overlooked in American studies' transnational turn. The condition of exile, Said argues, is not a romantic state of cosmopolitan belonging but, instead, an insecure place fixed between the loss of one home and the ex-clusion from a new home. Exile is not a "privilege, but an *alternative* to the mass institutions that dominate modern life. Exile is . . . not a matter of choice. . . . But, provided that the exile refuses to sit on the sidelines nursing a wound, there are things to be learned: he or she must cultivate a scrupu-lous (not indulgent or sulky) subjectivity."[39]

Interestingly, Said's insights into the condition of Palestinian exile were inspired by a genealogy of Jewish exilic intellectual thought. Specifically, Said was influenced by Theodor Adorno's autobiography, *Minima Mora-lia*, which was written during Adorno's exile. Through Adorno's recogni-tion of the "homes"' location within a politics of violent belongings, Said came to the recognition that "the exile knows that in a secular and contin-gent world, homes are always provisional." Indeed the condition of exile is the condition of understanding the contingent nature of attachments (to home) and belonging. Exile, then, "is predicated on the existence of, love for, and bond with, one's native place; what is true of all exile is not that home and love of home are lost, but that loss is inherent in the very existence of both."[40] For Said, the exile is aware of, and may be excluded from, at least two homes, and this produces a "plurality of vision" in which "both the new and the old environments are vivid, actual, occurring to-gether contrapuntally."[41] Contrapuntal modernities are exilic imaginar-ies in which the condition of homelessness produces emergent aesthetic politics.

In this project, I read modern histories of black Americans, Palestin-ians, and Jews relationally and in terms of shared histories of exclusion, exile, and countermodern political imaginaries. This may seem like an ar-bitrary linkage, produced by an idealistic wish for global third world leftist struggle. Yet this project is informed by the articulation of comparisons that emerge from American blacks, Palestinians, and some Jews at various historical conjunctures. I am not, therefore, merely imposing a comparative framework on disparate local histories. Rather, in this project I am interested in understanding how and why Palestine emerged in early pan-African writing, how the narrative of exodus informed black American conceptions of freedom, how Arab and Islamic intellectuals articulated expanded notions of belonging for black Americans, and how black American politics became meaningful to Arab Jews in Israel as well as Palestinian artists in Ramallah. In other words, the relational and interdependent world I outline in this project has been articulated historically through a global imaginary, Afro and Arab—Jewish, Muslim, and Christian—that I am calling the geographies of liberation.

There are, of course, limits to the transgressive potential of geographies of liberation. They are rooted in the languages, cultures, and norms of rule from which they seek liberation and therefore can reproduce those norms. Partha Chatterjee's theorizing of postcolonial politics is especially relevant here. Chatterjee argues that the process of claiming political sovereignty and national self-determination is always and already shaped by the political community from which groups seek liberation. Hence for Chatterjee as for Frantz Fanon, the colonial always shapes the postcolonial in complex ways. According to Chatterjee, anticolonial movements always reproduce the terms of postenlightened reason, and the postcolonial nation therefore mirrors certain forms of the colonial society. European Zionism, for example, was a form of postcolonial politics that reproduced particular forms of Eastern European nationalism—the very form of colonial power and racial modernism from which Jewish Zionists sought liberation.[42]

Organization of Book

Geographies of Liberation examines the history of African American engagement with the Arab world within the context of shifting colonial borders and racial ideologies in the United States and the Arab world, beginning in the mid-nineteenth century. Although the chapters are organized chronologically, there are places where there is considerable temporal overlap across chapters. Some chapters cover a chronology that might be most appropriate in the next chapter; this is a product, I contend, of studying comparative and overlapping global histories. Events that are transformative in one part of the world are not as transformative in another region. For example, the formation of Jim Crow laws in the United States in the wake of Reconstruction did not have much impact on the Arab world, and neither did the Sykes-Picot agreement that divided the modern Middle East into European mandates have much impact on the black freedom movement in the United States. Yet both of these transformations were profoundly important within their region and help explain the geopolitical contexts within which an early-twentieth-century Afro-Arab political imaginary formed. I have attempted to strike a delicate balance between local and global contexts, and this has required a narrative form less dedicated to strict chronology than to a more complex and kaleidoscopic story in which chapters sometimes bleed into each other, even as they describe distinct topics. Instead of thinking of the chapters as organized temporally, I have instead chosen to organize the chapters thematically (although these themes hew somewhat closely to a temporal chronology).

I focus on five conjunctural moments of encounter, each of which is analyzed through the lens of a specific geography of liberation. The history of early pan-Africanism and its relationship to European Jewish Zionism and Gilded Age Holy Land travel is understood through the concept of diaspora. Pan-African/pan-Oriental politics that took place in the imperial public sphere of London between the world wars is read through the term "pan-Islamism." African American writing about, and political participation in, the UN partition of Palestine is understood through the concept of binationalism. Arab-Jewish engagement with African American decolonization and black nationalism in the 1960s and 1970s is explored through the term "intercommunalism." The contemporary African American and Arab cultural representation of the refugee, produced in the context of post-Oslo neoliberal governance and the war on terror in America and Palestine, is described as an Afro-Arab international.

In Chapter 1, "Overlapping Diasporas," I discuss the formation of an African American diasporic imagination that was deeply influenced by Jewish diasporic politics and European Jewish Zionism. Beginning in the 1860s, African Americans traveled to Ottoman Palestine as slaves traveling with masters or as free black ministers in search of holy lands. I examine the politics of diaspora and early pan-Africanism by identifying the comparisons black intellectuals drew between the European "Jewish question" and the condition of blacks within the United States. Both groups developed political imaginaries that responded to racial modernity. As I discuss in the chapter, in the late nineteenth century, European Jews confronted the Dreyfus affair at the same time that black Americans witnessed how their nation failed to realize Reconstruction and allowed the ascendency of Jim Crow legislation.

In Chapter 2, "From Subject to Citizen: Dusé Mohamed Ali and the Afro-Orient," I examine the formation of pan-Africanist and pan-Islamic politics in Europe in the context of post–World War I League of Nations colonial formations in the Middle East. I explore the convergence of pan-African and pan-Arab politics by examining the career of Dusé Mohamed Ali, who claimed to be a Sudanese Egyptian intellectual and was the founder of the influential *African Times and Orient Review*.[43] Ali moved to London after the dissolution of the Ottoman Empire, and he confronted new nationalisms throughout the Arab world that were formed under the framework of the League of Nations' mandate system. I demonstrate how the League of Nations enshrined the logic of cultural pluralism as a framework of international governance. The league's system created the category "national minority" and in doing so established new conditions of possibility within which groups could be made legible within the international order.

In Chapter 3, "Black Marxism and Binationalism," I examine the decline of the League of Nations' trusteeship and mandate systems and the rise of national liberation and the United Nations as new frameworks of international governance. This chapter focuses on the UN's deliberations on the partition of Palestine. A central figure in this debate was the African American intellectual Ralph Bunche, who was a prominent member of UNSCOP. Although he never joined and ultimately rebuked the Communist Party, in the 1930s Bunche nevertheless embraced the party's Black Belt thesis (which conceived of black Americans as a colonized nation within a nation), and he was committed to a racially diverse labor movement in the United States. In the mid-1940s, as he considered the Palestine question, Bunche advocated a binational state in Palestine, uniting Arab Palestinian and European Jewish political interests. The binational movement, I demonstrate, was an attempt to imagine a different kind of political community beyond the nation-state.

Chapter 4, "The Black Panthers and the PLO: The Politics of Intercommunalism," examines the 1967 Six-Day War as a new condition of possibility for Afro-Arab political imaginaries. This chapter focuses on the formation of Black Panther intercommunalism as an anti-imperialist, trans-community politics that united the U.S. Black Panther Party, the PLO, and a group of Arab Jews in Israel who called themselves the Israeli Black Panthers. In this chapter I am interested in how anticolonialism emerged as a post-1967 response to the ascendancy of the Israeli colonial state as an occupying army. I focus in particular on the ways that the PLO and the U.S. Black Panthers drew comparisons between racial capitalism in the United States and in Israel, as well as between U.S. imperialism globally, in which Israeli politics in the West Bank and Gaza were implicated. Moreover, I demonstrate how the Panthers' political imaginary reverberated within Israel, where some Mizrahi Jews began to see themselves as members of a different sort of political imaginary, one that was shaped by the Afro-Arab politics of the Panthers.

Chapter 5, "Neoliberalism, Security, and the Afro-Arab International," turns to the Afro-Arab political imaginary rooted to the cultural politics of hip hop and poetry, as well as to the 2001 UN World Conference against Racism, Racial Discrimination, Xenophobia, and Related Intolerance in Durban, South Africa. I describe how the contexts of neoliberal governance, as articulated in the 1993 Oslo Peace Process and the 1996 transformation of "welfare as we know it" in the United States, in conjunction with the global security infrastructure established by the war on terror, became the conditions of possibility for Afro-Arab political imaginaries.

Geographies of Liberation is a transnational analysis that engages overlapping global histories. The risks of such an analysis are many. I may offend experts in fields in which I am a relative outsider, not to mention those committed to maintaining normative geographies and political arrangements as they currently exist in the Middle East. At the same time, however, I intend for this book to help map a new scholarly terrain within which to read political imaginaries that are not readily available to our disciplined (and disciplinary) eyes. In this way, *Geographies of Liberation* is meant to forge new directions and possibilities of the black radical tradition and its Arab and Palestinian coordinates.

CHAPTER ONE

Overlapping Diasporas

The question [of Zionism] is similar to that which at this moment
agitates thousands of the descendants of Africa in America, anxious to
return to the land of their fathers. —Edward Wilmot Blyden

In 1907 an African American Baptist minister from Atlanta, W. L Jones, articulated his longing to travel the world in order to connect with ancestry and lost culture. "For a long time," Jones wrote, "yes fifteen years, I have had a desire to visit the old world." For Jones, however, the location of the "old world" was ambiguous. Did black Americans belong to the African continent, as the emerging pan-African movement suggested? Or was Jones referring to Europe, America's "old world"? Or, given Jones's Baptist beliefs, was the old world rooted in a more sacred past and geography beyond Africa and Europe? According to Jones, "I first felt that it was my calling to Africa, and for several years I was troubled with that thought; afterwards my mind was disabused of that idea, for a new one, that of Jerusalem. And for more than ten years I have had a restless desire for the Holy Land and especially for Jerusalem."[1] What made Jerusalem a meaningful geography for Jones? Obviously, since Jones was a Baptist minister, Jerusalem was the home of his religious faith, and like many Christian ministers he may have traveled to the "Holy Land" in order to realize Bible lands and to develop religious authority.[2] Black Americans throughout the era of slavery and in the post-Reconstruction era employed "Holy Land" symbols and titles in order to imagine a "Promised Land" or "Zion" within the United States.[3] But did Jones's search for Zion represent more than a mere attachment to religious faith and a sacred geography? Did the geography of Ottoman Palestine and its location next to Egypt imbue the Holy Land with additional meanings?

Although there exists a small but emerging scholarship on African American engagement with Palestine in the post–World War II period, very little scholarship focuses on the complex identification of pan-Africanists with Palestine in the late nineteenth and early twentieth centuries.[4] And yet for many post–Civil War African American intellectuals, preachers, and pan-Africanists, Palestine was a generative site for articulating anti-racist politics, particularly at the moment when the future for blacks in the United States was severely attenuated by Jim Crow segregation and violence. In the period following emancipation, many Africa American intellectuals, religious figures, and political radicals sought to visit the Holy Land in order to forge a liberation politics that would enable them to engage a political community beyond the Occident. Moreover, in finding political meaning in visiting the Holy Land, black Americans engaged in a larger Western movement in Europe and the United States of countermodern intellectuals seeking to articulate a new future in a different homeland.

Little is known about W. L. Jones's motives for international travel, except what he wrote in his brief travel account of visiting Egypt and the Holy Land. What is clear, however, is that Jones encountered the Holy Land at a moment when Ottoman Palestine became a symbolic geography within American national culture as well as within European Jewish diasporic culture, and Jones, as well as many other African American travelers, could not help but encounter the Holy Land through the optics of Western imperial culture.[5] In seeking to visit the Holy Land, black Americans were like many American figures who traveled to the Holy Land during the Gilded Age and Progressive Era, including former Civil War generals, American writers, and religious leaders. Yet African American travelers to Palestine were also like many European Jews who similarly imagined Palestine as a geography of liberation and a destination to escape their inhuman treatment by European nations.

In this chapter I describe African American engagement with Palestine in the late nineteenth and early twentieth centuries and argue that this engagement was made meaningful within the context of Gilded Age American orientalism and U.S. national interest in "the Holy Land"; the ascendance of the Jewish Zionist movement, especially in the aftermath of the Dreyfus affair; and the growth of black nationalist interest in African settlement in Liberia. These contexts established the conditions of possibility within which a political imaginary cohered around concepts of diaspora and homelands. Palestine was a generative site for black American diasporic political imaginaries that confronted the dehumanizing politics of race within Europe and the United States. Yet, at the same time, pre–World War I black American engagement with Palestine illustrates the mostly elite and Western discourses of black countermodernity during this period of black liberation politics. Throughout this chapter I privilege a historical narrative rooted in political and social change in the United States and, to some extent, in Europe. Subsequent chapters look beyond the United States and will consider how global changes elsewhere produced different Afro-Arab political imaginaries. One of the important claims of *Geographies of Liberation* is that political imaginaries are always situated in particular spaces and times; hence, what may be radical in one geopolitical context can be much less so in another.

American Orientalism

African American travel to the Holy Land took place within a geopolitical context characterized by U.S. diplomatic, cultural, and scientific interest in the region. U.S. interest in the Levant began in earnest in the early nineteenth century and was inspired by a mixture of religious and affective interests. During the 1820s, the American Board of Missions in Massachusetts began sending Protestant missionaries to the Mount Lebanon region of Ottoman Syria in order to convert Eastern Catholics, a variety of sects that Protestants believed were not only misguided but also oppressed by Ottoman Muslim leaders. The Protestant missionaries, like most orientalists, did not understand the complex history of tolerance within the Ottoman Empire and therefore were incapable of comprehending the relative stability of Christian communities in places like Mount Lebanon, where Maronite Catholics were then a majority of the population.[6]

The American Protestant missionaries in Mount Lebanon encountered a diverse confessional environment that was majority Christian, with sizable Muslim, Jewish, and Druze populations. Moreover, American Protestant conceptions of religious conversion were foreign to the Levant, where stability among religious communities was highly prized. According to Ussama Makdisi, "The notion of rushing forth to evangelize the world because of the rapid passage of time was alien to an Ottoman Arab culture that prided itself on stability amidst heresy and its fidelity, and its uninterrupted political and religious lineages."[7] Failing to learn Arabic and misunderstanding complex Ottoman social norms, the American Protestant missionaries did not produce any religious converts, although they did manage to profoundly transform the society in which they conducted their missionary work.

By the 1860s, the missionaries realized they had failed at religious conversion and transformed their goal to modernizing the Levant via liberal education. The missionaries founded Syrian Protestant College in 1862 as a nonsectarian school located in Beirut. The college would be renamed the American University of Beirut in 1920. Although they failed at religious conversion, the missionaries nevertheless built an American institution in the Levant and, in doing so, helped make the Levant a place of interest for Americans, while also serving to represent America within the Arab world. Through the 1830s–1880s, the United States opened foreign consulates across the Middle East. The consulates signaled the operations of international diplomacy as well as the presence of services and support for American citizens who traveled and worked throughout the Middle East.[8]

During the decades after the Civil War, travelers and writers played a seminal role in making the Middle East accessible and interesting to American audiences. Travel writing played an important role in an expanding U.S. imperial culture by translating "foreign" geography into familiar terms and landscapes. The travel writer assumed an aesthetic authority to name and to know distant lands.[9] In this way, travel writing has the power to define a geopolitical map from the vantage point of the author's origins and to contribute to the formation of imperial culture.[10]

American travel to the Levant, or Holy Land, was popular especially after the Civil War when Americans attempted to forge national unity. Milette Shamir argues that in the wake of the national and familial violence of the Civil War, Americans sought to define a common national culture by identifying a common cultural ancestry. The Holy Land, as a Christian sacred geography, signified in American national culture a maternal figure that helped Americans reunite as a nation. Hence, in the years after the Civil War, many prominent Americans traveled or expressed an interest in traveling to the Holy Land. It was widely rumored after his assassination that Abraham Lincoln was planning a Holy Land sojourn after the war.[11]

Hilton Obenzinger has termed the U.S. interest in the Holy Land during the Gilded Age the "Holy Land Mania." Obenzinger is especially interested in the popularization of Holy Land travel in the literary work of Mark Twain and Herman Melville, both of whom published significant works dedicated to Holy Land travel.[12] Twain authored the 1869 *Innocents Abroad; or, the New Pilgrim's Progress*, in which he satirized American travelers' interests in the Holy Land. Twain drew much of his comedic effect from lampooning Protestant religious interests in the Holy Land and the arrogance of American travelers abroad. Melville published an 1876 epic poem about the Holy Land, *Clarel: A Poem and Pilgrimage in the Holy Land*, which he based on his 1856 travels through Palestine.

Popular fictional accounts of Holy Land travel joined a range of additional travel accounts from religious leaders who sought to represent a living bible to their parishioners and from American political leaders who used their Holy Land travel to authenticate their Protestant and American bona fides. During the Holy Land mania, the holy city of Jerusalem was understood, by some, as an American space. American national culture had always relied on a foundational narrative of providential destiny, especially in Puritan narratives of North America and the New World as "God's Chosen Israel."[13] In the nineteenth century, some Americans referred to Jerusalem as a quintessentially American geography; both Jerusalem and the United States were understood by these Americans as sacred geographies with a God-chosen destiny. Such was the understanding that the family of Anna Spafford brought to Jerusalem when she established the American Colony in 1890.[14]

Americans began to "know" the Holy Land through missionaries and travel writing. They also developed knowledge through military-scientific exploration. In 1848 American naval commander William Francis Lynch traveled overland across Syria en route to Palestine's Sea of Galilee in order to map and study the Jordan River valley from the Sea of Galilee to the Dead Sea. Lynch's expedition led to his publication of a detailed scientific study of the geography, biology, and cultures of the Jordan valley.[15] Following Lynch's expedition, the U.S. Army, believing the newly acquired U.S. Southwest and the Syrian and Egyptian deserts were similar, began to import Levantine camels through ports in Texas to constitute the U.S. Camel Corps. Taken together, American missionary work, travel accounts, and scientific study produced a discursive field we might call American orientalism. In his important study, *Orientalism*, Edward Said argued that Americans did not participate in orientalism until after World War II, when U.S. military power entered the Middle East. Said made this claim because he believed that orientalism was a discourse of direct imperialism, and U.S. imperialism in the Middle East began only in the mid-twentieth century. For Said, orientalism was not merely about producing a discursive field; it was also the material fact of imperialism in the Middle East.[16] Although the U.S. was not directly involved in military and other imperialist projects in the Levant until the twentieth century, American orientalism was nevertheless an important national narrative throughout the post–Civil War period that helped define U.S. geopolitical power throughout the era of the Mexican-American War and the Spanish-American War. I use the term "American orientalism" as a variation of Said's important framework in order to argue that orientalism helped Americans make meaning for U.S. imperial expansion across North America and in the Pacific during the nineteenth and early twentieth centuries. There is a deep archive of U.S. imperial literature that equates the North American Indian to the "oriental." For example, Mark Twain could not describe the "orientals" he encountered in *The Innocents Abroad* without referencing the indigenous subjects within the western United States, especially those he encountered in California's mining camps. William Francis Lynch described the Jordan valley in terms of the northern Mexico territories he conquered just two years earlier in the Mexican-American War.[17]

American orientalism played an important role in helping Americans to make sense of their imperial national culture. In 1904, just six years after the Spanish-American War, the United States hosted the World's Fair Exposition in St. Louis, Missouri. The fair marked an important moment for the United States. It commemorated the 100th anniversary of the Louisiana Purchase (which was the country's largest territorial expansion), and it signified the new status of the United States as an imperial global power, since it had engaged in wars in the Philippines, Puerto Rico, Guam, and Cuba. Like all world's fairs, the St. Louis exposition enabled the host nation to represent the world geopolitically, with the host serving as the center.[18] At the St. Louis exposition, Europe and America were prominently featured as bastions of modernity and innovation. Territories conquered by the U.S. and Europe were presented ethnographically as primitive curiosities. However, at the center of the 1904 World's Fair, situated outside geography on the midway, was a 1:1 scale model of the Old City of Jerusalem. The exhibit featured hundreds of "real Orientals" shipped in from the Holy Land. Guests paid a small entrance fee to visit the Holy Land, to get married in the Holy Land, and to shop the Holy Land's authentic bazaars and souks.[19]

That Jerusalem was disassociated from the Middle East exhibits at the fair illustrates the extent to which Americans claimed the holy city as their own. Claiming Jerusalem as American space characterized an American orientalism that helped the United States to make sense of its imperial status in the wake of the Louisiana Purchase, the Mexican-American War, and the Spanish-American War. Wars of territorial acquisition and conquest seemed to contradict a national culture that posed the United States as an "Empire of Liberty" and not similar to European empires.[20] One way to rationalize conquest was to view national expansion as providential destiny rather than as imperial hubris, and thus Jerusalem was an important symbol of American national "chosenness" and not its imperial violence.

Race and Western Modernity

How should we understand African Americans' complex relationship to Gilded Age and Progressive Era American orientalism? The decades in which the United States engaged the "Holy Land mania" were also the decades in which it undermined the possibility of black Reconstruction and instituted harsh Jim Crow laws that limited black futures. The history of racism in the wake of the Civil War is well beyond the scope of this chapter.[21] What concerns us here is how, during the Gilded Age and the Progressive Era, African Americans developed alternative political imaginaries that articulated political communities and belongings beyond nationalism. Moreover, I am interested in the relationship between black cultures of countermodernity, their geographies of liberation, and extant discourses of American orientalism. During the Gilded Age and the Progressive Era, African Americans developed countermodern geographic imaginaries that engaged the Middle East differently than American orientalism. If, for American orientalists, the Holy Land was an American geographic imaginary through which U.S. national culture could project fantasies of common heritage and providential destiny, for African Americans, the Holy Land was an abolitionist geography—a geography of liberation—through which to articulate new political communities. Palestine was an important location of black geographies of liberation because of its status in religious understandings of exodus and, by the turn of the twentieth century, because of the emergence of European Jewish discourses of countermodernity and Zionism.

Although domestic U.S. contexts of racism and Jim Crow profoundly shaped black internationalism, so too did European anti-Jewish racism powerfully, if indirectly, inform black political imaginaries. The 1894 conviction of Alfred Dreyfus in Paris reverberated throughout Europe and within African American intellectual circles. W. E. B. Du Bois was studying in Berlin during the Dreyfus affair and has identified it as a significant event in his growing political consciousness.[22] Black newspapers regularly focused on the Dreyfus affair and condemned the French government. The *Washington Bee* wrote, "The cowardly persecution of Captain Dreyfus will go down to posterity as the most outrageous persecution of an innocent man known to modern times."[23]

In November 1894, the Jewish captain Alfred Dreyfus was convicted of treason for the crime of having shared French military secrets with the German Embassy in Paris. Like many racial minorities accused of being disloyal to national interests, Dreyfus entered his case as a suspicious suspect, as the Jew who was not quite French. Dreyfus was convicted of treason and sent to the penal colony at Devil's Island in French Guinea, where he would spend the next five years. In response to the verdict, throughout France anti-Jewish rallies were held to condemn Dreyfus and, in some places, to call for "Death to the Jews." The case highlighted the plight of the Jew in European modernity. Intellectuals pondered at the inability of the Jews to receive a fair trial in "enlightened" Paris. In 1896, two years after Dreyfus's conviction, new evidence demonstrated his innocence. But the French government did not relent; instead it levied new charges. Dreyfus would not be exonerated until 1906, when he was reinstated in the French military, where he continued to serve through World War I.[24]

The Hungarian Jewish journalist Theodor Herzl was profoundly interested in the case, as he covered the trial for his newspaper. Herzl responded to the Dreyfus affair by publishing his influential 1896 book, *The Jewish State*, and by founding the World Zionist Organization. In *The Jewish State*, Herzl argued that Jews could never be included in European nations and that only through self-government, a Jewish state, could Jews achieve a modicum of freedom.[25] In this way, for Herzl, because of the ways European Jews had been racialized, Jewish sovereignty via state-making was the most appropriate response.

> The Jewish question persists wherever Jews live in appreciable numbers. Wherever it does not exist, it is brought in together with Jewish immigrants. We are naturally drawn into those places where we are not persecuted, and our appearance there gives rise to persecution. This is the case, and will inevitably be so, everywhere, even in highly civilised countries—see, for instance, France—so long as the Jewish question is not solved on the political level. The unfortunate Jews are now carrying the seeds of anti-Semitism into England; they have already introduced it into America.[26]

European Jewish Zionists argued that racial minorities could only gain recognition and freedom if they had a national homeland. This conclusion, as discussed in more detail in Chapter 2, was derived in the context of new international frameworks of governance established by organizations like the League of Nations. The Zionist movement did not immediately attach to the idea of settling Palestine, and Herzl was initially interested in Ugandan settlement as a possibility for Jewish statehood.[27]

Late-nineteenth-century African American political imaginaries were forged in the crucible of European Jewish Zionism as well as American orientalism. Black Americans were interested in the Jewish Zionist idea of creating a nation-state as a means to establish sovereignty, yet they were unable to shed American orientalist frameworks for viewing "the Orient." These complexities meant that black liberation geographies were an alchemy of multiple global political imaginaries, including pan-Africanism, Jewish Zionism, and black nationalism.

African American encounters with Palestine after the Civil War took many different forms. Some African Americans traveled to Palestine in order to make manifest a Protestant narrative of the Holy Land. In these cases, African American encounters were similar to those of many Holy Land travelers to the region during the Gilded Age, with an important difference. To black travelers, Palestine was not merely the location of Christian heritage; it was also the location of exodus and emancipation. Thus the Holy Land, for these black travelers, was not a salve to inspire U.S. national reconciliation after the Civil War but was instead something far more radical and perhaps countermodern.

To other black radicals, Palestine was made meaningful not through a Protestant understanding of Palestine as Holy Land but instead through a secular, abolitionist, and pan-Africanist politics that made comparisons between the history and experience of Western anti-Jewish anti-Semitism and what Paul Gilroy has called antiblack modernity.[28] To many black radicals, Jewish diasporic politics, including the politics of Zionism, have been useful frames for understanding the politics of black nationalism, pan-Africanism, and even black colonization movements in Africa, including, most prominently, those in Liberia.

In the remainder of the chapter, I discuss African American engagement with Palestine during a long historical period defined by the ascendancy of Jim Crow legislation in the United States. These examples foreground U.S. historical temporality because the key figures themselves are rooted in the Americas. In subsequent chapters, I move to different geographies that have their own temporality, and in this way, the chapters demonstrate overlapping and transnational histories. First, I discuss the African American Palestine travel narrative. Next, I turn to the location of Palestine in pan-Africanist political writing about Liberia. And finally, I conclude with a discussion of W. E. B. Du Bois's writing about Zionism and Israel.

Black Orientalism

During the second half of the nineteenth century, African Americans, like many other Americans, began to document their travel to "the Orient." The travel narrative was a medium for African Americans to narrate as Western travelers and thereby gain subjectivity and recognition as Western subjects. African American travel writing about Palestine took place during a period that was framed by the end of slavery in the United States, the colonial occupation of the Levant in the wake of World War I, and the genocidal Holocaust taking place in Europe. Pan-Africanists, African Americans seeking rights within the United States, and African American Christian Zionists rendered Palestine through the optics of American orientalism; yet because they were themselves oppressed within the West, they also viewed Palestine with a great deal of identification and longing because of its status as the site of exodus and abolition.[29] The travel narratives discussed here thus document the complexities of late-nineteenth- and early-twentieth-century black internationalist political imaginaries, which were simultaneously pan-African, orientalist, and Zionist.

The first African American Holy Land travel narrative was written by David Dorr, who as a slave accompanied his master to Europe and the Levant. Born in 1827 or 1828 in New Orleans, Dorr traveled between 1851 and 1854 through Europe and the Ottoman-controlled Syria. Upon returning to the United States, Dorr fled his master, who had failed to guarantee his promised freedom, and in 1858 he published *A Colored Man Round the World*.[30] As Malini Johar Schueller has suggested, Dorr's narrative is marked by a gentlemanly tone that establishes the authority of a slave to speak and define for American readers the non-Western world. In this way, Dorr participates in American orientalism through his construction of knowledge about the Orient and through his geographic and cultural descriptions of the Orient in comparison to the Occident.

For example, after describing a bucolic experience traveling through Europe, Dorr relates his journey from Paris to Egypt by juxtaposing Parisian civility with oriental savagery. "If you have, see me alike, pulling away from the festal abode of Paris' comfort, and loosening the tie of familiar smiles, for a hard journey over a rough see, dead lands, and a treacherous people."[31] In Egypt, Dorr's accommodations were "sickening," and he was continually appalled by what he considered Arab laziness. While traveling down the Nile, Dorr described "some places, when the boat was shoving out, some great, fat and lazy Arab would come blowing and panting to the edge of the Nile with one single egg, that he had been waiting for the hen to lay. . . . To believe what an Arab says when trying to sell anything, would be a sublime display of the most profound ignorance a man could be guilty of."[32] Dorr's frequent allusions to the backward Orient replicated one of the hallmarks of American orientalism and, in so doing, granted him the Western authority to gaze East.

Yet Dorr's narrative is not merely orientalist; it also makes subtle allusions to U.S. slavery, and in this way Dorr turns his critical gaze toward the West as he illuminates Western modernity's slavery and racial terror. The book is dedicated "to my slave mother." Dorr writes in the inscription, "Mother! Wherever thou art, whether in Heaven or a lesser world; or whether around the freedom Base of a Bunker Hill, or only at the lowest savannah of American Slavery, thou art the same to me, and I dedicate this token of my knowledge to thee mother, Oh, my own mother, Your David."[33] This dedication disrupts the travel narrative's occidental modernity by illuminating the practice of racial terror and backwardness within the West. It underscores that *this* purveyor of the Western gaze is himself the product of an enduring slavery and that travel in the Orient signifies a level of freedom unknown to the author in the United States. In this way, Dorr enacts American orientalism as well as a radical black countermodernity that reflects American barbarism back on itself.

In addition to highlighting the limits of occidental modernity, Dorr also celebrates the possibilities of a black modernity beyond the West, especially when he narrates his visit to the Egyptian pyramids, a destination he celebrates as a site of African self-rule. In Egypt, he notes the similarities between the rulers of the extant Ottoman Empire and the rulers of former Egyptian monarchies, "though black," Dorr reminds readers. In this way, Dorr exposes the black origins of Egyptian civilization, thereby locating blacks within the Occident as well as beyond. This doubleness allows Dorr to assume an authority not only over the Orient and its indigenous populations but also over the Christian sites of the Holy Land. Because he claims parts of the Holy Land as his ancestral homeland, Dorr is critical of Christian tourists who cannot "know" what he can. For Dorr, it was the white tourist, and not the black slave, who was a foreigner. In Jericho, for example, Dorr scoffs at a guide who explains that the source of a spring is "because the jawbone that Sampson fought so bravely with was buried here." Because he imagines a privileged place for himself in the biblical landscape of exodus, Dorr "was not inclined to believe anything I heard from the people about here, because I knew as much as they did about it. I came to Jerusalem with a submissive heart, but when I heard all the absurdities of these ignorant people, I was more inclined to ridicule right over these sacred dead bodies, and spots, than pay homage."[34] Dorr makes clear his belief that members of the African diaspora are not foreigners to Palestine when he compares the consistency of the waters of the Jordan to that of the Mississippi; both rivers share in the black imaginary as sites of emancipation, and the comparison links Dorr to the Orient.

By engaging the legacy of slavery in the context of an orientalist travel narrative, Dorr's story takes on the political significance of a slave narrative, but one routed not South to North but internationally, West to East. As Schueller has noted, Dorr challenges slavery through cultures of taste; his ability to assume Western respectability and to narrate the Orient gives him an authority to challenge slavery. Ultimately, however, Dorr's travel narrative is a call for a new modernity in the United States, one that locates exodus and the acknowledgment of black civilization at the center of the West, rather than in the Orient. Subsequent African American travel writers would employ orientalist travel accounts to similar ends, but those published after 1890 had only to look to the growing Zionist movement as a touchstone around which criticism of Western racial violence could be elaborated.

The late-nineteenth-century development of European Jewish Zionism, and the emergence of Jewish settlements in Palestine, contributed to black American understandings of the Levant's abolitionist potential. To many African American intellectuals, Zionism was a diasporic movement that developed in parallel to African diasporic politics. For some African American Christians, Jewish Zionism was part of a Christian narrative that believed the return of the Jews to Palestine, and their subsequent conversion to Christianity, was the first stage in the ultimate return of the Messiah. Hence, African American Christian Zionists' eschatological view of the Holy Land employed orientalism and Zionism to different ends than did Dorr.[35]

One year prior to Herzl's inauguration of the Zionist movement, an African Methodist Episcopalian minister named Daniel P. Seaton published a travel account espousing Jewish return to Palestine following Jewish conversion to Christianity. Seaton's 1895 *The Land of Promise; or, the Bible Land and It's Revelation* offered readers a history of the Bible's geography. Seaton had traveled to Palestine on at least two occasions, and he sought to describe for his congregation the geography of biblical lands. In this way, Seaton's book was not unlike many other Western travel narratives that sought to render biblical stories through geographic descriptions of Palestine, yet Seaton also sought to locate Africans and African Americans as the beneficiaries of Christian Zionism. Doing so, however, required Seaton to narrate as an orientalist and to describe Palestine and its people as primitive, exotic, and in need of Western intervention. Moreover, Seaton viewed Jews he encountered as misguided and pitiful. He advocated Jewish return to Palestine only if Jews first converted to Christianity.

Land of Promise constructs Palestine through orientalist tropes. Palestinians were, according to Seaton, stuck in biblical eras, thus lending authenticity to the place as a Christian site while also fixing Arabs as premodern. "These farmers have lived too greatly isolated from the modern people and so far behind the march of civilization they would not know how to use the farming implements used in modern times."[36] Seaton believed the natives required colonial intervention in order to improve their lot. "[In Joppa] the stranger finds himself in a most repulsively filthy place, with a wild looking people, of all complexions, among whom ignorance is dominant, excepting those who have settled there from countries of progressive civilization, and you can find but few natives who have been taught to appreciate a higher state of manhood."[37] Only at the American Colony did Seaton find any relief from the primitive landscape. "It should be stated concerning the American Colony at Joppa they are doing well, and have done much to change the habits of many of the natives, who, at the time they landed, were not far above the average heathen: they have built a commodious little village to themselves in the most healthy section of town, and have organized a church and school, which has done an incalculable amount of good."[38]

Although the Zionist movement had not yet formed, Seaton drew on a history of Christian Zionism that viewed Jewish return to Palestine as the precursor to the return of the Messiah. Thus, while he regarded the Jews he encountered in the same contemptuous way he did the Arabs, Seaton nevertheless saw them as redeemable due to their Western origins. "Their land" wrote Seaton, was "subordinate to foreign powers."

> But they have a hopeful future; the time is coming when they will fully accept Christ, whom their fathers nailed to the cross, and reverently come before Him in devout worship, return to their own land, and pay Him their tribute on the very summit where the pathetic prayer was offered by the Lord Jesus, in their behalf, while the arrows of death were piercing His soul. . . . If we have noticed the predictions concerning the future of this people, we cannot be otherwise then inclined to the opinion, that a restoration of the Jews will take place. . . . Christians are looking forward to this time, which to them will be a glorious event, both to Jews and Gentiles. . . . What a glorious time, what a blessed period when the people, once dispersed and unsettled, shall again "sing the Lord's song" in their own land![39]

But for Seaton's acknowledgment that Western pilgrims are packed into Greek steamships "like slaves" but with "choice," there is little discussion of slavery or the predicament of African Americans in the United States in *Land of Promise*.

For the Reverend W. L Jones, Palestine was not merely a metaphor for African American diasporic longing; it was the actual scene of African American restoration.[40] Jones began his 1907 travel account, *The Travel in Egypt and Scenes of Jerusalem*, "For a long time, yes fifteen years, I have had a desire to visit the old world. I first felt that it was my calling to Africa, and for several years I was troubled with that thought; afterwards my mind was disabused of that idea, for a new one, that of Jerusalem. And for more than ten years I have had a restless desire for the Holy Land and especially for Jerusalem."[41] Jones left for Jerusalem in 1897. Like Seaton's *Land of Promise*, Jones's travel account represents Palestine through orientalist tropes. "There is nothing beautiful about the little city Joppa. The streets are narrow and not as clean as they ought to be, and full of Arabs, Turks, Bedouins, donkeys, and camels."[42] The conflation of the native with the natural—people with animals—was a staple of orientalist travel literature.

Orientalist descriptions of geography also shaped Methodist Episcopalian bishop William Sampson Brooks's 1915 travel narrative *Footprints of a Black Man*.[43] Books was a pan-Africanist born in Maryland. During the first half of the 1920s, Brooks was the bishop of West Africa who contributed to the construction of Monrovia Normal and Industrial College in Liberia. By the time of Brooks's travel narrative, Jewish Zionists had begun establishing colonies in Palestine. Brooks observed these colonies and applauded the settler colonial movement, especially the German colony he encountered in Haifa. "It owes its progressiveness and beauty to the indefatigable industry and thrift of a small Germany colony nestling at the foot of the mountain." According to Brooks, the inhabitants of the colony were German Americans who combined "their American ideas, methods and tools with the incomparable German spirit for progress, and they have accomplished the salvation of the city. They have revolutionized the city from the filth and squalor of the Turks to its present condition."[44]

Brooks also supported European Jewish Zionists who were creating colonies in Jerusalem and other parts of Palestine. He distinguished between the "native" Jews who had lived in Jerusalem for centuries and the new settlers from Europe. "The [Jewish] quarter reeks with filth. About ten thousand men, women, and children live in its wretched tenements in the most abject squalor and wretchedness."[45] This native Jewish neighborhood, however, was in sharp contrast to the Zionist settlement outside the old city walls. There was, by the time of Brooks's travel, the "'Zion Suburb,' a new settlement of [European] Jews who live in comfortable homes, and commodious tenements, and enjoy real cleanliness and sanitation." Whereas the Jewish settlers were "making themselves respected in the business and commercial life of Palestine, in spite of the great obstacles and restrictions the Turkish Government place in their path . . . the Moslems of Jerusalem are among the most fanatic and rapacious in Palestine, and derive great profit from brisk traffic in souvenirs of the Holy Land and in showing tourists places of interest connect with the life of Christ and the days of the kings."[46] To Brooks, the Arabs he encountered were a people without history, merely there to provide a service industry for Christian travelers. While he looked forward to Jewish conversion to Christianity, he also believed that European Jewish settlement of Palestine would improve the land and make it more hospitable for Christian tourists such as himself.[47]

In her 1928 book, *My Trip through Egypt and the Holy Land*, the African American writer Carolyn Bagley encounters an English speaker on her tour bus. "I learned that he was a Jew living in the Jewish city of Tel Aviv near Jaffa. . . . Here the business was not so remunerative as before but he felt free and a man of an equal chance with others. . . . Passing along a ridge overlooking large plains below, we passed several villages containing many stone houses with pretty red tops, surrounded by a background of green hills and fertile, well-kept farms. All these belonged to the new Zionist districts, which America has done so much to promote."[48]

By the 1920s, the context for African American travel narratives like Bagley's had dramatically changed. As I will discuss in Chapter 2, in the wake of the imperial First World War, the British and French Empires expanded their reach in the Middle East as Palestine came under the rule of a British mandate government chartered by the League of Nations. Moreover, the Zionist movement gained momentum by the outcomes of the war, as many Zionist Jews fought on behalf of the British army in Palestine. In 1914 the Jewish population in Palestine was estimated at 7.5 percent. In 1922, the year of the British mandate over Palestine, the Jewish population was 11.1 percent. This proportion grew steadily to nearly 30 percent in 1941.[49] While these changing demographics meant many different things to different groups in the region, to the West's travelers, it appeared that Palestine was becoming more Western and, by extension, more modern.

The 1930s witnessed the development of a variety of internationalist, diasporic, and anticolonial movements, including the rise of the négritude movement routed through Paris and Marcus Garvey's black nationalist movement in the United States, which I discuss in more detail in Chapter 2. Many African Americans, especially those participating in what would be known as the Harlem Renaissance, organized politics that were not only based on inclusion and equality within the U.S. nation-state but also diasporic and spoke to the shared experience of blacks across the globe.[50] Within this context of black internationalist politics, the issue of Palestine, now framed as a solidly "Jewish question," took on new importance in African American intellectual thought.

It was within this black internationalist context that the famous pastor of Harlem's Abyssinian Baptist Church, Adam Clayton Powell Sr., traveled to Palestine, a country then under the British mandate. Like other travelers before him, Powell, already a public figure, wrote a travel narrative detailing his trip to Palestine. A two-volume work titled *Palestine and Saints in Caesar's Household*, the narrative is framed as a challenge to the growing trend of anti-Semitism sweeping the European continent. Powell was especially interested in Zionist settlements he saw in Palestine, and his view concerning debates over Zionist claims to Palestine was rather pragmatic; he believed that the British mandatory government had clearly promised the establishment of a Jewish national home in Palestine. At the same time, however, Powell was critical of Western imperial rule in Palestine and believed it had created animosity between Jews and Arabs that had not been in force prior to World War I. This is certainly open to debate; for our purposes, Powell's critique of Western imperialism *through* Zionism is most important and illustrates how countermodernist critique and orientalism could operate in the same text.

The preface to *Palestine* frames the travel narrative in orientalist terms as Powell attempts to dispel for his readers any romantic notions they may have had about the Holy Land.

> Before going to Palestine, he [Powell] thought it was a divine place and totally different from any other spot on earth. He expected to find all men and all things holy. This expectation was exploded almost immediately. Before he had spent a week in the Holy Land, he had met people characterized by all the bad qualities possessed by the worst in New York and in the mountains of Kentucky. That little strip of land between the Jordan and the Mediterranean produced more holy characters and more holy literature than any one of the five continents, but the men and their literature have had more influence for good upon the citizens of Chicago than upon the natives. It is still true that prophets are not without honor save in their own homes.[51]

Yet alongside his orientalist interpretation of Palestinians, Powell develops a critique of Christianity's interpretation of the Holy Land. Powell was unwilling to write a romantic story of the Orient, instead punctuating his travel narrative with references to the anti-Semitism and the regular abuse of African Americans in the United States. "If you want to hear birds of paradise sing in every tree, to see angels peeping from behind every rock and 'the spirits of just men made perfect' riding on every cloud, do not read these five chapters."[52] For Powell, the Orient's significance was in its sacred history as the site of exodus and as a counterexample to occidental modernity.

In addition to dispelling romantic myths about the Holy Land, Powell frames his travel narrative as an intervention into the West's disregard for Jewish victims of European racism.

> The second reason for writing . . . this book is to help stem the world's rising tide of fierce, ungodly anti-Semitism. The author admits that it is a very feeble effort, but it is the first he has seen from a member of his race. On the other hand, he has heard whisperings of indifference to the campaign to exterminate the Jewish race—if not approval of it. The colored people should be the last, even by their silence, to give consent to the brutal persecution of the Jews. For if this campaign of inhuman cruelty against the Jews should succeed, who knows by what the same evil forces would next attempt to put the colored people on the rack.[53]

Palestine thus offers a triangulated narrative in which geography is rendered through the narrative devices of orientalism, diaspora, and Zionism. These discourses allowed Powell to develop authority as orientalist narrator while also locating racism and violence at the center of Western imperialism.

Powell embraced Zionism as both countermodernist and Western at the same time. Powell describes his interaction with "the Zion movement" when he visits Tel Aviv, which by the time of Powell's writing was an all-Jewish colony. Zionist colonies, Powell believed, were more advanced than the rest of Palestine in terms of their technology, cleanliness, and civility. "The Zion movement, one of the most significant in the world today, is made up of Jews in all parts of the world, some of whom are moving back to Palestine to live the remainder of their lives. These settlers, who have met with such bitter antagonism, are more prosperous in the Jaffa section than in any other part of Palestine."[54] He was clear that "the Jews and all civilized people throughout the world" interpret the Balfour declaration as the creation of a Jewish state in the Holy Land. During his visit, Powell witnessed daily violence between settlers and indigenous Palestinians. He interpreted Arab animosity toward Jews only as anti-Semitic, without recognizing how the process of settler colonialism in the region shaped Arab responses to Jewish colonization. "Arab after Arab said to me, 'Before we will let the Jews come back here and rule the Holy Land they desecrated, every one of us will die with our shoes on.' They say this with a look of cruel murder on their faces and the hiss of serpent in their voices."[55]

Yet Powell also understood that prior to the British invasion of Palestine, "the Jews and Arabs lived side by side, in Palestine and other countries, without experiencing any serious trouble."[56] Moreover, Powell noted that "for 450 years under the powerful reign of Arab princes in Spain, the Jews experienced the happiest and most prosperous era of their racial existence."[57] Here Powell suggests that the Orient and the Arab world in general had not created the sort of racial horrors one could claim were central to the Occident.[58] More importantly, Powell's discussion of anti-Semitism might be read as more centrally concerned with a countermodernist reading of Western imperialism than with a fully formed endorsement of the Zionist movement. Zionism converged for Powell with his commitment to illuminating the acts of racial terror underpinning occidental modernity and with his own orientalist relationship to Palestine. *Palestine*'s conclusion firmly establishes Powell's political project of describing Palestine as a means to bring home to America a critique of antiblack racism. "As I stood there [in the Holy Land], I could not help but recall that both Moses and I represented an enslaved, persecuted and despised race. Moses was born a slave; he tramped and traveled and sacrificed for forty years to reach Canaan, but died without attaining the overmastering ambition of his life. I was born in a one-room log cabin in Virginia, twenty-six days after the chains of slavery were broken from the black man's wrist and the white man's conscience."[59] To a black American writer struggling with the daily abuse to black subjects, Zionism seemed an intervention into Western notions of progress and modernity.

Liberia's Palestine

Locating Palestine in a history of black global politics necessitates an analysis not only of how Palestine figures into the history of black politics and travel but also of how Palestine was an important imaginary for black political projects beyond Palestine. For example, thinking about, traveling to, and writing about Palestine were formative experiences for African American intellectuals seeking to better understand and to make a compelling case for Western blacks' emigration to Africa. Indeed the politics of homecoming and return that animated European Jewish politics throughout the early twentieth century were influential among African Americans who viewed their predicament in the West through the lens of exile and colonialism.[60]

Although black emigration from North America to Africa began as early as the eighteenth century with black Canadian emigration to Sierra Leone, the largest emigration movement took place in the early to mid-nineteenth century when black Americans set eyes on Liberia. African Americans looked to African emigration as a means to escape the brutalities of slavery, as well as to form sovereign black nations and new societies. As early as 1792, 1,200 "Black Loyalists" migrated from Canada to Sierra Leone. The Black Loyalists were former U.S. bondmen who had followed the North Star to their freedom in Canada. In 1811 the African American businessman Paul Cuffee initiated a Sierra Leone migration movement using his own ship for transport, yet this movement never fully materialized. Although initial efforts at emigration to Sierra Leone did not expand greatly, black Americans continued to look outside the United States for places to migrate to and build new black societies. They migrated throughout the Caribbean, with Trinidad being most prominent, as well as to Mexico, Ethiopia, and Canada.[61]

African American desires for emigration away from the United States sometimes converged with racist interests within the U.S. to remove blacks from the nation. In 1816, for example, northern businessmen, sympathetic to slaveholding interests in the South, formed the American Colonization Society (ACS), which sought to colonize free northern blacks to Africa in order to make more secure the system of southern slavery. In 1820 the ACS-funded ship *Elizabeth* traveled with eighty black migrants to Sierra Leone. The ship had planned to dock in Liberia but failed to secure requisite permission. One year later, the ACS funded the migration of thirty-three African Americans to Liberia.[62] The ship arrived at Cape Mesurado, which would be named Monrovia after U.S. President James Monroe. Over the course of the nineteenth century, the ACS transported approximately 16,000 African Americans to Liberia. The initial wave of U.S. migrants to Liberia consisted of free northern blacks. Eventually, however, the demographic of migrants shifted south, as some slaves were emancipated on condition of their migration to Liberia.[63]

Representatives from the ACS administered migrant communities in Liberia. Over time, however, as the number of African American migrants grew, Liberia's governance shifted to African American migrants. By 1837 Liberia was formed as a commonwealth, and in 1848 Liberia declared independence and became a state controlled by African American migrants. Although Liberia was, to the ACS, a solution to the "problem" of free blacks in the United States, to many African Americas, especially those who had been enslaved, Liberia was the promised land. Liberia promised black freedom and eventually all of the attributes of self-rule. What had begun as the malicious program of black removal from the United States would become, to African Americans, a movement of return to a homeland, with all of the trappings and nostalgia associated with "home" and "return."

The word, "colonization" figures prominently in the story of Liberia, not only because of the influence of the ACS in the development of black migration to Liberia, but also because the formation of the Liberian state would entail an act of colonialism over indigenous tribes in Africa. Many Western blacks encountered the indigenous African as a heathen in need of Western civilization. Indeed many migrated to Liberia not as bondmen but as missionaries. For example, the Reverend Henry Highland Garnet founded the African Civilization Society in order to bring "civilization" and "Christianity" to Africa. Garnet would eventually migrate to Liberia.[64]

The complex history of Liberia is, like Jewish settlement in Palestine, a story of exodus as well as colonialism, one that blurs the boundaries between liberation and oppression. Black Americans fled persecution and the strongest and most damaging forms of racial subjugation, but their emigration was understood in terms of the modernist and colonial categories of "return" and "home." As the cases of Martin Delany, Edward Wilmot Blyden, and W. E. B. Du Bois will illustrate, while Liberian migration entailed a flight from the West, black migrants took with them parts of the very imperial culture from which they fled, including a powerful geographic imaginary that assumed native African inferiority and Western superiority.[65]

But what does Palestine have to do with Liberia? As North American blacks developed a rationale for Liberian settlement, they regularly relied on comparisons between Jewish return to Palestine and African American return to Africa. These comparisons were productive in that they articulated black settlement of Liberia as a homecoming and as a just solution for modernity's Others. Jewish aspirations for a national homeland, which became rooted in an organized Zionist movement by the late 1890s, was, in short, the model for black emigration projects to Liberia. Martin Delany, Edward Wilmot Blyden, and W. E. B. Du Bois each drew comparisons to Jewish Zionism in order to understand and promote Liberian settlement.

Martin Delany was born in West Virginia in 1812 to an enslaved father and a free mother of Angolan descent. Delany was one of the first African American applicants accepted to Harvard University's medical school. Although his studies there were cut short, he developed a successful medical career. Delany was an active participant in the African Methodist Episcopal Church and in the abolitionist movement that was led by his peers Frederick Douglass and William Lloyd Garrison.[66]

Delany became an early black nationalist whose analysis of the condition of blacks in the United States led him to speak of them as a "nation within a nation" that would always be second class within the United States. Because he viewed blacks as a nation within the U.S. nation, he saw the condition of blacks as similar to that of European Jews, who were similarly positioned as a despised people within a nation. He thus compared U.S. blacks to minority groups throughout history, such as "the Israelites in Egypt, the Gladiators in Rome, and similar classes in Greece; and in the present age, the Gipsies in Italy and Greece, the Cossacs in Russia and Turkey . . . and the Welsh and Irish among the British."[67] Oppressed groups such as these, Delany argued, were inherent to the formation of modern nation-states. Indeed, Delany saw racism as part of the condition of modernity: "There have in all ages, in almost every nation, existed a nation within a nation—a people who although forming a part and parcel of the population, yet were from force or circumstances, known by the peculiar position they occupied . . . forming in fact, by the deprivation of political equality with others, no part, if any, but a restricted part of the body politic of such nations."[68] If, as Delany believed, "nations within nations" were themselves the predicament of modernity, he also believed that oppressed minorities could only become free through forming and obtaining sovereignty over a national homeland. Once again, Delany followed the model of European Jewish history by arguing that Jewish aspirations for a homeland represented the only possible route for black freedom as well. Jews were, Delany wrote, "scattered throughout not only the length and breadth of Europe, but almost the habitable globe, maintaining their national characteristic and looking forward in high hopes of seeing the day when they may return to their former national position of self-government and independence, let that be in whatever part of the habitable world it may."[69]

In his black-produced newspaper, *The Mystery*, Delany advocated the politics of black nationalism, which included creating a black-controlled economy and public sphere and, later, black emigration and resettlement of Africa. The politics of black emigration were complex, bringing together the political interests of black nationalists like Delany, as well as segregationists and slave-owners in the ACS, who sought to encourage free black migration to Africa in order to maintain racial purity in the United States as well as to limit the influence and power of the abolitionist movement.

Delany opposed the activities of the ACS, recognizing that racist motives were at its core. Moreover, he refused to advocate black emigration to Africa only for free blacks (as did the ACS), because he viewed as linked the condition of free blacks and southern bondmen. Indeed, Delany wrote, "the bondsman is disenfranchised. . . . So are we [northern 'free' blacks]. . . . They are ruled and governed without representation, existing as mere nonentities among the citizens, and excrescences on the body politic—a mere dreg in community, and so are we."[70] Delany's political commitments, then, entailed creating a politics of black nationalism that could unite black freemen and slaves across the United States, the people that Delany understood as a nation within a nation. Once the black nation was formed, Delany advocated a return to that nation's homeland, which meant black emigration to Africa. During his lifetime, the politics of black nationalism were central, while black emigration was secondary.

In 1859 Delany traveled to Liberia, where he held meetings with African tribes in order to discuss and negotiate the terms of black American settlement. He met with the eight tribal leaders and claims to have negotiated an agreement to allow U.S. blacks to settle in an undeveloped part of Liberia, although some dispute whether he actually reached an agreement. In 1877 he established the Liberian Joint Stock Steamship Line, which had its first and only voyage a year later, when the ship *Azor*, carrying 207 migrants, sailed from Charleston to Liberia. Delany died before he saw much interest in black American settlement of Liberia, yet he would help pave the way for a growing interest in the politics of diaspora and homeland, a politics that could not help but make comparisons to European Jewish interests in a Jewish homeland.

Delany's forays into black settlement in Liberia drew on a history of Jewish desires to create a Jewish homeland. Yet, during the era of Delany's interests in Liberia, there was not yet an organized political movement for Jewish Zionism in Europe. It should be pointed out that there were Jewish communities throughout the Ottoman Empire that preceded active Zionist settlement, including throughout Palestine. An estimate of population statistics in 1890 indicates there were around 43,000 Jews, 57,000 Christians, and 432,000 Muslims in Ottoman Palestine.[71] Known in Europe as Palestinian Jews, theirs is a history that has largely been forgotten in the modern era, in part because their presence undermines a modernist colonial geography that presumes the categories Arab and Jewish are mutually exclusive.

Arguably, the most sophisticated and articulate expression of early Zionism was articulated not by a European Jew but by an African intellectual form the Americas named Edward Wilmot Blyden. Blyden, like Herzl, had witnessed the Dreyfus affair in France, had grown up among Jews in the Danish colony of St. Thomas, and became one of the founding fathers of the pan-African movement. Although Blyden is frequently appropriated by scholars seeking to prove the historical similarities between African Americans and Jews, Blyden's history is far too complex to be contained in one national narrative or in a bipolar interfaith dialogue.[72] Blyden developed a global imaginary in which Christianity, Judaism, and Islam could each provide narrative grist for pan-Africanism. Ultimately, Blyden developed a liberation geography, but one that ultimately failed as anticolonial because of its investment in modernist constructions of civilization and the modern state.[73]

Blyden's travel narrative *From West Africa to Palestine* (1873), along with his essays "Mohammedism and the Negro Race" (1877) and *The Jewish Question* (1898), conveys the complex alchemy of orientalism, Zionism, and pan-Africanism within which he encountered the Levant. *From West Africa to Palestine*, like Dorr's travel narrative, is orientalist in the ways it establishes a Western authority to gaze at, and rank, the Orient. For example, the travel narrative is filled with geographic descriptions of the Orient's barrenness as well as its exotica. Blyden is "struck with the bareness of the mountains of all forest trees of natural growth" while also struck by the "sublimity of scenery—the overpowering charms of the *tout ensemble* of a summer-evening view from the summits of Lebanon."[74] Geographic observations helped Blyden establish a hierarchy of the Orient's inhabitants, with native Arabs on the bottom and recent settlers, including missionaries at the Syrian Protestant College in Beirut, on top. The Orient was, for Blyden, disorganized and poorly ruled. "There seems to be no law or order to regulate the tumultuous and boisterous crowds which overwhelm the new comer to these Oriental ports."[75]

Because Blyden viewed Arabs as irrational and Ottoman rule as insufficient, he advocated Western imperial administration of Palestine.

> When one is at a distance from Palestine, unless he makes the present condition of the country a subject of careful and special study, it seems but a small matter what political power holds possession of it. But when he visits the land and perceives how, under the misrule of the Turks—a misrule rather of negligence and omission than of elaborate design—everything lies waste and desolate—how the land is infested with thieves and robbers—how some of the most interesting localities cannot be visited without a strong and expensive guard—when he sees sacred places under the surveillance of Turkish solders who have no respect for that which the Christian venerates—he wonders why it is that the land has not passed long ago into the hands of one of the Great Christian Powers. . . . The land is desolate and overthrown by strangers.[76]

For Blyden, Western imperial rule over Palestine was the only means to secure the landscape's Christian sites. In this way, Blyden's orientalism

"Edward Wilmot Blyden, half-length portrait, facing front, holding book" (Anson Rufus Photography; courtesy of Library of Congress)

rests on his assumptions about the beneficent role of occidental imperial administration.

Yet Blyden also sought to challenge how Western cultures had assumed blacks' inability to be fully modern and to govern. Thus he embraced the politics of Zionism and pan-Islamism as alternatives to Western modernity and in order to argue that in the absence of Western racial slavery and racial terror, blacks were fully capable of being modern. *From West Africa to Palestine* begins with Blyden's admission that the orientalist fantasy of "Jerusalem on the Brain" was not his motivation for traveling to Palestine. "I was not proceeding to the Holy Land in obedience to any irresistible impulse—I had not seen a vision or dreamed a dream."[77] Blyden was critical of the Christian pilgrim who traveled to the Orient for some primordial, spiritual urge. Moreover, in searching out the Holy Land, Blyden attempted to render visible the legacy of slavery on Western civilization. While visiting Egypt, for example, Blyden narrates the region as a site of black civilization. "I felt lifted out of the commonplace grandeur of modern times; and, could my voice have reached every African in the world, I would have earnestly addressed him in the language of Hilary Teage—'Retake your fame.'"[78]

Blyden focuses on Egyptian history in order to demonstrate the African origins of Western civilization, as well as to show that Western blacks, as the descendants of Egyptians, are capable of self-government in places like Liberia "Now that the slave-holding of Africans in Protestant countries has come to an end, and the necessity no longer exists for stripping them of the attributes of manhood, it is to be hoped that a large-hearted philosophy and an honest interpretation of the facts of history, sacred and secular, will do them the justice to admit their [black Egyptians] participation in, if not origination of, the great works of ancient civilization."[79] If blacks originated "the great works of ancient civilization," Blyden argued, they were certainly capable of participating in the civilizing authority of colonial administrations.

Concurrent with his embrace of Zionism and pan-Islamism, Blyden's argument for self-rule in Liberia was based on his appropriation of Western discourses of colonialism and orientalism. For example, Blyden's choice of the travel narrative genre through which to articulate his argument for Liberian settlement demonstrates an engagement with Western orientalism and its related arguments about the benefits of Western colonialism in the Levant. Moreover, in the context of his travel narrative, Blyden made comparisons to examples of settler colonialism in North America as a useful analog for African American colonization of Liberia.

> While the American Indians, who were, without doubt, an old and worn-out people, could not survive the introduction of the new phases of life brought among them from Europe, but sunk beneath the unaccustomed aspect which their country assumed under the vigorous hand of the fresh and youthful Anglo-Saxon and Teutonic races, the Guinea Negro, in an entirely new and distant country, has entirely delighted in the change of climate and circumstances, and has prospered, physically, on all that great continent and its islands, from Canada to cape horn.[80]

African Americans, unlike American Indians, had prospered in North America; thus according to Blyden, they were fit to rule. Thus in his choice of genre and in his admiration for settler colonialism in the U.S., Blyden engaged with Western discourses of power.

From 1885 to 1919 the British and French Empires acquired vast areas of Liberia's original 1821 territory. In Zionism, Blyden saw a useful model for black self-determination during a time when Liberian independence was in question. His 1898 essay, *The Jewish Question*, links the Jewish and black diasporas as having "a history almost identical of sorrow and oppression." In Zionism, Blyden saw a movement of suffering people to a national homeland, and given his interest in bringing African Americans to Liberia, Zionism seemed to him a "marvelous movement."

> The question [of Zionism] is similar to that which at this moment agitates thousands of the descendants of Africa in America, anxious to return to the land of their fathers. It has been for many years my privilege and my duty to study the question from the African standpoint. And as the history of the African race—their enslavement, persecution, proscription, and sufferings—closely resembles that of the Jews, I have been led also by a natural process of thought and a fellow feeling to study the great question now uppermost in the minds of thousands, if not millions of Jews.[81]

Although Blyden believed "[all] recognize the claim and right of the Jew to the Holy Land," he did not believe that the Zionist movement required settlement of Palestine. A Jewish national home could be created anywhere where there was available land, including in Africa.

Importantly, he did not support Western imperial intervention on behalf of Jews. "The 'ideals of Zion' can be carried out only by the people of Zion. Imperial races can not do the work of spiritual races." Here we see that Blyden endorses a Zionist cause that can "bring about the practical brotherhood of humanity by establishing, or rather propagating, the international religion in whose cult men of all races, climes, and countries will call upon the Lord under one name." Blyden was not merely a Zionist but also part of a black Atlantic tradition that looked beyond the nation-state in order to find freedom.[82] Therefore, while he saw the nation-state as the most appropriate rubric for black self-rule, Blyden also believed that the Zionist movement need not be rooted in a particular geography; indeed, he advocated African settlement for Jewish Zionists. "If what I have here written should have no other effect than to attract the attention of thinking and enlightened Jews to the great continent of Africa . . . I should feel amply rewarded."[83]

In addition to articulating a geography of liberation rooted in Western discourses like Zionism and orientalism, Blyden embraced epistemologies beyond the West when he advocated that black liberation would be most possible under Islam. Although his writing about Liberia was steeped in racialist understandings of "primitive" Africans, he nevertheless recognized that Arab colonial powers for whom Islam was the main religion created relative equality among their colonized subjects. In his 1877 essay, "Mohammedism and the Negro Race," Blyden challenged the Christian teleology of empire embodied in the Crusades and British and French Empires and wrote to a Methodist audience about Islam as a humanistic faith. Islam was not, for Blyden, as advanced as Christianity, yet it was better than African paganism. Moreover, colonial powers guided by Islam were far less oppressive, at least in Africa, than were those guided by Christianity. "Wherever the Negro is found in Christian lands, his leading trait is not docility as has often been alleged, but servility. He is slow and unprogressive. . . . There is no Christian community of Negroes anywhere which is self reliant and independent."[84]

On the other hand, Blyden viewed Arab colonial powers, and Islam, as less degrading to Africans. "If the Mohammedan Negro had at any time to choose between the Koran and the sword, when he chose the former he was allowed to wield the latter as the equal of any other Moslem; but no amount of allegiance to the Gospel relieved the Christian Negro from the denigration of wearing the chain which he received with it, or rescued him from the political and, in a measure, ecclesiastical proscription which he still undergoes in all the countries of his exile."[85] For Blyden, who learned Arabic but never converted to Islam, Arab Islam was less violent in its administration of colonial rule. Moreover, even for Blyden, the Christian minister, embracing aspects of Islam and Zionism were not contradictory; each facilitated a counterdiscursive maneuver through which he was able to identify and challenge the racial violence and terror that constituted the West while also making a case for Western forms of colonialism in Liberia.

W. E. B. Du Bois and Afro-Zionism

W. E. B. Du Bois's relationship to Zionism and to Liberian colonization is complex and demonstrates how black liberation geographies could be rooted in the imperial cultures from which they emerged. Du Bois was not only a formidable scholar of U.S. domestic race relations, which he so intelligently theorized as the problem of the color line; he was also an anti-imperialist who criticized U.S. intervention in Haiti and identified the roots of World War I in the European scramble for colonial acquisitions in Africa. As Amy Kaplan has argued, in expanding his analysis of the color line globally, Du Bois was able to link domestic history of racial formation to international and imperialist geopolitical moments. Focusing on Du Bois's often overlooked *Darkwater: Voices from within the Veil* (1920), Kaplan argues that the text is "a linguistic form of imperial cartography that uses language to draw overlapping maps of the emerging postwar world. *Darkwater* expands the meaning of 'world war' beyond the battlefields of Europe to encompass and interlink the colonization of Africa and Asia, the struggles of the post-Reconstruction United States, and the overseas propulsion of the U.S. empire."[86] Kaplan's brilliant analysis of Du Bois's "imperial cartography" speaks to the ways that Du Bois made connections between domestic and international concerns and the ways he imagined international collectivities that linked distant geographies united by shared struggles with imperialism.

Du Bois's analysis of the anarchy of empire, particularly in the years before World War II, was rooted in an imperial world in which elite intellectuals, most often males, had authority to speak and to read maps. As such, Du Bois frequently reproduced orientalist and colonialist discourse, particularly in his understanding of Zionism and Liberia. Du Bois fully supported the idea of a Jewish state in Palestine as the appropriate solution to European Jewish exile. At the same time, Du Bois was complicit in the early-twentieth-century Liberian colonization movement, in which he found himself working on behalf of U.S. economic and diplomatic interests in African natural resources and labor.[87] Like Blyden, Du Bois made frequent comparisons between blacks and Jews in order to suggest that both groups sought liberation from Western modernity. At the same time, Du Bois frequently reproduced American orientalism as he described Arabs as primitive and in need of Western tutelage. Although he did not travel to Palestine, he made frequent reference to it in his writing, beginning in the early twentieth century. Du Bois compared the African movement—the migration of Western blacks to Africa—to the Zionist movement. "The Africa movement," Du Bois wrote in 1915, "means to us what the Zionist movement must mean to the Jews."[88]

Du Bois's support for Zionism put him at odds with many of the Jewish intellectuals, activists, and donors who helped organize the National Association for the Advancement of Colored People (NAACP). The most influential donors and contributors to the NAACP, a list that included Louis Marshall, Franz Boas, Melville Herskovitz, and the Spingarns, all opposed Zionism because they were politically committed to the notion of complete Jewish assimilation. For these and many other Jewish intellectuals, Zionism seemed antithetical to the American dream of complete ethnic assimilation.[89] Du Bois's support for Zionism, which went far beyond his Jewish NAACP colleagues' support for Zionism, confounds the argument that black Americans advocated Zionism because of Jewish American support for civil rights. Du Bois demonstrates how, for some black internationalists, Zionism was regarded as a leftist internationalist movement similar to pan-Africanism; Jewish support for black American causes mattered little in this case.

Du Bois's embrace of Zionism echoed his support for Liberian coloni-zation, and in this way, we can see how his politics never escaped the co-lonial world in which he lived and worked. In 1923, U.S. President Calvin Coolidge appointed Du Bois to represent the United States at the inau-guration of Liberian president C. B. King. Du Bois was the U.S. "envoy ex-traordinary," and he publicly supported U.S. stewardship and protection of Liberia. While in Liberia, Du Bois toured the country with executives from Firestone Rubber Company and later gave support to Firestone's invest-ment in Liberian land that had been coveted by Marcus Garvey's Universal Negro Improvement Association (UNIA). Du Bois advocated U.S. corpo-rate investment in Liberia as a countermeasure to British and French im-perial ambitions. He assumed that U.S. investments could be benevolent, provided native Africans benefited materially.[90]

Du Bois supported the pan-Africanist aspirations of black settlers in Af-rica while also seeming to support the imperial aspirations of U.S. corpo-rations in Africa. Similarly, as I will show in Chapter 3, Du Bois embraced Zionism, early in the 1940s, as emancipatory, while ignoring altogether the implications of the Zionist movement on Arab Palestinians. Du Bois's ini-tial embrace of Zionism focused not on the possibilities of a Jewish state in Palestine but on the benefits that would accrue by the formation of global Jewish peoplehood. Zionism, for Du Bois, was a politics of diaspora, just as pan-Africanism was the formation of black peoplehood globally. Zionism and pan-Africanism were both countermodern geographies that reconsti-tuted the world from the vantage point of the West's outcasts. In Chapter 3 I will elaborate on Du Bois's understanding of Zionism, especially in the wake of the 1948 creation of the State of Israel.

Conclusion

As scholars contemplate what Earl Lewis has called "overlapping dis-courses of Diaspora," they will need to attend to the complexities of Pales-tine in the late-nineteenth-century African American global imaginary.[91] A complex alchemy of orientalism, Zionism, and pan-Africanism structured turn-of-the-twentieth-century African American internationalist politics centered in Palestine. There is a relationship between African America and Palestine that is at once orientalist and internationalist. African American travel writers represented Palestine as an exotic destination in need of co-lonial intervention, yet they were also attached to the region as a geogra-phy of liberation. For these writers, Zionism, orientalism, and even pan-Islamism were political imaginaries that responded to African Americans' need to engage global antiblack politics. Within African American travel writing Palestine affirmed blacks' belonging in the West, while also signaling blacks' belongings elsewhere, beyond the West.

For some the Jewish Zionist movement to Palestine was an analog for Liberian colonization efforts. To these intellectuals African settlement and Zionist settlement were each anti-Western movements through which racial minorities could at last obtain freedom and self-government. At the same time, however, the Liberian and Zionist cases both ultimately reproduced the logic of racial modernity from which they were intended to escape.

This chapter has examined how African American geographies of liberation engaged Palestine and the Middle East through the Western optics of American orientalism and European Zionism. The focus of this chapter has been on the political uses of Palestine within the context of a U.S. social and political history in the decades after the Civil War. I have therefore limited my analysis here to the ways that a small group of mostly elite black Western men imagined the Middle East in order to articulate new political communities. In this chapter I've focused on the rise of European Zionism and African American pan-Africanism as the "engines" of this historical narrative. Yet within the Middle East during much of the period of this chapter, dramatic and transformative political and social changes were taking place that were influential in shaping Afro-Arab political imaginaries that were developed elsewhere. In the next chapter I move the analysis to London in the years before and after World War I in order to show how the changing landscapes of European empire and nationalism shaped the contours of Afro-Arab geographies of liberation.

From Subject to Citizen

DUSÉ MOHAMED ALI AND THE AFRO-ORIENT

Herein will be found the views of the coloured man, whether African or
Oriental from the Pillars of Hercules to the Golden Horn, from the Ganges to the
Euphrates, from the Nile to the Potomac, and from the Mississippi to the Amazon
East, West, North, or South, wherever the Oriental or African may found a
congregated habitation from thence shall our information spring.
—Dusé Mohamed Ali

On May 16, 1918, the British Foreign Office considered the complex matter of Dusé Mohamed Ali's petition for a British passport. Ali claimed to be an Egyptian national living in London, and in support of his petition he spoke of his "anomalous position in this country regarding the question of nationality."[1] At the time of the petition, Egypt was a British protectorate, and Ali, who had lived in London for over three decades, believed himself eligible for British travel documents.[2] The British authorities, however, were uncertain of Ali's origins—which some officials believed were in Turkey, others in America, and still others in Egypt—and of how the empire ought to determine the citizenship status for people like Ali who were former members of dissolved empires and current protectorates abroad.

Well before his request for a passport, Ali had raised suspicions for MI5 officials in Britain. At the outset of World War I, Ali had been interviewed by Britain's secret service to determine his allegiance to the Ottoman Empire and Turkey, in particular. In the wake of World War I, Ali was forced to register his identity within the United Kingdom. "Like all other Egyptian residents in England I registered as an Egyptian subject when the order for such registration was issued by the Government."[3]

After World War I, Ali remained in Britain, where he would become a well-known newspaper publisher and supporter of Islamic and pan-Arab causes. In support of his petition for a passport, Ali enlisted the support of a British Foreign Service official, Aubrey Herbert, who had become Ali's acquaintance when the two were members of the Anglo-Ottoman Society, an organization Ali had helped to found that sought to improve trade relations between the British Empire and Turkey. Herbert wrote to the Foreign Office in support of Ali's petition for a British passport: "There is a Negro called Dusé Mohamed. He is by way of being an Ottoman subject, though actually I believe he is American born and does not talk either Turkish or Arabic, but he is, or calls himself Mohammedan. In the past he was quite useful at Moslem meetings, when a number of people used always to try and make anti-Government speeches. I don't think that there is any harm in the man. He is anxious to go to West Africa for trade purposes, and has been refused a [British] passport."[4]

Herbert's brief memorandum of support locates Ali on a vast imperial map linking him to the Ottoman Empire, to the United States, and to West Africa. Moreover, the memo recognizes various forms of juridical and affective belonging, including to the nation ("he is American"), to language ("does not talk either Turkish or Arabic"), and to religion ("he is, or calls himself Mohamedan"). Underscoring his indeterminate status, Ali wrote, "[I am] at present politically suspended between Egypt and Turkey. . . . The unenviable position in which I find myself makes it absolutely impossible to carry on my business, because neither the people with whom I have business relations nor myself are able to determine whether I am an Egyptian, Turk or Briton."[5]

The British Foreign Office ultimately refused Ali's requests for a British passport. In its final decree, the Foreign Office wrote, "Dusé Mohamed was only known to the Anglo-Egyptian Authorities through articles formerly published by him in the British Press. . . . In view of his long absence from Egypt, he cannot be regarded as an Egyptian entitled to British protection abroad."[6] Thus, the Foreign Office denied Ali a British passport because he was not verifiably Egyptian—and certainly not British—at the time of the empire's rule over Egypt.

The court decision underscores how colonial changes in the wake of World War I effaced the complexities of Ali's belongings. Ali's participation in a London-based pan-African newspaper, the *African Times and Orient Review*, became "the British Press." Moreover, it was Ali's *lack of connection* to Egypt that precluded "British protection abroad." The British officials were unable to legibly read Ali as British or Egyptian and therefore attached him to the former Ottoman Empire, then defined by the Turkish nation-state.

While Ali's passport drama was likely repeated by countless others caught in the tides of imperial change marked by world war and the imposition of new imperial configurations, Ali's case nevertheless animates a particularly rich imaginary that underwent transformation in the wake of World War I and the dismantling of the Ottoman Empire. Ali inhabited a world being transformed by new international frameworks of governance, new understandings of race, and pan-African and pan-Arab awakenings. Within a period of two decades, Ali belonged to multiple places as an Egyptian member of the Ottoman Empire, a British subject living in a "foreign protectorate," and then finally as a member of either the Turkish or British nation-state. Dusé Mohamed Ali is important to this study because of the ways he articulated a transnational imaginary that got produced in the ruptures of colonial and nation-state formations during the first three decades of the twentieth century.

In the previous chapter I considered the ways that African Americans based in the United States (and the Caribbean) engaged the Middle East throughout four decades after the Civil War through the optics of American orientalism and European Zionism. I privileged U.S. (and to a lesser extent, European) history as the significant context within which to understand African American engagement with the Middle East. This chapter, however, moves to a different geography and temporality as I consider the contours of Afro-Arab political imaginaries as they were formed outside the United States and in response to social and political events occurring in Europe and the Middle East. African Americans circulate throughout this chapter's narrative, but the key figure here is Dusé Mohamed Ali, who founded the most influential Afro-Arab newspaper of the early twentieth century, the *African Times and Orient Review*, and contributed to the formation of Black Muslim societies in the United States.

How did being governed from the imperial metropolis of Europe and not the Ottoman Empire reconfigure the ways that Arabs encountered the West and African Americans in particular? How did European governance over the Middle East impact the changing relationships of African Americans to imperialism and to orientalism? What sorts of political imaginaries were possible within this changing geopolitical context? In this chapter I locate an Afro-Arab political imaginary that was forged in the context of post–World War I geopolitics, including the dissolution of the Ottoman Empire and the ascendance of liberal internationalism. I argue that the transformation within the Middle East of the Ottoman Empire into European mandate governments and the rise of cultural pluralism as a paradigm of liberal internationalism established the context within which early-twentieth-century Afro-Arab political communities were formed. In this way, I read Afro-Arab political imaginaries in dialectic relationship with hegemonic discourses of race and governance that were articulated in places like the 1912 Universal Races Congress in London and the 1919 Treaty of Versailles, which established the League of Nations' mandatory system.

Although the geopolitical transformations brought by imperial war, the ascendancy of the nation-state, and the transformation of racial formations to cultural pluralism shaped the contours of the Afro-Arab world, its geography and imaginaries were ultimately forged not from above—by the imposition of new colonial borders and frameworks of colonial governance—but perhaps more profoundly by the political imaginaries of the inhabitants within the colonized world who often worked within contexts not of their own making. After describing the ascendancy of discourses of cultural pluralism and liberal internationalism as contexts within which Afro-Arab political imaginaries were formed, I turn to an analysis of Dusé Mohamed Ali's *African Times and Orient Review* and the social movements of pan-Arabism and pan-Africanism that Ali worked within and helped to inspire.

Who Was Dusé Mohamed Ali?

A biography of Ali's Zelig-like life deserves a monograph of its own; for now, however, I am content to present Ali's life as he presented it in his autobiography, *Leaves from an Active Life*, which was serialized in the newspaper *The Comet*, in Lagos, Nigeria, where Ali ended his professional career as an editor.[7] The autobiography begins with a fabulous account of his 1866 birth. Ali writes that the midwife was absent during his delivery, making it impossible for him to obtain any certificate of his Egyptian birth. This fact is important to Ali's autobiography because it allowed Ali to explain how he could be Egyptian without any documentary evidence of his birth. Ali's father was an Egyptian soldier, dedicated to maintaining Egyptian sovereignty amidst European colonialism. Ali's mother was Sudanese (and is never named). Ali claims that his father arranged for him, at age five, to learn English from a Scots missionary woman in Egypt, because his father predicted that Britain would someday rule Egypt and that English language skills would enable Ali to "be of service to my country." He claims that he was later sent to England for boarding school but at age fifteen (in 1882) was sent back to Egypt, where he witnessed the British bombardment of Alexandria. In other published accounts, Ali claims that in 1875 his parents, fearing war in Egypt, sent him to London under the care of a French official named Dusé. During the upheaval of British attacks on Egypt, Ali claims that his mother and sister fled to Sudan, never to be seen again. In 1882, Ali's father was killed in the British bombardment of Egypt. "I found myself, at the age of sixteen, a stranger in my own land and was compelled to return to England where, at least, I had many acquaintances and some few friends."[8] Hence Ali had reason for not knowing his parents and, for that matter, for not knowing Egypt.[9]

From 1883 to 1921 Ali lived in London, where he began a successful career as an actor and, eventually, a journalist, a businessman, and a political agitator. Having narrated himself into Britain, Ali describes a fantastic life of global travel and radical possibilities. According to Ali, he abandoned formal education (despite claiming in some places to have earned a degree from King's College) in order to find a job. His first employment was as an actor in the Royal Princess Theater on Oxford Street, London, in the Roman drama *Claudian*. Because he was a stage success, he was invited to tour the United States with this production. In the United States, he was hired by Major Pond, "the great lecture agent," to tour America as "The Young Egyptian Wonder Reciter of Shakespeare." After his stint in the U.S., Ali claims, he toured the United Kingdom, playing "dark parts" or being cast as "Nubian slave" in numerous productions.[10]

In the 1890s, according to the autobiography, Ali traveled the world in search of adventure and job opportunities. He was invited to publish a newspaper in Bombay, India, but not liking the climate in Bombay, he says he traveled to Hong Kong for one month. Next he returned to the United Kingdom, only to eventually find himself aboard a steamer headed toward the West Indies and South America a few months later. This itinerary is difficult to verify; what is known is that he lived for a brief time in Florida— after allegedly returning from South America. Ali very briefly edited a local newspaper in Osceola, Florida.

From 1909 to 1911, Ali worked in London for the Fabian newspaper the *New Age*, edited by the socialist A. R. Orage.[11] Orage encouraged Ali to publish in the newspaper and to assume a public role in support of Egyptian sovereignty and against British imperialism. In 1911, with Orage's mentorship, Ali published an anti-imperialist monograph, *In the Land of the Pharaohs* (which was largely plagiarized from similar works by Theodore Rothstein, Wilfred Sacwan Blunt, and the Earl of Cromer).[12] Despite his predilection for borrowing from other scholars, Ali's book won him some notoriety from the British public as a defender of Egyptian nationalism.[13]

If working at the *New Age* politicized Ali, it was the 1912 Universal Races Congress that radicalized him. Ali claims to have performed the third act of *Othello* for the conference attendees and to have been given a copy of

W. E. B. Du Bois's *Souls of Black Folk*. Ali disliked Du Bois, most likely because they disagreed intellectually about the direction of pan-African politics and because Du Bois gave only tepid support to Ali's newspaper. Moreover, in the debate between Booker T. Washington and Du Bois, Ali clearly sided with Washington's "bootstrap" approach to racial advancement. Hence Ali remembers that he was "not impressed" by Du Bois's *Souls of Black Folk*.

> The book is beautifully written but throughout there was a wail about the ostracism to which the author had been subjected by his white school-mates, particularly the women, after his graduation. Booker T. Washington realized that his people were neglecting the realities of life by an obsession for mere academic advantage which was of scant service to them in a super-materialistic country where the Dollar is the prime consideration. He did not deride education, as Tuskegee Institute amply demonstrates. That institution, where academics run par passu with manual labor, will remain an enduring monument to Booker T. Washington's vision when the ephemeral academic and social efforts of Bughardt Dubois [*sic*] will have been forgotten. America is already over-run by Afro-American academic idlers, down-at-the-heel preachers and an abundance of unemployed lawyers.[14]

Despite his criticism of Du Bois, Ali found the Universal Races Congress enlightening; it was precisely the sort of transnational gathering that made his own complex history intelligible. The conference would be the model for Ali's forging of an Afro-Arab political imaginary. Yet the congress reverberated in many contexts; it could inspire Ali's political imagination, but it also helped enshrine a new international order—governed by liberal internationalism—through which mostly Anglo-American interests could mediate global conflict in ways that benefited Anglo-American interests.

Universal Races

Gustav Spiller and Felix Adler, both of whom were active in the Humanist movement, convened the Universal Races Congress in London July 26–29, 1911. According to the papers of the Congress, the gathering was intended to address "the problem of contact of European with other developed types of civilization. . . . The object of the congress will be to discuss in the light of science and the modern conscience, the general relations subsisting between the peoples of the West and those of the East, between so-called coloured peoples, with a view to encouraging between them a fuller understanding, the most friendly feelings, and a heartier cooperation."[15] The congress was organized to address ethical, and not political, questions. It developed arguments against scientific racism and race purity in favor of a new field of understanding called comparative race relations.[16]

Many U.S. intellectuals and activists were included in the congress, including Jane Addams, the organizer of Hull House in Chicago; the noted anthropologist Franz Boas; and the southern historian Ulrich B. Philips. The African American sociologist W. E. B. Du Bois was appointed to lead the U.S. delegation. The conference was intended to promote understanding among global nations and races and to establish an international vision of intergroup relations. It was held at a critical time in the history of racial formations, as the field of race studies was dominated by anthropologic arguments about polygenesis. Gobineau's racial science, which classified human races into distinct species and types, was still dominant.[17] Yet by the first decade of the twentieth century, new anthropological studies committed to cultural pluralism and monogenesis were ascendant.

The Universal Races Congress was among the first international conferences aimed at defining cultural pluralism, which argued that racial difference was produced through environmental factors and that the core of the human species was essentially similar. Racial differences were therefore to be understood in terms of cultural and environmental differences rather than inherent, biological traits. In preparation for the conference, Gustav Spiller asked participants to prepare presentations that responded to a lengthy list of questions about the nature of racial difference and the origins of international and intergroup conflict. Among the questions asked were those that gestured toward the rise of cultural pluralism.

1. (a) To what extent is it legitimate to argue from differences in physical characteristics to differences in mental characteristics?
2. (ii) To what extent does the status of a race at any particular moment of time offer an index to its innate or inherited capacities?
3. (a) How would you combat the irreconcilable contentions prevalent among all the more important races of mankind that *their* customs, *their* civilisation, and *their* race, are superior to those of other races?
4. (a) What part do differences in economic, hygienic, moral and educational standards play in estranging races which come in contact with each other?[18]

The anthropologist Franz Boas presented what was at the time perhaps the most important intervention in the study of racial difference. In his lecture "The Instability of Human Types," Boas argued that there was nothing

inherent or biological to racial inferiority; instead, he argued, racial difference, or what he called the "plasticity of human types," could be explained
by environmental and geographical influences, and not any inherent ge-
netic or biological conditions. "I believe . . . that the mental make-up of
a certain type of man may be considerably influenced by his social and
geographical environment. . . . The old idea of absolute stability of human
types must, however, evidently be given up, and with it the belief of the
hereditary superiority of certain types over others."[19]

Boas's lecture set the stage for other presenters to offer detailed socio-
logical evidence of the local and material conditions that shaped global
"cultures." Among the most rigorous of these presentations was W. E. B.
Du Bois's "The Negro Race in the United States of America," in which Du
Bois illustrated that contexts shape black inequality in the United States.[20]
Gesturing toward the sweeping social history he would publish in *Black Reconstruction in America*, Du Bois detailed the history of the slave trade, its
economic impact on the United States, and the implications for black slaves.
He also described the abolitionist movement and the democratic potential
he found in the self-emancipation of the slaves. Next he discussed the betrayal of black freedom. The largest section of Du Bois's address contained
painstakingly detailed data on rates of black inequality in the early twentieth century. These data were used in order to recast the "Negro problem"
not as a problem of black inferiority but, instead, as a problem of economic
inequality and social injustice. In his conclusion, having laid bare the history of racial brutality and injustice in the United States, Du Bois returned to
the "Negro problem" and revised its normative usage. "Whether at last the
Negro will gain full recognition as a man, or be utterly crushed by prejudice
and superior numbers, is the present Negro problem of America."[21]

The conference leaned toward an elite and Eurocentric orientation
and represented knowledge produced entirely within the West. Although
there were representative speakers from the Ottoman Empire, these were
often the most westernized voices. For example, the lead delegate for the
Turkish/Ottoman region of the globe was the president of Syrian Protestant College (soon to become the American University of Beirut), Howard
Bliss. The elite caste of intellectuals at the congress conformed to Du Bois's
talented-tenth philosophy.[22] Du Bois was therefore enthusiastic about the
potential of the congress, which he called the "greatest event of the twentieth century so far." He wrote in the *Crisis*,

It was more significant than the Russian-Japanese war, the Hague Conference or the rise of Socialism. . . . [It was] great because it marked the

first time in the history of mankind when a world congress dared openly and explicitly to take its stand on the platform of human equality—the essential divinity of man. For the first time in history the representatives of a majority of all nations of the earth met on a frankly equal footing to discuss their relations to each other, and the ways and means of breaking down the absurd and deadly differences that make men hate and despise each other.[23]

In addition to his presentation, Du Bois wrote and recited "A Hymn to the Peoples" before the Congress.

> O Truce of God!
> And primal meeting of the Sons of Man,
> Foreshadowing the union of the World!
> From all the ends of earth we come!
> Old Night, the elder sister of the Day,
> Mother of Dawn in the golden East,
> Meets in the misty twilight with her brood,
> Pale and black, tawny, red and brown,
> The mighty human rainbow of the world,
> Spanning its wilderness of storm.
> . . . .
> Save us, World-Spirit, from our lesser selves!
> Grant us that war and hatred cease,
> Reveal our souls in every race and hue!
> Help us, O Human God, in this Thy Truce
> To make Humanity divine![24]

Despite Du Bois's celebration of the congress's importance, his assessment was overblown and may say more about Du Bois's Progressive Era "talented-tenth" philosophy of racial uplift. The congress had limits as a framework for radical politics, as I will argue, because of its investment in the nation-state as the basis of belonging and recognition.[25] At the same time, however, there is little doubt that for Dusé Mohamed Ali, the congress inspired something very different from what members of the conference had intended.

The *African Times and Orient Review*

Although the Universal Races Congress, and the liberal internationalism it helped create, was, for most of its attendees, a tribute to cultural pluralism and the humanistic values of international brotherhood, the conference had unintended reverberations beyond the meeting hall. Although he was absent from the official program of the Universal Races Congress, Dusé Mohamed Ali was present nevertheless; he helped organize the conference, and he provided entertainment to official conference attendees with his performance of the third act of *Othello*. To Ali, the congress represented the possibilities of a new political imaginary that could unite the interests and dreams of Arabs contending with the imperial powers of Ottomans and Europeans and of black diasporans, who were dealing in ways similar to those of the Arabs with the contingencies of imperialism and colonialism. Indeed, Ali, in ways similar to Edward Wilmot Blyden in the late nineteenth century, linked the politics of pan-Africanism and pan-Arabism through the political imaginary he helped foster. In the following section I discuss the formation of an Afro-Arab political imaginary through Dusé Mohamed Ali's newspaper the *African Times and Orient Review* and Ali's political organizations. Ali's political imaginary was shaped by a combination of social and political movements, including Arab nationalism, pan-Africanism, and pan-Islamism.

In addition to the Universal Races Congress, Ali had been politicized at the turn of the century in London via his political engagement with pan-Islamic and Arab nationalist organizations. For example, Ali collaborated with the Egyptian nationalist Mohamed Farid Bey, who was an influential follower of Mustafa Kamil, the leader of Egyptian nationalism.[26] Bey, along with Ali, organized a variety of anti-imperialist meetings in London that attracted, according to Ali, a global left that would become the audience for his newspaper. Ali described attending a lecture by Bey in front of an Afro-Arab audience he would hope to engage in his press.

> It was a curious motley crowd, and typical of the problem which their nationality presents. Turks, Arabs, men of Sudanese blood, and men who have inherited unchanged the feature that we see on the walls of the temple and tomb at Karnark and Luxor—every cast and hue of countenance from Levantine to Negro. Indeed, the only common symbol of unity was the fez, which nearly all wore. It was indeed a varied crowd, and proved the popularity of the man [Bey], for this "motley crowd" included all shades of Egyptian religious thought[;] in addition to Muslims both Jews and Copts were present.[27]

In addition to his work with Egyptian nationalists like Bey, Ali had been politically active in London's Islamic society and, according to Kambiz GhaneaBassiri, associated with the mission of Ahmadiyya Muslims in

Cover of *African Times and Orient Review*

Britain, which was led by Khwajah Kamel-ud-Din. Ali and Kamel-ud-Din frequented the Central Islamic Society, and Kamel-ud-Din would contribute two essays to Ali's newspaper.[28] His work with the Ahmadiyya would play a significant role in his political work in the United States in the 1920s, when he became an intermediary between Marcus Garvey's UNIA movement and a growing U.S.-based Black Muslim movement.

Despite his contemporaries' suggestion that Ali knew little about Islam, was not a practicing Muslim, and didn't speak Arabic, Ali nevertheless founded Islamic organizations in London. For example, he founded London's Universal Islamic Society, and in November 1912 he cofounded, with British orientalist Dr. W. MacGregor Reid, Persian intellectual Syed Abdul Majid, and the Anglo-orientalist Charles Rosher, the Oriental, Occidental, and African Society, which sought to integrate Islam into a liberal internationalist vision of cooperation.

Ali's participation in the Universal Races Congress as well as his activism in Islamic societies and Arab nationalist politics inspired him to see the need for an "Afro-Oriental" newspaper that could articulate the internationalist and Afro-Arab political imaginary in which he was engaged. Inspired by the global dimensions of racial politics in the United Kingdom and the possibilities of Afro-Arab solidarity they inspired, in 1912 Ali began publishing the *African Times and Orient Review* (*ATOR*). According to the first edition of newspaper, "The recent Universal Races Congress, convened in the Metropolis of the Anglo-Saxon world, clearly demonstrated that there was ample need for a Pan-Oriental Pan African journal at the seat of the British Empire which would lay the aims, desires, and intentions of the Black, Brown and Yellow races—within and without the empire—at the throne of Caesar."[29]

In addition to providing the intellectual inspiration for his newspaper, the Universal Races Congress also provided Ali with the resources—human and material—he would need to undertake producing a globally distributed newspaper. *ATOR* received financial backing during its first year from J. Eldred Taylor, a Sierra Leonean businessman Ali had met at the Universal Races Congress. Ali used the attendance list from the congress to distribute the newspaper. John Edward Bruce (Arthur Schomburg's colleague) as well as J. E. K. Agrey and Richard B. Moore distributed *ATOR* in the United States.[30] As a result of his work with *ATOR*, Ali was elected corresponding member of the Negro Society for Historical Research, which was founded in 1911 by John Bruce and Arthur Schomburg.[31]

During its first year of publication, the newspaper was primarily focused on British and West African affairs. However, after the first year of publication, Taylor's financial support fell through, and Ali turned to new donors to help support the paper. With new financial backing, *ATOR* became much more internationalist and focused its news coverage on questions of anti-imperialism across the Arab world, East Asia, Europe, and the United States. Ali sought to map an internationalist order different from that of the Universal Races Congress. If the congress sought to establish universal norms in order to reach liberal harmony, *ATOR* was interested in creating an international field from the perspective of what Vijay Prashad has called the "darker nations."[32] Ali's internationalism thus drew comparisons between global regions suffering similar forms of colonialism and racism, and in doing so, he would begin to outline the contours of what would become a "third world left."[33]

During a sporadic ten-year publication history, the newspaper's London office became a hub of pan-African activism. For example, Marcus Garvey joined the *ATOR* staff and published his first article, "The British West Indies in the Mirror of Civilization: History Making by Colonial Negroes," which told the history of the slave trade to Jamaica.[34] While in London, Garvey relied on Ali's assistance to gain access to the British Museum, where Garvey sought to read Edward Wilmot Blyden's manuscript collection. Ali wrote to the museum on Garvey's behalf, "I bid to recommend Mr. Marcus Garvey as being a fit and proper person to use the reading room of the British Museum."[35] *ATOR* brought Ali into contact with a global network of activists, including W. E. B. Du Bois, Booker T. Washington, Garvey, C. L. R. James, and others.[36]

The first issue of the newspaper illustrated the global dimensions of Ali's vision; it featured news about Moroccan culture (while Morocco was partially a French protectorate), a Negro conference at Tuskegee, and colonial conditions in the Hawaiian Islands. In linking these sites of colonialism, Ali sought to identify and to unite into a singular imaginary the wisdom of decolonial thinkers across the globe. "Herein," Ali wrote in the newspaper, "will be found the views of the coloured man, whether African or Oriental from the Pillars of Hercules to the Golden Horn, from the Ganges to the Euphrates, from the Nile to the Potomac, and from the Mississippi to the Amazon East, West, North, or South, wherever the Oriental or African may found a congregated habitation from thence shall our information spring."[37]

In an effort to fill the pages of the first issue, as well as to advertise itself, *ATOR* presented a symposium in which it printed responses to a survey about the desirability of a pan-African, pan-Oriental newspaper. Respondents ranged from British businessmen and newspaper publishers to East

Indian and American intellectuals who had attended the Universal Races Congress. By presenting supportive (as well as unsupportive) comments about the paper, Ali was able to shape reader reception to the paper as well as to locate its politics within extant intellectual and social movements. W. E. B. Du Bois responded to Ali's request for feedback to *ATOR* by offering tepid support: "I think it would be a good thing if a review like yours could be supported in London, but I do not see how it could possibly pay."[38] Ali responded that Du Bois's letter was "disappointing and pointless." H. G. Wells indicated that he "would support [*ATOR*] highly." Gustav Spiller, the co-organizer of the Universal Races Congress, wrote, "I believe there is a growing body of opinion in the Empire, especially in England, in favour of friendly relations between those of lighter and darker hue, and a magazine such as you propose to publish would thus meet an increasing want." Booker T. Washington cautioned against publishing stories critical of white people, as doing so would not achieve racial equality. Instead, he advocated "a paper that devotes itself to emphasizing and promoting the common fundamental interests of the white people and coloured, which advocates measures which will win the sympathy of the wisest and best people in both races."[39] Support for *ATOR* also came from intellectuals beyond the Anglo-American world, including Tengo Jabavu of South Africa, M. Siri Nanissara Therea of Ceylon, Sir Krispina G. Gupta of India, and Tongo Takebe of Japan.

Ali argued that the newspaper, which began before World War I, was needed as a response to growing European and U.S. imperialism: "Europe stretches forth her arms on every side to squeeze the darker races to her own advantage, because she knows the people of Africa and the people of Asia to be divided. Her aim has ever been to promote division. It therefore behoves [*sic*] you, men of Asia, and you, men of Africa, to join yourselves in one common bond of lasting brotherhood."[40] Ali hoped to forge bonds of brotherhood by revealing the global reach of imperialism and racism and by suggesting alternative political communities through which to combat global powers. As a means to create a "common bond of lasting brotherhood," Ali needed to compare global sites of imperialism in order to foster a reading public engaged in shared struggles of anti-imperialism. Ali helped create this sort of readership by focusing on global sites of colonial violence and then by posing pan-Islamism as one model of global anti-imperialist community.

In order to form an anti-imperialist and international reading public, Ali's newspaper focused on global sites of imperialism, including those within the United States. For example, the paper featured regular stories on questions of U.S. dependencies within the nation—indigenous peoples—as well as in places like Puerto Rico and the Philippines. In November 1912, *ATOR* republished a report written by Henry S. Haskins, the secretary of the Lake Mohonk Conference, in order to demonstrate to readers the international dimensions of U.S. settler colonialism. In presenting large portions of Haskins's imperialist rant concerning "backward races" and the fanaticism of "Muhammadans," *ATOR* brought the United States into the fold of its analysis of imperial and racist states. In doing so, the paper likely encouraged American readers to begin to see the United States as part of a global history of imperialism and racism, and therefore to see global anti-imperialist struggles as their own.

The Lake Mohonk Conference on International Arbitration was the precursor to the International Court of Arbitration at The Hague, Netherlands, and was founded in 1895 in order to arbitrate international conflict. In 1912 the conference considered the question of "tutelage" for the Filipino Islands under American guidance. Although the League of Nations mandate system was not yet developed, Haskins's report revealed the racist discourse of U.S. overseas expansion as well as the participation of the United States in imperial projects. *ATOR*'s readers encountered Haskins's worry that the U.S. occupation of Moro Province would bring the U.S. into conflict with "Muhammadan fanatics." According to Haskins, there was a "special problem" in the case of U.S. engagement with the Philippines: "A problem within a problem is Moro Province. This southern Philippine province contains over a quarter of a million fighting Muhammadan fanatics. The Spaniard fought them for centuries without conquering them. . . . The question is—if we should give independence to the Philippines, what about Moro Province?" In presenting Haskins's concern for the "special problem" of Muslim independence, *ATOR* was able to illustrate that anti-Islamic sentiment extended beyond European empires to the United States.

Haskins's article also exposed *ATOR* readers to the U.S. position on the "problem" of "Porto [*sic*] Rico." Like the Philippines, Puerto Rico sought independence from the United States, but in this case, the U.S. sought incorporation of the dependency into the nation in some capacity. Yet, Haskins wrote, "if Porto Rico is to become a State of the Union it must be Americanised." Underlying Haskins's writing on the Philippines and Puerto Rico was his understanding that the U.S. had successfully incorporated its first dependent people, Native Americans. "Progress" in incorporating the native North American population, "has been made. The general principles upon which efforts for the uplift of this backward race should be based have been determined. The aim is not the incorporation of the Indian into the body of American citizens." In closing, Haskins extolled the virtues of "first world" tutelage of "backward" peoples: "This is the age of wonderful growth among backward races."[41]

Typical of *ATOR*'s attention to British imperialism was Sundara Raja's 1913 article about British-controlled India. In August 1913 Raja published "The Real Situation in India," in which he attempted to dispel racist British media representations of Indians as unfit for self-rule and an impoverished race. British rule in India had been justified by biological arguments about Indian fitness for self-government. In the wake of movements like the Universal Races Congress, however, biological racist arguments were being challenged. Raja argued that Indians were "emaciated, unconcerned, impoverished, poverty-stricken" due to their subjugation, and not due to anything related to their customs and culture. Moreover, he argued that the "civilized" British and their imperialist policies should be blamed for Indian dependency: "It is curious that at a time when millions of human beings are struggling vainly to liberate themselves from the horrible and atrocious customs which have stemmed the tide of progress for generations, a body of civilized men, on whose whim and caprice depends the fate of these myraids [*sic*] of men and women, should endeavor to dissuade them, by active and passive methods, from awakening."[42]

In addition to focusing on global examples of imperialism and anti-imperialist struggles, *ATOR* attempted to create an international political imaginary. Ali sought to translate the cultural pluralism of the Universal Races Congress into an anti-imperialist politics guided by pan-Islamism. Typical of this attempt was an article in *ATOR* written by Tajuddin Peer, ex-Naib Tesildar of Punjab, titled, "Muslim Unity." Peer articulated an alternative vision for universality, rooted in a sense of pan-Islamism and not race. "We [Muslims] allow no distinction of colour and creed, and we place no restrictions and obligations on the unity of our world-wide brotherhood. Our religion is the only true 'leveller' in the real sense of the word; and we are free from the benedictions and blessings of priesthood."[43] Peer argued that a pan-Islamic movement should take root in London, as it was "geographically and politically, the center of the world."[44]

Existing sporadically for ten years, *ATOR* never realized its full potential. Funding was difficult to secure, and creating a global distribution network proved difficult for Ali, who was long on vision but short on business skills and tact. Moreover, British imperial policies limiting foreign distribution of journalistic publications further impeded the progress of the newspaper.

From Empire to Nation

Although he attempted to illuminate the global order from the perspective of the "darker nations," Ali formed political organizations that fostered cultural understanding and dialogue rather than advocate for radical social change. In this way, *ATOR* engaged anti-imperialist politics within the organizing logic of cultural pluralism that had been developed in places like the Universal Races Congress. Publishing during the last decade of the Ottoman Empire, *ATOR* existed during a moment when cultural pluralism was expanded into a theory of international relations; Ali witnesses in his newspaper the ascendance of liberal internationalism.

The Universal Races Congress fostered a global and transnational politics rooted in a conception of race as culture and, ultimately, as nation. Cultural pluralism understood race as a product of culture, defined as national type. Thus the political implications of cultural pluralism were that groups would gain political recognition within an international order on the basis of belonging to a culture-as-nation. Minority groups within nations would gain recognition through their attachment to a national homeland. This framework posed political problems for national minorities like Christian Arabs and European Jews, who were not necessarily defined by their connection to a distant national homeland but were minoritized within their national homeland (European nations or new Arab states). We can best understand the evolution of cultural pluralism into liberal internationalism by examining the post–World War I creation of nations and mandate governments out of defeated empires in the Levant.

At the turn of the twentieth century the ascendancy of European nationalism began to impact the multiethnic and multiconfessional world of the Ottoman Empire, a world that had shaped Ali's early political consciousness. In the first two decades of the twentieth century the Ottoman Empire's political and territorial influences were in rapid decline and were fully defeated by 1922. European colonial powers imposed the nation-state and its rubric of governance on former Ottoman territory. This transformation was profound, carving up Ottoman territory into new geopolitical entities that created new social subjects—citizens, foreigners, foreign protectorates—where there had previously only been subjects of imperial authority. Indeed, in the Levant, the imposition of the nation transformed non-Muslim Ottomans into national minorities and, in doing so, altered the terms of recognition and rights.[45]

In 1919 the League of Nations enshrined into international law the term "national minority."[46] The category of the minority radically transformed the nature of intergroup relations in former Ottoman territories. Under the Ottoman system, non-Muslim groups were tolerated—while also unequal to Muslims—under a system of Islamic rule. The transformation to "national minority," however, reset the terms of recognition under the sovereign state; within the nation-state national minorities gained recognition by virtue not of their membership in a vast and diverse empire but by virtue of their confessional background or ethnicity/race. Indeed, the ascendancy of the nation-state as the sovereign rubric within which international recognition could be attained meant that in order to claim minority rights, groups needed to highlight their linguistic and cultural differences from majority cultures. Thus it became more difficult for them to ever live with the people from whom they were minoritized.[47]

Although a full discussion of the implications of the transition from imperial subject to national citizen is beyond the scope of this chapter, it is important to note how the ascendance of the nation-state within former imperial territories profoundly transformed belonging. As Saba Mahmood has written,

> The establishment of the nation-state as the dominant political form [within former Ottoman territories] put into play a new rationale of governance that divided up the governed differently from the logic of empires; instead of recognizing parallel and contiguous communities distinct by virtue of their confessional, denominational, or tribal/ethnic affiliation, the nation-state sought to represent "the people," united by a shared history, culture, and territory, wherein each individual qua citizen was tied to the state through a legal system of rights and obligations.[48]

The legal codification of the "national minority" contained an inherent contradiction, however, in that the category itself recognized that the national project of creating a unified "people" was always incomplete; there would always be a group (or groups) of people who would be excluded from "the people" by virtue of their racial/ethnic/religious particularity. Moreover, the terms by which the national minority could be recognized within the nation-state were through appeals to ethnic/religious/linguistic particularity. As Mahmood demonstrates, throughout the former Ottoman territories, under the international conventions of the nation-state, religious minorities were required to emphasize their differences from majority Arab Islamic communities (at least in the Levant), over their much longer history of conviviality.

The League of Nations and Liberal Internationalism

The cultural pluralist logic of the Universal Races Congress established one of the contexts within which the international community engaged questions of international relations. While I do not claim that the Universal Races Congress was solely responsible for shaping the future of international governance, the congress's international articulation of cultural pluralism was one among many contributions to emerging understandings of liberal internationalism. The politics of cultural pluralism were made manifest in the intergovernmental organization formed at the January 15, 1919, Paris Peace Treaty that ended World War I, a war in which 10 million people perished. The League of Nations was established to create an international framework to maintain world peace, prevent war via disarmament and arbitration, and guarantee minimal global labor and health standards. During its peak, the league had fifty-three members. Because the league lacked its own military, it was dependent on the Great Powers and therefore often reproduced an international order favorable to imperial powers.[49]

The creation of the League of Nations was important to U.S. President Woodrow Wilson's Fourteen Points for Peace, in which Wilson's fourteenth point outlined the need for an international body that could mediate global conflict.[50] Yet the United States never joined the League of Nations due to Republican Party opposition to Article 10 of the league's charter, which required the participation of member states in threats to the national sovereignty of any league member. Republican senators believed that Article 10 would require the United States to be dragged into international disputes that had nothing to do with U.S. interests or sovereignty.

A key feature of the League of Nations was its articulation of a mandate form of governance for territories formally ruled by imperials powers, such as the non-Turkish Ottoman territories and the former African territories of Germany. Operating against the internationalist spirit of the league, the most powerful European powers, Britain and France, pushed forward a mandate system that benefited their own imperial ambitions.[51]

Article 22 of the Covenant of the League of Nations, drawing on the logic and language of cultural pluralism articulated at the 1911 Universal Races Congress, discussed when and how it was appropriate for certain nations to "assist" and help manage the affairs of peoples residing within areas of the former Ottoman Empire "which are inhabited by peoples not yet able to stand by themselves under the strenuous conditions of the modern world." According to the international conventions approved by the 1919 League of Nations convention, "The best method of giving practical effect to this principle is that the tutelage of such peoples should be entrusted to advanced nations who by reason of their resources, their experience or their geographical position can best undertake this responsibility, and who are willing to accept it, and that this tutelage should be exercised by them as Mandatories on behalf of the League."[52]

The League of Nations mandate system developed into international relations the logic of cultural pluralism, in that it grouped nations as "peoples" or races in a spectrum of development. Where the racial politics of the Universal Races Congress assumed fundamental equality among races, once environmental conditions could be improved, so, too, did the League of Nations embody the presumption that certain classes of people could be educated to equality through exposure to, and the rule of, more advanced people. The emphasis in the league system on the presumption that tutelage would emancipate ignored the obviously colonialist and racist presumption that certain peoples *needed* training form more *advanced* peoples.

The league's mandate system, as well as the Universal Races Congress, developed a geography of advanced peoples and races and those who were in the developmental stages. Yet maps can be read in many ways; for those looking at the mandate system from the outside, or from the perspective of the "developing" races, the League of Nations drew a new map of the third world. The articulated politics of "third world-ism" was not yet developed in the 1910s and 1920s; yet the geographies of third world-ism were being drawn in the politics of Afro-Oriental solidarity that emerged in the wake of the Universal Races Congress and the League of Nations.[53]

The colonial history of the Middle East in the first three decades of the twentieth century is well documented.[54] It is a history that involves European orientalist assumptions about the capacity (or lack of it) for Arab self-rule as well as private concessions and promises to European Zionists, who saw in European colonial rule over the Arab world an opportunity to establish a Jewish state in Palestine. What remains hidden in this story, however, are the ways that colonial change redrew the boundaries of Afro-Arab encounters and produced new Afro-Arab political imaginaries. In the next section I address these questions by exploring the worlds of pan-Arabism and pan-Africanism within the context of global imperial changes. Ultimately these social movements, as well as geopolitical understandings of race, shaped the Afro-Arab world that Ali sought to forge and document.

The Contingencies of Pan-Arabism

In response to European imperialism, Arab members of the declining Ottoman Empire (now allied with Germany) initiated a social movement for pan-Arab nationalism, a movement that was not unlike the growing pan-Africanist movements in the Anglophone and Francophone worlds, which I will describe momentarily.[55] During the early decades of the twentieth century, Arabs rebelled against imperial rule as well as colonial occupation. The Arab revolt of 1916–18 sought to unify Arab lands from Syria to Yemen, and its leaders took up arms against Ottoman Turks. The leaders of the Arab revolt received material support from the British and French Empires, which viewed the revolt as a useful challenge to Ottoman powers during World War I. The famed Briton T. E. Lawrence—known popularly as Lawrence of Arabia—supported the Arab revolt. In a series of correspondence between the United Kingdom and the leaders of the Arab revolt between 1915 and 1916, known as the McMahon-Hussein Correspondence, the United Kingdom entered an alliance with the Arab revolt, with the understanding that the UK would recognize Arab independence. Lawrence wrote to officials in the UK that the McMahon agreement to recognize Arab independence in exchange for the Arab revolt against the Ottomans would be "beneficial to us, because it marches with our immediate aims, the break up of the Islamic 'bloc' and the defeat and disruption of the Ottoman Empire, and because *the states [Sharif Hussein] would set up to succeed the Turks would be . . . harmless to ourselves. . . .* The Arabs are even less stable than the Turks. *If properly handled they would remain in a state of political mosaic, a tissue of small jealous principalities incapable of cohesion.*"[56]

Following the presumed agreement with the British, Arab leaders began their rebellion in June 1916, when 70,000 Arab infantry attacked Ottoman forces. The revolt led to the capture of Aqaba (now in Jordan) and the severing of the Hejaz railway that led through the Arab peninsula and was one among many Ottoman innovations. The Arab revolt enabled General Edmund Allenby to enter, and eventually capture, the Ottoman territories of Palestine and Syria. Despite promises to support Arab independence in exchange for the Arab allegiance in the war with the Ottomans, however, the British signed an agreement with the French, the Sykes-Picot agreement, just three years after the McMahon-Hussein Correspondence, to establish

European colonial mandatory governments over Arab lands. The Sykes-Picot agreement would be codified in the internationalist language of the League of Nations.[57]

In 1920, just one year after the imposition of the British mandate in Iraq, Iraqis initiated a second Arab revolt. The rebellion united Sunni and Shia Iraqis in opposition to the British. The revolt was quickly crushed, however, and approximately 9,000 Iraqis and 500 British soldiers were killed.[58] In Syria, under a French mandate, an Arab rebellion took place between 1925 and 1927. The rebellion united Arab religious factions, including Druze, Christians, and Sunnis, across Lebanon and Syria and fostered early, and somewhat cosmopolitan, iterations of Syrian nationalism.[59]

To Jewish Zionists, British colonial rule over Palestine made possible increased immigration to Palestine, as the region was now controlled by the British military. In 1917, three years before the British mandate, the United Kingdom's foreign secretary, Arthur James Balfour, promised the leading British Zionist, Baron Rothschild, that the UK would create a Jewish state in Palestine. In what has become known as the Balfour declaration, Balfour wrote, "His Majesty's government view with favour the establishment in Palestine of a national home for the Jewish people, and will use their best endeavours to facilitate the achievement of this object, it being clearly understood that nothing shall be done which may prejudice the civil and religious rights of existing non-Jewish communities in Palestine, or the rights and political status enjoyed by Jews in any other country."[60] Palestinians—Muslim and Christian—opposed the Balfour declaration, seeing it as a move toward colonialism. In 1918 a group of Palestinian dignitaries responded to the Balfour declaration in a letter to the mandatory government: "We always sympathized profoundly with the persecuted Jews and their misfortunes in other countries . . . but there is wide difference between such sympathy and the acceptance of such a nation . . . ruling over us and disposing of our affairs."[61] As the region came under European hegemony, Palestine entered a European orbit of influence and interest, much to the detriment of Palestinian Muslims and Christians. According to the 1937 census collected by the British mandatory administration, from 1922 to 1937 the Jewish population increased precipitously (from 83,790 to 386,084), while the non-Jewish population during this same period increased only minimally (from 668,258 to 997,236).[62] These figures suggest that British control over mandatory Palestine enabled migration to Palestine for Jewish Zionists who were likely inspired by British promises, in the Balfour declaration, to create a Jewish state in Palestine as well as the protection British soldiers provided.

Lost in the transition from Ottoman Empire to British and French mandates were the political desires of pan-Arabism and its call for an indigenous Arab nationalism. Instead, Arabs were legally and culturally interpolated into mandatory governments that brought with them new configurations of identity and belonging. Moreover, the particularities of national belonging began to overshadow the political imaginaries of pan-Arabism as the new international order recognized the rights of national minorities, rather than the diasporic belongings that had been recognized under older political regimes. And yet pan-Arab politics and its geographic imaginaries were not fully surpassed and would emerge throughout the twentieth century as well as intersect at times with pan-African politics.

We can begin to understand, in the context of pan-Arabism, some of the complexities of Dusé Mohamed Ali's belongings as he approached the British government for citizenship papers. Within the span of thirty years Ali saw his world dramatically transform as he moved from Ottoman subject to Egyptian national to British protectorate to Turkish citizen. Yet throughout this change, Ali witnessed—and sometimes participated in—pan-Arabist calls for Arab sovereignty and anti-imperialism. Moreover, Ali would similarly be called to anti-imperialism within the context of his engagement with pan-Africanism.

The Contingencies of Pan-Africanism

Although the decline of the Ottoman Empire had its greatest impact on the peoples of the empire, it also shaped the contours of imperial subjects across the globe. The end of World War I is not merely a story of the replacement of empires with nation-states; it is also the story of the expansion of British and French imperialism. Black internationalist politics within the West were therefore shaped directly and indirectly by the watershed changes wrought by the declining Ottoman Empire, leading to the imperial war. New internationalist and diasporic movements emerged as early as 1900 in places like London and Paris, where colonial metropoles became administrative—and sometimes actual—homes to foreign "subjects."[63] The metropoles of the imperial world fostered imperial public spheres; they became crossroads of goods and people from global imperial outposts and nurtured diasporic and international consciousness and solidarities. Indeed, a brief overview of the diverse array of pan-African politics during the first three decades of the twentieth century illustrates how an internationalist black consciousness—along lines similar to those causing transformations within the Arab world—emerged as a consequence of imperial change.

The colonial world of the twentieth century made European imperial metropoles spaces of pan-Africanist and diasporic black politics. There was no singular pan-African movement but, instead, multiple movements that took place over two centuries. My goal here is to briefly sketch how imperial transformations during the first three decades of the twentieth century shaped pan-African politics and to gesture toward the ways that pan-Africanism intersected with pan-Arabism. Pan-Africanism is a belief that African people constitute a diaspora that shares a common past and destiny. In the United States, pan-Africanism could describe how African religious traditions were incorporated into U.S. Christian traditions. Indeed the formation of "African" churches in the United States constituted a pan-Africanist project. In 1892 there could be found Ethiopian churches in the U.S. South, and in 1893 the U.S. hosted in Chicago a "conference on Africa," which included presentations by Henry McNeal Turner, Alexander Crummel, and the Egyptian Yakub Pasha. Yet a sustained social movement called pan-Africanism would develop in the early years of the twentieth century in the imperial public spheres of Europe.

In 1897 in London, Henry Sylvester Williams formed an African Association, which convened the first pan-African congress during July 23–25, 1900. Williams's association was soon renamed the Pan-African Association and produced a monthly magazine titled *Pan-African*. The formation of a magazine helped forge an internationalist consciousness, or an "imagined community," to use Benedict Anderson's term, that helped produce a black diasporic readership. The Pan-African Association fostered an emphasis on black history and pan-Africanist archives. In the United States, the Pan-African Association would inspire John Bruce and Arthur Schomburg to form the Negro Society for Historical Research, an association that included Dusé Mohamed Ali as a member.

Pan-African politics in London attracted black members of the British Empire to the city, where they would participate in the active publishing world of the pan-Africanist movement. In 1911–12 4,540 Africans lived in the United Kingdom.[64] In 1912 the Jamaican Marcus Garvey traveled to London, where he would work for two years in the offices of Dusé Mohamed Ali's *African Times and Orient Review*. Garvey returned to Jamaica in 1914 and established the Universal Negro Association and African Communities League. Garvey's initial attempt at building a "Negro Association" were mostly unsuccessful until, in 1917, the East St. Louis riots led Garvey to reform his association into the United Negro Improvement Association. The

UNIA emphasized black nationalism and black-owned businesses, including a shipping company that could transport African Americans to Africa. Garvey's pan-Africanism included the desire to "strengthen the imperialism of independent African States" while also "civilizing the backward tribes of Africa." Garvey's UNIA, like the pan-African movement, emphasized print culture, and the press, as a means to forge a diasporic imaginary. Garvey's organ was the *Negro World*, a publication to which Garvey's first mentor, Dusé Mohamed Ali, would contribute.[65]

By the mid-1920s, literary and cultural movements in the United States, such as the Harlem Renaissance and other variations of pan-Africanism, flourished.[66] In 1927 the pan-African congress was held in New York City. At this meeting, Cyril Briggs, the leader of the African Blood Brotherhood, called for a resolution supporting Egyptian, Chinese, and Indian liberation, suggesting the global dimension of pan-Africanist politics. The African Blood Brotherhood, as I will discuss in the next chapter, advocated the Communist Party's Black Belt thesis, which conceived of black Americans as a colony within the United States.[67]

France's vast imperial holdings across the black world in Africa and the Caribbean made Paris a nexus of black anti-imperial and decolonial politics. In the 1930s, French-speaking black graduate students in Africa and the Caribbean began to contest French imperialism by affirming a black nationalist aesthetic rooted in pride in African heritage. The Afro-French anti-imperialist movement drew inspiration from pan-African congresses held in previous decades that emphasized the importance of African self-determination and race pride.[68]

The leading intellectuals of what became the négritude movement were the Martinicans Jane and Paulette Nardal and the much-better-known men of the movement, Aimé Césaire, Léopold Sédar Senghor, and Léon-Gohntran Damas. The Nardal sisters were instrumental in linking a global Francophone anti-imperial movement to the growing political work of the Harlem Renaissance writers who had fled to France. Langston Hughes, James Weldon Johnson, Richard Wright, and Claude McKay would all participate in the négritude movement while living in France. By 1934 Senghor, Césaire, and Damas had developed a newspaper, *L'Étudiant Noir* (*The Black Student*), that articulated the political imaginary of what Jane Nardal would call Internationalisme Noir (Black Internationalism).[69]

By the time that Ali published the last issue of *ATOR* in 1921, the world had changed in profound ways. New internationalist pan-African and pan-Arab movements confronted new geopolitical realities in the forms of European mandate governments and increasing European Zionist settlement in Palestine. For Ali, London was no longer a hub of pan-African and pan-Arab politics; instead he believed the future of his Afro-Arab political imaginary lay in the United States with Marcus Garvey's UNIA and a growing Black Muslim movement.

The American Dusé Mohamed Ali

In 1921, after ten years of work on *ATOR*, Ali traveled to the United States, where he reunited with Marcus Garvey. Ali became a regular contributor to the UNIA's newspaper, the *Negro World*, and served as the head of the newspaper's Africa section. While working with the UNIA Ali drew on his experiences in Britain and was asked to organize a United Kingdom tour for UNIA officials. Ali's success in the organization led him to be appointed the UNIA foreign secretary, and in this capacity Ali drafted the UNIA's 1922 petition to the League of Nations requesting that German colonies in Africa be given to the UNIA in order to create a black nation-state. According to Garvey biographer Robert Hill, some UNIA members saw Ali as a potential successor to Garvey. By 1924, however, Ali appears to have left the Garvey movement as he turned his attention to rebuilding a Muslim international.[70]

After working with the UNIA, Ali moved to Detroit, Michigan, at the invitation of a group of Indian Muslims. Ali writes that he had traveled to Detroit because "I was requested to organize a Muslim Society which would be the means of establishing a prayer room with a regular system of weekly prayers which had been sadly neglected."[71] According to Ghanea-Bassiri, the Indian Muslim who had invited Ali was likely the Ahmadiyya missionary Muhammad Sadiq, who served as imam of the Highland Park mosque.[72]

GhaneaBassiri suggests that Ali may have been an intermediary between Garvey's movement and the Ahmadiyya movement. According to this argument, Ali's commitment to pan-Islamism provided a meaningful analog to Garvey's black nationalism. Muhammad Sadiq made this connection explicit when he argued that "the spread of El Islam cannot help but benefit the UNIA.... With millions of Moslems in India, China, Arabia, Persia, Afghanistan, Turkey, Negroes would find valuable allies."[73] Sadiq's advocacy of a Muslim international that would serve an Afro-Arab political imaginary would eventually be taken up by the Nation of Islam; Dusé Mohamed Ali's future, however, would not be in a Muslim international but in Lagos, Nigeria, where he was invited to publish a newspaper in which he turned his attention back to the United States.

Curiously, Ali's autobiography almost completely ignores his years as a Garveyite. Moreover, he describes his activities in Detroit as mostly apolitical and seems to suggest that his goals were to improve Americans' perceptions of "orientals" as well as to advance his stage career.

> Owing to frequent discussion on Oriental subjects emanating from our social activities, I conceived the idea of founding an American Asiatic Association which would call into being more amicable relations and a better understanding between America and the Orient in general than had previously obtained.... By way of introducing the Association to Detroit, I gathered a company of local dramatic and musical talent and produced two short Oriental costume a [sic] plays of my own interspersed with selected musical numbers form compositions by Lisa Lehmann and Woodford Finden, adequately costumed within an Oriental setting designed by myself and executed by the scenic artists at the local theater.[74]

After living in the United States and working on behalf of the UNIA, Ali moved to Lagos in 1931, primarily to work in the cocoa business. Yet he would make his mark in Nigeria by becoming the editor of the Lagos *Comet*. In addition to editing the newspaper, Ali contributed short fiction and a novel, titled *Ere Roosevelt Came: A Record of the Adventures of the Man in the Cloak*.[75] Having built a career as one of the foremost intellectuals of the Afro-Arab world, in one of his final acts Ali wrote a novel set in the United States about an impending international race war. In his most "American" moment, Ali's novel is an allegory of U.S. domestic race relations and the contingencies of World War I. By the 1930s, Ali seems to have abandoned his desire for pan-Islamism and instead was interested in global antiracism. Yet, curiously, he focused his attention on the struggle of black Americans to represent the United States, while the novel parodies black nationalists and intellectuals like Marcus Garvey and W. E. B. Du Bois. In this way, while Ali's novel demonstrates a global analysis of racial imperialism, it ultimately embraces a sort of U.S. exceptionalism by posing African American airmen as the saviors of his racial drama.

The novel was published in the Lagos *Comet* between February 24 and October 13, 1934. Despite the title's reference to President Theodore Roosevelt, whom Ali had scorned in his book *In the Land of the Pharaohs*, in *Ere Roosevelt Came* Ali invoked the president in name only. In *Ere Roosevelt*, Roosevelt is "the man in the cloak," or Emperor Blood, the supreme leader of a white supremacist organization modeled on the Ku Klux Kan. The central drama of the novel involves Emperor Blood's attempt to mobilize a global race war—against the Afro-Asian world—on behalf of the "Nordic empire." In defense of African American interests opposed to Emperor Blood are two thinly veiled allegories of Marcus Garvey and W. E. B. Du Bois. Napoleon Bonaparte Hatbry, Garvey's allegory, leads a Negro association dedicated to developing black-owned businesses, including a black line of aircraft that can be used to train black airmen for impending global war against the Nordic empire. Hatbry's approach to the Nordic empire is posed in opposition to that of Dr. De Wine (a thinly veiled reference to Du Bois), who is a moderate integrationist beholden to the wishes of the black bourgeoisie.

Ultimately world war breaks out between the Nordic empire, black nationalists—here conceived as their own nation—Russia, and Japan. The white supremacists form an allegiance with the Russians and Japanese—despite their reticence about the "yellow" peril in the United States. The black airmen defend the United States against the un-American Emperor Blood and his Russian and Japanese allies. Ultimately it is the Negro airmen trained by Hatbry who are most cunning and successful; they stage a sneak attack on Russian forces in Siberia launched from their Alaskan air base.

The Negro airmen are embraced as ideal citizens in the United States, and they contribute to the victory of the Republican candidate for president, who promises to guarantee full black inclusion in the nation. In the end, the white supremacists are roundly criticized, and their arguments for white supremacy are fully undermined not least because their self-declared "racial purity" is revealed as a lie. Throughout the novel, Ali creates a subtext of miscegenation, interracial rape, and passing. By the end of the novel we learn that Emperor Blood is the father of a disgraced mixed-race member of the Nordic empire who had been passing. The presence of Emperor Blood's mixed-race child and the revelation that he had raped the child's mother before eventually murdering her undermine the emperor's avowed racial purity and expose the Nordic empire's misguided theories of racial superiority.[76]

Ali's American turn in *Ere Roosevelt* focused on the possibilities of black nationalists in the United States creating a new world in which they represented not only the dreams of national inclusion but also the fate of the black world against imperial Nordic empires. Yet the black nationalists in Ali's novel have a less internationalist view of global racial politics than that offered in *ATOR*. Instead, Ali's protagonists struggle globally, but ultimately in the name of the United States and in order to gain full inclusion. Perhaps this shift—from the anti-imperialist, pan-Islamist Ali to the civil rights Ali—illustrates something about the hardening of nationalism throughout the post–World War I era.

Conclusion

Dusé Mohamed Ali lived with a complex set of belongings. At the turn of the century, he was an Ottoman subject living in the United Kingdom. By 1915, four years after he founded *ATOR*, Ali had become identified as a member of a British foreign protectorate. In 1922, while Ali was in the United States working on behalf of the Garvey movement, he became identified with a sovereign Egyptian state. Ali died in Nigeria in 1945. His complex attachments contributed to his understanding of Afro-Arab political imaginaries and a geography of liberation.

Ali sought to draw global comparisons between the plight of Afro-Arab peoples contending with Anglo-American imperialism. *ATOR* therefore focused on a geography of anti-imperialism that linked the struggles of black Americans and Arab nationalists. This linkage was made possible because of the overlapping histories of pan-Arabism and pan-Africanism Ali encountered throughout his lifetime.

Like all geographies of liberation, however, Ali's mapping of the Afro-Arab world was located in a particular culture and standpoint. Ali never developed a revolutionary political theory within which to understand imperialism; he never embraced a Communist approach to the problem of imperialism, nor did he embrace the radical poles of pan-Africanist and pan-Arab social movements. Instead, Ali viewed the Afro-Arab world through the optics of liberal internationalism that had been enshrined in places like the Universal Races Congress and, later, in the League of Nations. This lens showed geopolitical inequality as something that could be mediated via greater cross-cultural understanding and not structural transformations. Thus, while Ali focused on a different sort of universal brotherhood than that envisioned by the Universal Races Congress, he nevertheless reproduced the congress's logic of cultural pluralism—but among the Afro-Arab world. Despite his limits, however, Ali did contribute to the making of an Afro-Arab political imaginary that would become fully realized, and less imaginary, during the 1940s and in another geography.

In 1936–39, the "Great Arab revolt" began in mandatory Palestine, this time against British mandatory powers and their Zionist supporters. Over 10 percent of the Palestinian Arab male population between the ages of twenty and sixty was killed during this rebellion.[77] The revolt was ultimately unsuccessful and exacted a harsh toll in terms of loss of property, land, livelihoods, and life. Yet the revolt in Palestine is credited with creating early Palestinian nationalism and with forcing the British, at least momentarily, to reconsider their support for Jewish emigration to Palestine.

In 1939, Malcolm MacDonald, the British colonial secretary, issued a policy paper advocating the abandonment of the partition of Palestine and the formation of a binational state, controlled by Palestinian Arabs and Jews, based on census figures in 1939. Moreover, the policy paper recommended limiting Jewish migration to Palestine for four years, after which time the Arab majority would decide on immigration quotas. Restrictions would also be placed on Jewish purchase of Arab lands, which was a key strategy of the European Zionist movement. The House of Commons approved the so-called white paper on May 23, 1939. Arab and Jewish political leaders opposed the white paper—the Arabs because it threatened their political sovereignty and the Jews because it limited their vision for a Jewish state. Ultimately, Zionist militancy, illegal immigration, and terrorist raids on Palestinian villages, coupled with the rise of Nazi racism and fascism in Europe, led to the abandonment of the white paper.[78]

The possibilities of radical Afro-Arab politics during the first half of the twentieth century did not lie in the United States or in Europe, but in the Arab world. Throughout the 1940s, the politics of binationalism, which echoed the call of the 1939 white paper, shaped radical Palestinian Arab and Palestinian Jewish political activism. In the next chapter I shift geographic focus again and move the analysis to Palestine in the 1940s, where the Communist-inspired politics of binationalism converged with European Jewish antinationalism and African American Popular Front Communism.

CHAPTER THREE

Black Marxism and Binationalism

*A home that my neighbour does not recognize and respect
is not a home.—Hannah Arendt*

In his 1929 essay, "Marxism and the Negro Question," the African American intellectual Ralph Bunche argued that black inequality in the United States could only be addressed through the development of a broad interracial class movement that could establish a "dictatorship of the proletariat." The term "dictatorship of the proletariat" came directly from Karl Marx, who saw working-class control of the means of production, followed by control of the state, as an integral stage to working-class liberation and eventual classlessness.[1] Bunche drew on Marx in order to envision a radical class consciousness in which working-class whites and blacks would confront a system of racial capitalism, a concept Bunche, along with many other black radicals, employed in order to demonstrate how capitalism benefited from the division of labor along lines of racial difference.[2] Racial capitalism was, for Bunche, a global phenomenon that defined an imperial order that oppressed blacks in Africa and the United States.[3]

Bunche's global analysis of power led him to view black American inequality in the United States as the result of similar forces at work in colonial Africa. Hence he argued that African Americans were a caste that resembled similar castes produced under conditions of colonialism: "The organization of Negro society bears, in certain important aspects, a significant resemblance to the organization of society in a colony or a subject nation."[4] Throughout the 1930s, Bunche embraced the Communist Party's approach to the so-called Negro question that advocated interracial class consciousness to overcome the hegemony of the black and white bourgeoisie, although he never joined the party.[5] "The submergence of national and racial differences within the proletariat in the firm ties of class solidarity is an indispensable requisite for the triumph of the revolutionary struggle against capitalism. . . . In the Communist movement, in which all inner-class distinctions vanish, any open or disguised manifestations of race prejudice, which come as a result of the pressure of bourgeois ideology of the class, must be deliberately and consciously eliminated."[6] In making a case for a class-based revolution opposed to imperialism and racial capitalism, Bunche rejected black nationalist politics like Marcus Garvey's that were rooted in racialism. Combating racial capitalism meant imagining a future in which class and not blackness formed the bonds of solidarity. "It is clear," Bunche wrote,

> that the racial, that is, caste, emancipation of the Negro cannot come as the result of any "purely racial" movement of [sic] any movement deliberately aiming to subordinate, in the name of an unreal racial unity the masses of the Negro people to the narrow interests of the Negro bourgeoisie (who work hand in glove with their white paymasters), of any movement conscientiously striving to divorce the liberation struggle of the Negro people from the chief social movement of our time, the class war of labor against capital.[7]

In "Marxism and the Negro Question" Bunche offered a more radical critique of global imperialism than the one offered by Dusé Mohamed Ali in the *African Times and Orient Review*. The world that constituted *ATOR* was very different from the world that formed Bunche's life in the 1930s. The 1917 Russian revolution happened toward the end of *ATOR*'s run, while the rise of black Communist politics in the United States was a significant component of Bunche's milieu. For Ali, pan-Islamic politics led him to early Arab nationalist and anticolonial politics, while for Bunche the politics of American Communism were formative. Although the Communist Party's approach to the Negro question would change over time, in the 1930s, the Comintern's approach to organizing was the most internationalist and anti-imperialists it would ever be.[8] If, for Dusé Mohamed Ali, the Afro-Arab world could be united under the banner of pan-Islamism, for Ralph Bunche, at least in the early years of his public career, the Afro-Arab world could be united under the banner of black Marxism and anti-imperialism. Bunche would articulate this view in his approach to the Negro question in the United States, in his understanding of racial capitalism and colonialism in his doctoral work, and in his initial approach to the question of Palestine, when, as an employee of the United Nations, he initially advanced the idea of a binational union of Jewish and Arab labor interests in Palestine as an alternative to partition.

Bunche's political imaginary was also shaped by his participation in global organizations confronting massive geopolitical change. By the middle of the 1930s it had become clear that existing governmental frameworks to establish international peace and conflict resolution were inadequate, as the League of Nations was incapable of halting Germany's persecution of Jewish minorities. One of the many consequences of the Holocaust was the illustration of the limitations of the ability of the League of Nations to protect national minorities and the need for a different sort of international community that could mediate, as well as police, the global sphere.

At the same time, World War II brought an era of new nationalisms and decolonization across Africa and the Middle East. This was an era that saw the United Nations partition of former British colonies in India and Palestine, thereby creating new national entities in Pakistan and Israel. Moreover, African states emerged as newly sovereign with the defeat of colonial powers in World War II. Within former European colonies, national liberation and postcolonialism established new imaginaries.[9]

Throughout the 1930s and 1940s, Bunche's political analysis of the Negro question, of colonialism, and of the question of Palestine rested on his attempt to imagine political community beyond nationalism, regardless of whether nationalism meant black nationalism or, as in the case of the Zionist movement, new national homelands. During a political moment when much of the world was focused on national liberation and on establishing new homelands for national minorities, a range of Afro-Arab intellectuals and activists, as well as European Jewish activists, embraced a politics of binationalism (or antinationalism) as a potent counterdiscourse to the international logic of nationalism. Binationalism describes the attempt to create a political system capable of unifying two national peoples in one land. The politics of binationalism, as it emerged most prominently with regard to the question of Palestine, was a politics of conviviality that recognized the multinational possibilities of the land of Palestine.[10] Advocates of binationalism offered many different models for addressing questions of sovereignty and Jewish immigration; as I will show, these political models indicated that a "Jewish homeland" could mean something other than a Jewish state, and it could exist within an Arab-majority society within Palestine.

In this chapter I focus on Ralph Bunche's political involvement in three interrelated ethical questions during the era of World War II: the Negro question, the Jewish question, and the question of Palestine. In the process of discussing Bunche's engagement with these questions, I illuminate the making not so much of a singular Afro-Arab political imaginary as a series of Afro-Arab conjunctural and contingent moments that were produced in the crucible of the pre–World War II era and were being transformed by modern nationalist movements and the reordering of the imperial world. It would be a mistake to argue that Bunche's 1930s analysis of racial capitalism and his Communist-focused call for a dictatorship of the proletariat inspired his plans for binationalism in Palestine. This argument both ignores Bunche's own disavowal of black Communism and casts binationalism in too radical a light. Binationalism was a leftist position only for some; to Palestinians, however, it was a colonialist politics only slightly better than the colonial plan advanced by the Zionist movement. What I endeavor to show in this chapter are the global conjunctures that shaped the politics of binationalism, of which Bunche's changing political views, Palestinian Communists, and Jewish antinationalists were a part. Bunche developed an analysis of binationalism through his interactions with antinationalist Jewish intellectuals as well as with Communist organizers in Palestine. In order to trace the geographies of the Afro-Arab world from the 1930s to the outset of the Cold War, I focus here on Bunche's participation in international debate concerning the partition of Palestine.

From Black Marxism to Binationalism

To those who only know Ralph Bunche as the peacemaker who successfully mediated four armistice agreements during the 1947–48 Arab-Israeli war, or who know him as the first person of color ever to win the Nobel Peace Prize (1950), Bunche's 1930s writing may seem out of place. Bunche is, of course, regularly memorialized as the negotiator of the United Nations partition of Palestine and the mediator during the Arab-Israeli war. The Public Broadcasting Service lionized Bunche's life narrative in a miniseries subtitled *An American Odyssey*.[11] How did Ralph Bunche, who in the 1930s analyzed the Negro question in terms of racial capitalism and colonialism, become recognized by the 1950s as the champion of the ability of the nation-state (U.S. and Israeli) to address problems of racial minorities?

Bunche grew up in a working-class family and was not politically active until he began working at Howard University in 1928. Before working at Howard, Bunche studied political science at Harvard, where he was interested in the system of mandates established by the League of Nations. Bunche took an interest in whether European mandates were beneficial to developing nations, as the league's system of mandates presumed, or whether they merely reproduced the norms of colonialism. Bunche's 1934 dissertation, which won the Toppan Prize for the year's best dissertation in the field of government, was a comparative analysis of the French mandate over Togo and colonial Dahomey. Bunche compared colonial Dahomey to mandatory Togo in order to measure the efficacy of the League of Nations' mandate system and argued that there was little distinction between the mandatory system of the league and normative colonialism. In areas of education and the destruction of indigenous culture, colonial Togoland and mandatory Dahomey were similar. Bunche concluded that only an appropriate decolonial approach, one in which developed countries might offer tutelage to developing nations for a designated period of time, was useful. The dissertation criticized the implementation of the mandate system, yet it also supported the logic of liberal internationalism in that it advocated Western tutelage as an appropriate development policy. Thus Bunche would be at the forefront of international efforts to articulate the proper role for what has become known as the first in the third world. For Bunche, uneven global development was not due to the primitivism of developing nations; rather, it was due to the developing nations' inadequate exposure to Western englightenment.[12]

> It is important that the mandate principle assure to these territories an unselfish, helpful administration, which will offer them an opportunity to properly prepare themselves for the eventual day when they will stand alone in the world. The African is no longer to be considered a Barbarian, nor even a child, but only an adult retarded in terms of Western civilization. This Western civilization now surrounds him in his daily life, and he consumes it greedily. Assured of strong and helpful government under a sound mandate system and a liberal colonial policy, he will be assured a balanced diet and be spared the pains of social indigestion.[13]

After completing his dissertation, Bunche took a position at Howard University, where he became radicalized through his regular political discussions with colleagues that included Abram Harris, Sterling Brown, E. Franklin Frazier, Charles Thompson, Alain Locke, Charles Wesley, and Ernest Just. While at Howard, Bunche wrote *A World View of Race*, in which he argued that future class conflict would surpass racial conflict in global affairs.[14] Bunche's analysis was based on his belief that racism was a symptom of capitalism. Hence the way forward for blacks as well as whites was via labor organizing and, later, antifascism, since Bunche embraced Lenin's position that imperialism was the highest stage of capitalist development.[15] In his 1936 address to the Twenty-Seventh Annual Conference of the NAACP, titled "Fascism and Minority Groups," Bunche told his audience, "Fascism is the last desperate effort of capitalism to preserve itself at all costs, and to do so, therefore, it must destroy labor groups, labor organizations, all the rights that labor has won for itself over a long period of years of struggle—that alone gives sufficient reason for the Negro . . . to bend all his energies to fight against this monster."[16]

In 1935, while at Howard, Bunche joined John P. Davis and A. Philip Randolph, among others, in forming the National Negro Congress (NNC). The NNC was a New Deal era project of the Communist Party intended to unite the white and black working classes in the fight for racial justice. Bunche never joined the Communist Party, although he clearly participated in organizations formed by the party. After the NNC's 1936 inaugural meeting in Chicago, at which Randolph was elected president, Bunche declared that the NNC was the "first sincere effort to bring together on an equal plain Negro leaders, professional white collar workers with the Negro manual workers and their leaders and organizers."[17] The NNC emphasized interracial cooperation, working-class unity, and mass struggle.[18]

Because he embraced the Communist Party's approach to the Negro problem, if not the party itself, Bunche was critical of African American leaders who approached the question of black freedom through black nationalism or even nation-based civil rights. Black nationalism was, for Bunche, a reproduction of racial nationalism that failed to address the capitalist roots of racial inequality. The mainstream struggle for civil rights, on the other hand, seemed overly focused on assimilating to the norms of the capitalist state rather than undermining them. In his 1935 essay, "Critical Analysis of Tactics and Programs of Minority Groups," Bunche identified two forms of "minority" responses to conditions of inequality: violent and nonviolent. The violent approach to inequality included armed rebellion and global anti-imperialist solidarity. The nonviolent approach, according to Bunche, consisted of "Zionism and Garveyism, involving migration to new and foreign soil, economic resistance, conciliation via interracial organizations, and demands of political inclusion." Bunche rejected Garveyism, which he claimed was "an essentially reactionary philosophy based on an inverted form of the 'white supremacy' gospel of the white charlatanism."[19]

Given that Bunche would become an integral figure in international deliberations concerning the fate of Palestine, it is interesting that he linked the Garvey movement to Zionism and labeled both as impractical. According to Bunche, "For the American Negro the Garvey program may be characterized as the black counterpart of the Zionist movement." Like Zionism, argued Bunche, Garveyism offered followers an "emotional escape" from oppression and, like Zionism, was impractical, "for attractive land for such ventures was no longer available, due to the consuming greed and the inexorable demands of imperialist nations."[20] While serving on the United Nations Special Committee on Palestine, Bunche would hear similar positions articulated by Palestinian Communists who argued that Zionism was a form of European colonialism.

In 1937 Bunche enrolled in a seminar on comparative cultures led by the famed anthropologist Bronislaw Malinowski at the London School of Economics. There Bunche interacted with an international cohort of black intellectuals and pan-Africanists such as Jomo Kenyatta, Paul Robeson, and George Padmore, whom Bunche had taught at Howard. Bunche disagreed with pan-Africanism on the grounds that he believed African liberation could only derive from class struggle within imperialist nations. He preferred the approach of the NNC because it forged a path of interracial class solidarity and revolution rather than the more conciliatory—for Bunche—politics of civil rights within the framework of the liberal state.

Yet in 1940 Bunche and Randolph broke ranks with the NNC over that group's affiliation with Communism and the radical labor union, the Congress of Industrial Organizations. The 1939 Hitler-Stalin Pact dealt a death blow to the NNC, and by the 1940s, Bunche's politics had shifted away from the work of black Communism, although he maintained the belief in interracial class solidarity as the best model of advancement of African Americans for "subject" people. During World War II Bunche's scholarship on trusteeships and colonialism, and his status as a prominent African American intellectual engaged in international affairs, made him an attractive candidate to the U.S. State Department. Bunche was successful in convincing the U.S. government that his support for Popular Front causes was not un-American and would not undermine the mission of the U.S. State Department.[21] He eventually took a job in the Office of Strategic Services as a senior social analyst on colonial affairs. He joined the U.S. State Department in 1943 and in 1945 participated in meetings that led to the formation of the United Nations.

Among the Popular Front radicals of the 1930s, it is important to note, Ralph Bunche was a relatively minor figure. We should not, therefore, overemphasize his role in what is known as the Popular Front or in black Communist politics. By the 1940s Bunche clearly embraced the norms of liberal internationalism as he increasingly saw the League of Nations trusteeship program as a beneficent, if limited, program for African decolonization. Furthermore, by 1946, as he entered the workings of the United Nations, the "black Marxist" Bunche would be hard to locate, as he had by this time disavowed black Communism and joined the ranks of liberal nationalists in the UN. Nevertheless, as we will see, his stance on binationalism echoed his 1930s approach to the question of racial uplift in the United States.

Mandates, Trusteeships, and Partitions

Bunche entered the field of international relations at the precise historical moment that liberal internationalism, from the League of Nations to the United Nations framework, was undergoing transformation. Recognizing the limitations of the League of Nations and its failure to prevent World War II, the Allied powers in the war convened a series of international meetings in order to develop a new international body that could maintain international peace and resolve international conflict. In 1944 at Dumbarton Oaks in Washington, D.C., the international community, with Ralph Bunche in attendance, met to articulate goals for a new organization that could maintain international peace and security by taking collective action to suppress and prevent acts of aggression, develop amicable international relations, and encourage collective international action in the face of international, economic, social, and humanitarian problems. In short, the political leaders at Dumbarton Oaks envisioned an international body that had the authority to deploy international peacemakers, to put international pressure on states that violated international norms, and to protect states that were vulnerable to social and economic upheaval.[22]

In 1944 Bunche was hired by the State Department to oversee policies on "trusteeships" over "dependent territories" to replace the League of Nations mandate system. In his capacity as the head of the UN trustee program, Bunche advocated for universal rights for colonized peoples, rather than the existing framework of colonial rule. He believed that international governance had an important role in creating equality among nations. "International machinery will mean something to the common man in the Orient, as indeed to the common man throughout the world, only when it is translated into terms that he can understand: peace, bread, housing, clothing, education, good health, and, above all, the right to walk with dignity on the world's great boulevards."[23]

The work of Dumbarton Oaks was fully articulated in the April 25, 1945, United Nations Conference on International Organization, held in San Francisco. The UN was conceived of as an international body intended to stop wars and to provide a platform for international dialogue and conflict resolution. The UN would accomplish its mission through the establishment of a number of subsidiary bodies dedicated to security, world health, and human rights. Among the most lasting and important legacies of the UN was the establishment of the Universal Declaration of Human Rights in 1948.

The Universal Declaration of Human Rights asked member states to promote certain human, economic, and social rights as the foundation for peace in the world. Chaired by Eleanor Roosevelt, the UN's Human Rights Commission was tasked with articulating universal norms of rights. In order to establish norms to which every member state could aspire, the Human Rights Commission consulted with lawyers and activists from across the globe, including anticolonial leaders like Mohandas K. Gandhi. The Universal Declaration of Human Rights enshrined a set of universal values and rights, including the right to life, freedom from torture, the right to a fair trial, freedom of speech, and freedom of thought, conscience, and religion.[24]

In the aftermath of his participation at the UN conference, Bunche's analysis of race and colonialism began to change. By the mid-1940s Bunche disassociated the problem of racism in the U.S. and colonialism and, in doing so, rejected the 1930s Popular Front position he had embraced in "Marxism and the Negro Question." This shift had as much to do with transformations within the Communist Party, as it moved away from its Black Belt thesis, to Bunche's own move into the framework of national governance as a member of the U.S. State Department.[25] "There is utterly no connection," Bunche now argued, "between the two problems [colonialism and black American inequality]. . . . The Negro is an American, and his struggle is directed exclusively toward one objective: the full attainment of his constitutional rights as an American citizen. Unlike the colonial peoples, the American Negro, who is culturally American, has no nationalist and no separatist ambitions."[26]

During the UN conference, in which Bunche was instrumental in drafting the U.S. position on dependent territories, he encountered members of the Jewish Agency for Palestine, who sought to ensure that the United Nations would honor the Balfour declaration (see Chapter 2) and guarantee the formation of a Jewish state. Due to his scholarly and policy work on trusteeship programs in Africa, Bunche was appointed a special assistant to the United Nations Special Committee on Palestine, a body established to study the question of Palestine and to make recommendations to the UN General Assembly. Bunche provided research and considerable direction to the eleven appointed officials of UNSCOP and would later be head of the secretariat of the Palestine commission charged with implementing the UN's partition of Palestine. Following the outbreak of the Arab-Israeli war, Bunche was appointed a senior aide to the UN mediator, Count Folke Bernadotte, and was ultimately responsible for negotiating a series of armistice agreements that brought an end to the war.

The trusteeship council was established in 1945 to oversee the process of decolonization in "dependent territories." Under the framework of trusteeship, UN member states would oversee the transition of colonized states to independence. From the start of the UN, eleven territories were placed under trusteeship, seven in Africa and four in Oceana. Palestine was not dealt with under the trusteeship system because it did not fit the pattern of decolonization or European colonization. Instead, the question of Palestine was referred first to the Anglo-American Committee of Inquiry in 1946 and then to UNSCOP. The Anglo-American Committee heard testimony from Palestinian Communists—Jewish and Muslim—who argued for a binational or confederated state in Palestine. Bunche witnessed the Anglo-American Committee's work and was convinced of its conclusions that only binationalism would guarantee Jewish and Arab freedom in Palestine.

Throughout his work on the question of Palestine, Bunche encountered Zionist supporters of a Jewish state who ultimately convinced the UN to support the partition of Palestine and creation of a Jewish state. Yet what has been largely forgotten with time is the voluminous amount of testimony, on the part of Palestinian Communists and Jewish antinationalists, against partition and in support of binationalism. These arguments were so powerful that the U.S. State Department, due in part to Bunche's advocacy, proposed a binational solution to the question of Palestine before quickly changing course and recognizing the Jewish state. In the following sections, I discuss the binational argument and its resonances with Bunche's Popular Front past.

The Anglo-American Committee and Binationalism

The Anglo-American Committee of Inquiry was established in 1946 in order to study the question of Jewish refugees and their desired emigration to Palestine. Comprised of members representing the United States and the United Kingdom (which still maintained a mandate over Palestine), the committee conducted research and interviews in the United States and the United Kingdom and across the Eastern Mediterranean. Based on its research, the committee advanced a series of recommendations dealing primarily with how to address the tensions posed by the Jewish refugee problem across Europe. Although the committee was not established to recommend a framework for Jewish-Arab governance in Palestine, it clearly gestured toward an integrated political model of shared governance. Moreover, the committee's work established a framework for resolving territorial disputes in Palestine that would help influence the work of Ralph Bunche.[27]

A significant recommendation of the Anglo-American Committee was that European Jewish immigrants should not regard Palestine as the only destination for emigration. Hence the committee recommended that Jewish victims of Nazi persecution, who were displaced persons, should continue to live in Europe with the full protection of the United Nations charter, which called for "universal respect for, and observance of, human rights and fundamental freedoms for all without distinction as to race, sex, language or religion."[28] Given that the committee saw Europe as the most likely home for displaced Jews, it recommended significant, but limited, Jewish emigration to Palestine. The committee recommended that "100,000 certificates be authorized immediately for the admission into Palestine of Jews who have been the victims of Nazi and Fascist persecution."[29] This recommendation enraged Zionist organizations that felt that the committee had succumbed to the influence of Arab leaders. Moreover, the Anglo-American Committee was, rightly, perceived as the work of imperial powers that were, again, managing the affairs of colonized peoples.[30] Despite criticism of its recommendations, however, the committee's research revealed that increased Jewish immigration beyond the recommended 100,000 persons would mean Arab land loss and dispossession, and the committee felt that it was untenable for Palestinian Arabs to suffer dispossession due to a European atrocity.

In addition to recommending significant but limited Jewish emigration to Palestine, the Anglo-American Committee also made recommendations about Jewish-Arab shared governance, even though these recommendations went beyond its mission. In its third recommendation, the committee eschewed the formation of a state dominated by either Arab or Jew. Instead the committee advanced the following guidelines for future governance in Palestine: "I. That Jew shall not dominate Arab and Arab shall not dominate Jew in Palestine; II. That Palestine shall be neither a Jewish state nor an Arab state; III. That the form of government ultimately to be established shall, under international guarantees, fully protect and preserve the interest in the Holy Land of Christendom and of the Moslem and Jewish faiths."[31] The committee's recommendation was not *for* any particular form of government; it was most certainly not advocating binationalism. Yet the committee's recommendation seemed a clear statement against partitioning Palestine.

Although the British government was a participant in the work of the Anglo-American Committee—it was still the mandatory power in control of Palestine—Britain refused Jewish emigration to Palestine, despite estimates that more than 250,000 Jewish refugees were stranded in displaced persons camps in Europe. The mandate authorities believed that 100,000 new Jewish immigrants would only provoke a violent Arab response, one that the British occupying army was loath to mediate. Zionist militant cells in Palestine, in response to British obstruction to Jewish emigration, targeted British officials and military in a series of terrorist attacks and assassinations.[32] The British public, unhappy with the human and financial resources required to maintain the mandate in Palestine, forced its government to announce that it would relinquish the mandate by May 1948.

The recommendations of the Anglo-American Committee of Inquiry were delivered to UNSCOP, which would make the final determination on Palestine and the contentious politics of a Jewish national homeland. UNSCOP was comprised of representatives from eleven countries and was tasked with developing a political solution for Palestine. On August 31, 1947, after conducting a broad survey of Palestine, UNSCOP issued its report. Seven members (Canada Czechoslovakia, Guatemala, Netherlands, Peru, Sweden, and Uruguay) recommended partition, which meant the creation of independent Arab and Jewish states, with Jerusalem administered by an international body. Three UNSCOP member states (India, Iran, and Yugoslavia) supported the creation of a single federal state containing Jewish and Arab territories or nations united in a shared political confederacy.[33] The General Assembly approved UNSCOP's recommendations by a vote of 33 to 13. All of the Arab League member states voted against the partition.

The outcome of UNSCOP's work is well known. Yet what has been largely forgotten today are the intermediary stages leading to the partition vote and the radically different possibilities that existed leading up to the eventual partition of Palestine. Testimony offered to the Anglo-American Committee and UNSCOP from Palestinian Communists and Jewish antinationalists such as Judah Magnes constitute a taboo memory of the process of partitioning Palestine.[34] These groups argued passionately that the question of Palestine was not primarily a question of ethnic or racial antipathy but, instead, of racial capitalism and imperialism. Moreover, Ralph Bunche, who would ultimately be credited with overseeing the partition of Palestine, was actually sympathetic to and supportive of the binational idea and was nearly successful in winning U.S. State Department support for binationalism. In order to illuminate Bunche's work in UNSCOP, I turn

Left to right: Gen. William E. Riley, chief of UN truce observers in Palestine; Lt. Col. Trippett, aide to General Riley; and Dr. Ralph J. Bunche, acting UN mediator in Palestine, November 12, 1948 (UN Photo NICA 102542).

now to the arguments he encountered in Palestine during the UN hearings on the question of Palestine.

Comintern Binationalism

Jewish Communists associated with Eastern European radical movements, including members of the Jewish Poalei-Zion Left Party, some of whom participated in the 1917 Russian revolution, founded the Palestinian Communist Party (PCP) in September 1920.[35] Initially the PCP was exclusively Jewish and expressed only moderate criticism of Zionism. However, the Comintern in the Soviet Union encouraged the PCP to increase Arab participation in order for the PCP to join the Comintern. The Comintern's thesis on Zionism, as articulated by Lenin, was that Zionism was a bourgeois-nationalist ideology that promoted imperialism. The role of the PCP, according to the Comintern, would be to obstruct British and French imperialism while radicalizing peasant masses across the Arab world. In addition to taking up the Comintern's anti-Zionist position, the PCP also criticized Jewish immigration to Palestine, not due to a critique of colonialism but because European Jewish immigrants were labor competition for Palestinian workers. The PCP also began to criticize Arab landowners who sold property to Zionists; indeed they often suggested that the Arab landowner and the British imperialist were co-evil oppressors in Palestine.[36]

By 1923 the PCP had increased its Arab membership, but to the detriment of its Jewish and overall membership. According to Tarik Ismael, "Once Arabization became a primary focus of the party during 1923–1924, the party claimed to have only 20–30 percent of the number of members it had claimed just a year earlier."[37] Eventually the Workers' Faction of the PCP was expelled from the Jewish labor federation, the Histradrut, in April 1924, but it was also admitted to the Comintern at the same time. By 1924 the PCP was transformed from a predominantly Jewish organization to a predominantly Arab organization, but with Jewish leadership. Arab workers were trained for three years at the University of the Toilers of the East in Moscow. Soviet Communism in 1924 emphasized the binational nature of Palestinian society and recognized progressive and regressive actors among Jewish and Arab communities. For example, Arab landowners and British colonists were equally chastised, while the Communist impulses of some Jewish immigrants were recognized and celebrated. Thus, the Comintern saw the possibilities during this era of a united Jewish/Arab front in Palestine. By 1925 the Soviet Union denounced Zionism, the British occupation of Palestine, and the Jewish Labour Party.[38]

By 1929 the PCP had become more radical, calling for land redistribution, agrarian revolt, and support for the establishment of a government led by workers and peasants. Between 1930 and 1932, Arab leadership emerged within the ranks of the PCP. Jewish leaders of the PCP were recalled to Moscow and replaced with Arab leaders. Under Arab leadership, the PCP took a harder line in opposition to Jewish immigration. The PCP urged Arabs "to guard the ports, prevent Jews from landing and force the ships carrying Jewish immigrants to go back where they came from."[39] In its 1931 theses approved by the secretariat of its Central Committee, the PCP characterized Zionism as "the expression of the exploiting and great power oppressive strivings of the Jewish bourgeoisie, which makes use of the persecution of the Jewish national minorities in Eastern Europe for the purpose of imperialistic policy to ensure its domination."[40]

By the 1940s, Britain's preoccupation with World War II had led to a loosening of colonial restrictions on political activism in Palestine. The PCP's ranks grew as Marxism clubs emerged among the Palestinian intelligentsia and increasing proletarianization led to the formation of new trade unions. Some of the younger Arab members of the PCP began to break away from the PCP and formed an organization called the National Liberation League (NLL), which was committed to Communism but also to Arab sovereignty in Palestine. The NLL accepted that Jews had rights in Palestine, but they rejected the position of Jewish PCP members that these rights were national rights (i.e., rights to a Jewish state). The NLL sought redress and recognition in the United Nations by demanding the immediate termination of the British mandate and the formation of a Palestinian state with sovereign authority to determine immigration and land sales. The NLL was anti-Zionist but was not opposed to Jewish inhabitants of Palestine, especially those who were anti-imperialist.

In September 1945 the Ninth Congress of the PCP determined that Palestine was a "country with a binational character" and called for establishing a "democratic and independent Arab-Jewish state." In 1946 the editor of the PCP newspaper *Kol Ha'am* (*The People's Voice*) issued a pamphlet articulating the binational ideal: "Two national communities live in Palestine. Any program from the resolution of the problem of the country must take into consideration this fact and guarantee both nations equal rights and possibilities for free national development. The national question in Palestine is *sui generis*. Palestine is a binational country, but the Arabs and Jews do not live in separate territories."[41] The PCP, which in 1945 was mostly Jewish, and the NLL, which was entirely Arab, were, according to Joel Beinin, "united in their ideological opposition to Zionism and to the demand for a Jewish state in Palestine; both believed that only through anti-imperialist solidarity could Jews and Arabs in Palestine end British colonial rule, establish the political independence of Palestine, and secure Arab-Jewish coexistence."[42]

Shmu'el Mikunis, head of the PCP, argued in March 1947 that "the central national problem in Palestine was 'how to liberate the inhabitants, both Arabs and Jews, from the imperialist yoke.'"[43] Mikunis sought UN support for a democratic state with equal rights for all inhabitants. The PCP and the NLL disagreed over the role of Arab landlords, who, the PCP argued, were just as bad as the British, while the NLL included them in a nationalist cause.

In July 1947 Mikunis testified before Bunche and UNSCOP. Mikunis's advocacy of the binational ideal articulated a critique of racial capitalism and imperialism that echoed Bunche's similar analysis in "Marxism and the Negro Question." Mikunis told UNSCOP, "We emphatically reject the idea of partition, as it is contrary to the economic and political interests of the two people. We advocate the plan that Palestine should be constituted as an independent, democratic, bi-unitary state, which means a single state inhabited and governed by two peoples, Jews and Arabs, with equal rights."[44] Mikunis derided the history of international commissions regarding Palestine because, he argued, these international organizations tasked with studying the question of Palestine upheld an imperialist logic that protected the interests of British or American interests. Moreover, in the analysis of the PCP, Arab-Jewish antipathy had been sewn by imperial powers in order to undermine a popular Arab-Jewish front against European imperialism. Mikunis presented evidence of Arab-Jewish labor solidarity that illustrated the possibilities of a different political imaginary than the ones envisioned by UNSCOP or the Anglo-American Committee that had preceded it.

For example, Mikunis discussed an organization founded in 1930 called Workers' Brotherhood that organized Arab and Jewish workers in common trade unions. Arab and Jewish workers signed the charter for the organization. Yet, according to Mikunis,

> The Government reaps its political fruits from the policy of "Divide and Rule" and its support from reactional [*sic*] forces among both Arabs and Jews in that it has not [had] to face a united struggle of the Arabs and the Jews in Palestine for the abolition of colonial rule, independence and democratization of the country; instead, the Government has succeeded in fomenting hostilities on national lines around such problems as [Jewish] immigration, fear of national domination, purchase of land, employment in Government service and public works, import policy, industrial agricultural development, taxation, education and health.[45]

In the question-and-answer period of the PCP testimony, Mikunis reiterated his contention that it was imperialism that most threatened the possibilities for peace in Palestine. "The strongest weapons of imperialism in Palestine are not the tanks and the bombers," argued Mikunis, "it is the Arab-Jewish antagonism. In every case where Arabs and Jews unite and fight together they always succeed."[46]

Mikunis's politics are remarkable on a number of fronts. First, the position of the PCP suggests the possibilities of a political imaginary uniting working class Arabs and Jews against common enemies, including British imperialists, Arab landowners, and bourgeois Zionists. In this way, Mikunis's politics register a radical departure from the normative history of Israel's creation, which presume transhistorical Arab-Jewish antipathy.

There was, indeed, a social movement in support of a national government that could accommodate Jewish and Arab political desires.

At the same time, however, Mikunis articulated a remarkable sense of "at-home-ness" in his address to UNSCOP. The Jewish members of the PCP were unwilling or unable to confront the colonial conditions that produced their own presence in Palestine, instead focusing on the sins of British imperialism in Palestine. As a consequence, the PCP regularly succumbed to factionalism between Arab and Jewish members of a kind not sown merely by British imperialists but by the Jewish members' inability to recognize the colonial conditions that enabled a Jewish working class in Palestine.

Mikunis and his brothers and sisters in the PCP rejected the partition of Palestine and the creation of a Jewish state because they recognized that this would merely serve the interests of British and American imperialists eager to use a Jewish state as a proxy for their own geopolitical interest. Moreover, the PCP did not insist on encouraging Jewish immigration to Palestine in order to create demographic parity between Jews and Arabs (a position that Judah Magnes came to embrace). The PCP advocated the creation of "an independent, democratic, bi-unitarian state, which means, a single state inhabited and governed by the two peoples, Jews and Arabs, having equal rights."[47]

Antinationalist Jewish Binationalism

If Arab-Jewish proletarian unity and anti-imperialism were the hallmarks of the PCP's binational vision, for cultural Zionists binationalism was based in an ethical belief about the appropriate manner in which Jewish cultural life could be preserved and made to thrive.[48] To these Zionists, some of whom provided testimony in front of the Anglo-American Committee and then Bunche's UN committee, the modern state was a fiction that promised an illusive security and sovereignty. In actuality, the cultural Zionists believed, the modern state would threaten Jewish cultural life primarily because the state was secular and because it would enter Jewish cultural life into the unholy realm of the international order, an order that would require Jews to take up arms against competing nations. It is important to describe the conjuncture between the Jewish antinationalists, the Palestinian Communists, and Ralph Bunche's liberal internationalism at some length, as I contend that it is in this conjuncture that a political imaginary beyond nationalism was formed.

A small but influential group of critics of the formation of a Jewish state formed an organization in Palestine called Ihud (the Hebrew word for unity), which grew out of a similar group, Brit Shalom, formed in 1925.[49] Ihud was a small binationalist Zionist party headed by Judah Leon Magnes, Martin Buber, Ernst Simon, and Henrietta Szold. Ihud addressed the Anglo-American Committee and UNSCOP and advocated binationalism in its newspaper, *Hebrew Monthly*, which regularly demonstrated examples of Jewish-Arab cooperation in fields like citrus production and municipal governance in places like Haifa or in trade unions. Moreover, Judah Magnes, the president of Hebrew University, was someone whom Bunche personally relied on as an intellectual interlocutor on the question of Palestine.

In his testimony to UNSCOP as a representative of Ihud, Judah Magnes argued that Arab-Jewish cooperation in Palestine was both necessary and possible.[50] In making this case, Magnes argued that both Arabs and Jews had legitimate claims to Palestine; the Arabs had "natural rights" to Palestine, presumably through their presence and use of the land of Palestine, while the Jews had "historical rights," presumably derived from biblical and historical sources. For Magnes, both of these rights made legitimate Jewish and Arab national claims to Palestine. Therefore, he argued, the only possible solution to the question of Palestine was the creation of a binational state that embraced the claims of the Anglo-American Committee when they argued that "Palestine shall be neither a Jewish State nor an Arab State."[51]

Unlike his peers in the PCP, Magnes believed that it was crucial that demographic parity exist within the proposed binational state. Parity, for Magnes, meant that there needed to be equal numbers of Jews and Arabs in order for an amicable and just binational government to form. Hence, Magnes advocated a carefully regulated Jewish immigration policy that would encourage Jewish emigration to Palestine in order to achieve demographic parity with Arabs. In this way, we can see that a radical position in one context—binationalism—could simultaneously be a colonial position in the context of greater Palestine. Palestinian Arabs likely saw little utility in debates concerning the acceptable degrees of colonization.

Magnes's advocacy of "parity" derived from his belief that nations were incapable of protecting so-called national minorities. In order to make this case, Magnes reminded UNSCOP members of the failure of the Treaty of Versailles—which created legal norms to protect "national minorities"—in shielding European Jews form the Holocaust. "Minorities," Magnes argued, "can be protected only through parity, and the Jewish case, the Jewish cause in Palestine, can be protected here upon the basis of binationalism with two equal nationalities, so that they are in Palestine not a minority—to be sure, not a majority, and they, too, can have full national rights equally with their Arab fellow citizens."[52]

In addition to articulating a vision for a binational state based on demographic Arab-Jewish parity, Magnes argued that binationalism would lead to a renaissance in Arab-Jewish cultures. In this way, Magnes appealed to a political imaginary outside nationalism, rooted in what he called the "Semitic world."

> We think that a binational Palestine based on parity has a great mission to help revive this Semitic world materially and spiritually. The Jews and the Arabs are the only two peoples remaining from Semitic antiquity. We are related. We have lived and worked together. We have fashioned cultural values together throughout our history. We regard it as the mission of the binational Palestine to bring about once again, within the Semitic world, this revival of the spirit which has characterized Semitic history from antiquity.[53]

In addition to Magnes's argument, Ihud presented to UNSCOP testimony from Martin Buber, an Austrian-born Jewish philosopher who, in the early twentieth century, edited the Zionist Newspaper *Die Welt*.[54] Although he remained a cultural Zionist throughout his career, Buber withdrew from the formal Zionist movement because of these organizations' focus on the formation of a Jewish state and due to his own questioning about Jewish ethics and faith. Buber diverged from territorial Zionists, such as Theodor Herzl, who emphasized the primacy of a state over the importance of Jewish religion and culture.[55] Buber, on the other hand, believed that Jewish religion and culture could only be sustained outside the state. Indeed, he believed in a "Hebrew Humanism" that would always disavow war and territorial disputes but that would always emphasize Jewish faith and culture.[56]

The problem with territorial Zionism, according to Buber, was not primarily its emphasis on a national homeland; rather, it was the framework of internationalism, which superseded "intra-nationalism," or conviviality among the peoples of the land of Palestine. "Prevailing Zionist policy hitherto adhered to the axiomatic view that international agreement had to precede, nay, determine the intra-national agreement with the Arabs. It is imperative to reverse this order: it is essential to arrive at an intra-national agreement, which is later to receive international sanction."[57] Moreover, it was possible, Buber argued, for there to be a Jewish national home that was interdependent with Palestine. "We describe our programme as that of a binational state—that is, we aim at a social structure based on the reality of two peoples living together." Buber sought an economic unification with designated Jewish and Arab centers of culture and habitation. "This will lead," he wrote, to "Jewish-Arab cooperation in the revival of the Middle East. . . . This cooperation will allow development in accordance with an all-embracing cultural perspective and on the basis of a feeling of at-oneness, tending to result in a new form of society."[58]

Following Buber's testimony was that of H. M. Kalvaryski, a cultural Zionist who had studied agriculture at the University of Montpellier. Long before the atrocities of the Jewish Holocaust began, Kalvaryski immigrated to Palestine in 1895, where he served as an administrator of Zionist settlements and their colonization projects. He was the founder of the Zionist colonies of Kfar Tabor, Yavneel, and Menahemia. From 1923 to 1927 he served as an expert on Arab affairs from the Zionist institutions, but he eventually resigned due to the hard-line national approach assumed by Zionist organizations. Kalvaryski believed that Zionism could only exist in the context of peaceful coexistence with Palestinians and neighboring Arabs. In 1919 he met with King Feisal and the Pan-Syrian Congress in order to work out a plan for a binational state. He became the president of the League for Jewish-Arab Rapprochement and Cooperation and a member of the Presidential Board of Ihud.[59]

In the pages of Ihud's newspaper, Kalvaryski confronted the logic of international relations as enshrined by the League of Nations framework of self-determination and national minorities. Upon learning of the UN plan to partition Palestine, he lashed out at what he called the "empty splendor of sovereignty" and the "fictitious glory of a dwarfish state."

> Can we resign ourselves to this calamity of partition—even if the pill be coated with the emblem of sovereignty? We are confronted by the question, What comes first, the reunion—even if incomplete—of the remnants of the Diaspora in their Homeland, or the empty splendour of sovereignty, the fictitious glory of a dwarfish state, whose absorptive capacity will be very limited?
>
> We must recognize the kinship existing between the two branches of Semitic race, and the duty of both parts to act in accordance with principle: "that which it would not have the other branch do unto him, that it should not do unto the other." From this follow the principles of equality—parity—and of non-domination of either people by the other. Both these principles were accepted and proclaimed by various Zionist Congresses.[60]

Echoing the political philosophy of members of Ihud was Hannah Arendt, who studied philosophy with Martin Heidegger and Karl Jaspers, and who articulated what was perhaps the most philosophical and theoretical argument against the formation of the Jewish state.[61] She began to address "the Jewish question" with the rise of national socialism in Germany in the 1930s. Arendt appreciated the cultural Zionism of Bernard Lazare (1865–1903) over the territorial Zionism embraced by Theodor Herzl. Lazare deemphasized the importance of a Jewish homeland, instead focusing on the necessity of Jews to combat anti-Semitism through social movements and protest. As Arendt wrote about Lazare, "The territorial question was secondary. What he sought was not an escape from anti-Semitism but a mobilization of the people against its foes. . . . He did not look around for more or less anti-Semitic protectors but for real comrades-in-arms, whom he hoped to find among all the oppressed groups of contemporary Europe."[62] Arendt focused on the need to defend the Jewish people, and not on the need for a nation-state. In 1933 she fled from Germany to Paris, where she worked for Youth Aliya, a Zionist organization helping Jewish teenagers immigrate to Palestine.

Hannah Arendt viewed the Holocaust not as exceptional but as the normative process through which the nation-state confronts the problem of the national minority. Hitler's program of transforming "German Jews into a non-recognized minority in Germany," expelling the Jews as "stateless people across the borders," and the gathering of them "back from everywhere in order to ship them to extermination camps was an eloquent demonstration to the rest of the world how really to 'liquidate' all problems concerning minorities and the stateless." In this way, the problem of the nation-state and, by extension, the international framework of international relations was that the nation-form itself produced not only "the people" but also those who do not belong to "the people."

As Arendt argued in *The Origins of Totalitarianism*,

> After the war it turned out that the Jewish question, which was considered the only insoluble one, was indeed solved—namely, by means of a colonized and then conquered territory—but this solved neither the problem of the minorities nor the stateless. On the contrary, like virtually all other events of the 20th century, the solution of the Jewish question merely produced a new category of refugees, the Arabs, thereby increasing the number of stateless and rightless by another 700,000 to 800,000 people. And what happened in Palestine within the smallest territory and in terms of hundreds of thousands was then repeated in India on a large scale involving many millions of people.[63]

Hence, for Arendt, the nation and the international frameworks for addressing national minorities produced the condition of statelessness and expulsion. She therefore sought to imagine political communities beyond a nation, communities that could accommodate Jewish and Arab rights. She was unsure about binationalism, fearing that it might give the Arabs too much power over Jews; but she was also a staunch critic of Jewish sovereignty over Palestine, which she believed could only be obtained through Western military authority. Moreover, Arendt argued that a Jewish state formed against the will of the Arab majority would lead to permanent military conflict. "But if the Jewish commonwealth is proclaimed against the will of the Arabs and without the support of the Mediterranean peoples, not only financial help but political support will be necessary for a long time to come. And that may turn out to be very troublesome indeed for Jews in this country, who after all have no power to direct the political destinies of the Near East."[64]

As an alternative to the creation of a Jewish state, Arendt envisioned a Jewish federation existing within Europe as a possible answer to the Jewish question. In this she echoed the thesis of Lazare, who had considered the Jews as a "nation within a nation." Arendt was not a binationalist per se; she thought that the binational plan envisioned by Magnes relied too heavily on Anglo-American support and participation. Moreover, she felt that the binationalist movement had placed too much emphasis on state sovereignty. As an alternative to binationalism, Arendt initially looked to the Soviet Union, which she embraced as a different sort of collective of sovereignties and governance. "There are many problems unsolved in Soviet Russia, and I for one do not believe that even the economic problems have been resolved there, let alone the most important question of political freedom; but one thing has to be admitted: the Russian Revolution found an entirely new and—as far as we can see today—an entirely just way to deal with nationality or minorities. The new historic fact is this: that for the first time in modern history, an identification of nation and state has not even been attempted."[65] Arendt also imagined other configurations of confederation modeled on a "United States" approach or even a trans-Mediterranean confederation uniting Italy, France, Spain, and their North African extensions, and eventually other European countries and the rest of the Near East, bringing the Arabs into union with the Europeans.[66] Even after the partition of Palestine and the creation of a Jewish state, Arendt continued to advocate for forms of confederation across the Arab world.

Arendt criticized the forced removal of Arabs from their homes. Writing the week of the Deir Yassin massacre, Arendt predicted that the Zionist state would forever be haunted by its actions to forcefully expel and make stateless another people.[67] For Israel, Arendt argued, the "Palestine question" would become the central moral question, replacing the Jewish question.

> A home that my neighbour does not recognize and respect is not a home. . . . [The State of Israel will be] quite other than the dream of world Jewry, Zionist and non-Zionist [Israel will become a State in which] political thought would centre around military strategy [degenerating into] one of those small warrior tribes about whose possibilities and importance history has amply informed us since the days of Sparta, [leaving the Arabs] homeless exiles, [and the Arab problem as] the only real moral and political issue of Israeli politics.[68]

Ultimately, Arendt criticized nationalism as a power that creates statelessness and exile, while being rooted in an imperialist world order. The Zionist state, Arendt argued, was inevitably connected to the imperial powers that contributed to its creation and would therefore depend for its survival on continued military force.

> A nationalism that necessarily and admittedly depends upon the force of a foreign power is certainly worse. . . . The Zionists, if they continue to ignore the Mediterranean peoples and watch out only for the big faraway powers, will appear only as their tools, the agents of foreign and hostile interests. Jews who know their own history should be aware that such a state of affairs will inevitably lead to a new wave of Jew-hatred; the antisemitism of tomorrow will assert that Jews not only profiteered from the presence of the foreign big powers in that region but had actually plotted it and hence are guilty of the consequences.[69]

Many American Jewish intellectuals supported the formation of a Jewish state. But some notable members of the American Jewish intelligentsia refused to support the creation of a Jewish state, not because they embraced the politics of binationalism, but instead because they feared that the Jewish state would inspire accusation of Jews' "dual loyalties" (with the United States and Israel) at a time when Jews were not yet fully included in the normative bonds of whiteness.[70]

Partition or Binationalism?

The fate of Palestine, however, was not in the hands of Jewish and Arab proponents of binationalism, but with UNSCOP, which was created in May 1947 to study the Palestine issue and to submit recommendations to the General Assembly of the UN. UNSCOP was comprised of officials from eleven member states, including Australia, Canada, Czechoslovakia, Guatemala, India, Iran, Netherlands, Peru, Sweden, Uruguay, and Yugoslavia). Between June 15 and July 20, 1947, UNSCOP members toured Palestine and held meetings with representatives of the Jewish Agency (which represented the Zionist organizations) and various interest groups, including members of the PCP and intellectuals like Judah Magnes. The Jewish Agency was disproportionately influential because the Arab High Commission refused to cooperate with UNSCOP, believing that the Arab states and parties should boycott an agency whose sole mission was to dispossess Arab Palestinians of their land. Moreover, the British, the mandatory power occupying Palestine, similarly refused to cooperate with UNSCOP.

Although a majority of UNSCOP members held negative views of Arab capability for self-government, Bunche was concerned that the creation of a Jewish state would have negative consequences for Palestinian Arabs. As the UN official charged with overseeing "subject races" through the UN trusteeship program, Bunche was loath to create additional global dispossession. Yet Bunche was also highly influenced by the arguments he heard while working with UNSCOP, especially those of the PCP and of Judah Magnes, both of whom made an intellectual and practical case for the binational ideal.

UNSCOP ultimately recommended the partition of Palestine, with the creation of a Jewish state and an Arab state. Jerusalem would remain an international sovereign, monitored by the UN. However, events on the ground in Palestine illustrated the difficulties of creating a sovereign Jewish state on Arab land. Increasing attacks by Zionists on the British and by Arabs on the Zionists illustrated the need for further UN work. Hence the association established the UN Palestine Commission (UNPC), which was intended to further study the Palestine issue. Once again, Bunche played a prominent role as the senior advisor to the UNPC. Arab states again refused to participate in the UN process; hence the UNPC abandoned the question of an Arab state and focused entirely on how to create a Jewish state. But by February 1948, it was abundantly clear that creating a Jewish state in Palestine would lead to war and dispossession. Hence at its February 24, 1948, meeting, the UNPC, largely influenced by Bunche, began to revise its position on partition. The U.S. contingent was especially wary of partition, and on March 14, the U.S. informed the Security Council that the partition could not be implemented and that the UN ought to establish a trusteeship program. Moreover, U.S. officials began to embrace Bunche's ideas of a federated state with power sharing between Jews and Arabs. The U.S. went so far as to bring Judah Magnes to the United States in order to help convince American Jews of the importance of binationalism.[71] Ultimately the U.S. failed to convince other UNPC members that a trusteeship program was necessary.

Fearing that UN support for partition would waver, Zionists unilaterally declared a Jewish independent state on May 1948. The declaration led to war, requiring further UN actions. The UN appointed Count Folke Bernadotte to mediate an end to the Arab-Israeli war and to determine boundaries for the future Jewish state and a Palestinian state. Bernadotte knew little about the Palestine issue and therefore appointed Bunche as his senior advisor.[72] According to Bunche's biographer, Brian Urquhart, Bunche had unrivaled access to Bernadotte and was the actual author of Bernadotte's initial plan for a successful mediation of the Palestine issue.

At its April 1, 1948, meeting in Lake Success, New York, the United Nations trusteeship council heard a proposal from the United States demanding UN intervention in Palestine in order to secure an armistice agreement. Moreover, the U.S. delegation to the UN hinted that it believed a new plan for Palestine was required, as it was apparent that the creation of a Jewish state would only lead to war in Palestine. The U.S. delegation had increasingly embraced Ralph Bunche's position on Palestine, that the only amicable and just solution to the Palestine question was the formation of a binational or confederated state that gave equal rights to Arabs and Jews. The Jewish Agency vociferously opposed the U.S. plan to reconsider its support for the Jewish state. In front of the UN, the Jewish Agency's Moshe Shertok (who would later change his surname to Sharett) argued that the Arab-Israeli war was caused by Arab aggression that should not derail the lengthy work of the UN in planning for the partition of Palestine.

The UN approved the U.S. proposal to commission a mediator to negotiate a truce and to plan, again, for Palestine's future. Count Folke Bernadotte was appointed the mediator for Palestine in May 1948, making Bernadotte the UN's first mediator. Bernadotte appointed Ralph Bunche as his top advisor, and it has been widely documented that Bernadotte, who knew very little about the history of the Palestine question, relied on Bunche to draft his plan for Palestine.

The first Bernadotte plan introduced a position that echoed the work of the Anglo-American Committee. Bernadotte proposed that mandate Palestine be converted to a "Union comprising two members, one Arab and one Jewish." "The purpose and function of the Union should be to promote common economic interests, to operate and maintain common services, including customs and excise, to undertake development projects and to co-ordinate foreign policy and measures for common defense."[73]

Recognizing the importance of self-determination as a demand of Jews and Arabs, Bernadotte's plan articulated full sovereignty for Jews over Jewish territory and of Arabs over Arab territory. The vexed matter of immigration (particularly Jewish immigration) would be addressed within the sovereign body of the Jewish or Arab territory, with the stipulation that the council of the union could request modification of immigration policy if immigration was seen to disrupt the union. If the council of the union were unable to negotiate immigration policy, the matter would be referred to a ruling body in the United Nations.

Bernadotte recognized that the war had displaced hundreds of thousands of Arab Palestinians from their homes and that it would therefore be unjust to draw boundaries that would exclude Arabs from their homes and property. He therefore enshrined in his proposal the right of Palestinian Arabs to return to their homes, whether they were located in Arab or Jewish territories. "Recognition [should] be accorded to the right of residents in Palestine who, because of conditions created by the conflict there have left their normal places of abode, to return to their homes without restriction and to regain possession of their property."[74] Bernadotte's plan was roundly criticized by the Jewish Agency and by Zionist groups in the United States and Europe. By September 16, 1948, just one day before he would be assassinated, the UN mediator on Palestine issued his final progress report on Palestine. By this time, his first plan, which called for binationalism, had been soundly rejected. In his conclusion to the progress report, Bernadotte lamented the lost opportunity for an amicable and binational approach to Palestine. "I hold the opinion," Bernadotte wrote, "that [my first plan] offered a general framework within which a responsible and workable settlement might have been reached, had the two parties concerned been willing to discuss them. . . . However desirable a political and economic union might be in Palestine, the time is certainly not now propitious for the effectuation of any such scheme."[75] The task for the UN Security Council, if no binational union could proceed, was therefore to adjudicate boundaries and to determine the status of the 360,000 Palestinian refugees.

On the question of the refugees, Bernadotte was most resolute; the refugees had a right to return to their homes or to receive compensation for lost property if they chose not to return. Moreover, it was the UN's responsibility, and not neighboring Arab states', to care for the displaced refugees until they returned home.[76] On September 17, 1948, just three months after proposing his first plan and just one day after proposing a partition with Jewish and Arab states, Bernadotte was assassinated in Jerusalem by a Jewish terrorist organization called the LEHI (Lohamei Herut Israel, in English referred to as the Stern Gang) that was led by Israeli prime-minister-to-be Yitzhak Shamir.[77] Bunche was charged with presenting to the UN a revised proposal, taking into account the new facts on the ground created by the unilateral declaration of Israeli independence. Bunche was ultimately forced to submit to the UN a plan for partition that ultimately won the support of the General Assembly.

Although he would eventually be celebrated as a champion of peace in Palestine, Bunche was initially accused of anti-Semitism in Jewish and African American media due to his support for binationalism. According to Urquhart, "Bunche . . . found himself being written up as anti-Semitic in the Hebrew press in Palestine on the fantastic grounds that he didn't want a Jewish independent state because Black Americans would then ask for their own state too."[78] Moshe Shertok of the Jewish Agency theorized that racial politics in the U.S. had distorted Bunche's positions on Palestine. In his rejection of the Bernadotte plan, Shertok speculated that "the black man's complex was affecting [Bunche]. . . . If a Jewish state were established the question of a black country would arise [in the U.S.]. They would start shouting at the blacks to go to Liberia. . . . We are dealing with black people who are afraid that the Jewish State will harm their own standing."[79]

Bunche also received scorn from Jewish organizations in the United States that claimed that Arabists in the U.S. State Department and British Home Office had influenced Bunche. Walter White, then secretary of the NAACP, drafted a letter to Bunche in which he reported on ways that Bunche had been treated in the media. As Urquhart documents, White wrote "to say that in New York he had found 'one of the damnedest campaigns I have ever run into—of an apparently organized Jewish attack on you regarding the Negev.' White had been pointing out to his Jewish friends that the whole cause of the Jews 'was being damaged by their prompt assertion that anyone who does not do precisely as they wish is therefore guilty of having sold out to the British, the Arabs, or somebody else.'"[80] Bunche replied:

Most of my fan mail (chiefly from New York) is not pleasant reading these days. I am neither surprised nor hurt by it. In the sort of work on which I am now engaged this kind of attack must be rated as an occupational hazard. The purpose, of course, it to discredit me and also the Bernadotte report. It is not inconceivable that it may have a substantial measure of success. As long as I am on the job I shall continue to call each play just as I see it. When the Arabs are wrong I put the finger on them, and I'll do precisely the same with the Jews come hell or high water, and despite the fact that I have had a purely personal sympathy for their cause. That's the only way I know how to play the game.[81]

Bunche wrote to his friend Alain Locke, "I don't like misrepresentation, of course, and I am aware that in some quarters I am labeled as anti-Semitic. But all that is an occupational hazard in this controversial job. Trouble is the public gets political settlement mixed up with the truce supervision, and unfortunately I have been handling both, and walking just as straight a line as I know how."[82]

Israel/Palestine in the Black American Public Sphere

On the eve of Israel's declared independence, W. E. B. Du Bois added his own criticism of Bunche in a speech at Madison Square Garden to the American Jewish Congress. Du Bois apologized "in the name of the American Negro for the apparent apostasy of Ralph Bunche . . . to the clear ideals of freedom and fair play, which should have guided the descendant of an American slave."[83]

The subject of Du Bois's position on Zionism and Israel is complex and deserves its own study. As Eric Sundquist has identified, in 1940 and 1941, in the context of "As the Crow Flies," his regular column for the African American *New York Amsterdam News*, W. E. B. Du Bois engaged head-on the complex political topic of a Jewish state in Palestine. He marveled at the creation of Jewish sovereignty over Jewish cities and schools in Palestine. Even though "modern Jewish Palestine is only twenty years old," he wrote, Zionists had already created Jewish cities, like Tel Aviv, and Jewish-run school and universities. Du Bois also marveled at the Jewish cooperative societies—kibbutzes—which represented a capacity of "twenty million" dollars. According to Du Bois, "The only thing that has stopped the extraordinary expansion of the Jews in Palestine has been the Arab population and the attempt on the part of English and Arabs to keep Palestine from becoming a complete Jewish state."[84]

The Zionist movement was, for Du Bois, the realization that a group who had been brutalized by Western racism could guarantee their freedom via the modern state. Although Du Bois generally disagreed with nationalist projects that entailed segregation, he nevertheless believed that "the only refuge that the harassed Jewry of Europe has today is Palestine. They are therefore going to make segregation in Palestine possible and profitable and at the same time they are going to work for an unsegregated humanity. If this teaches the Negro of the United States nothing, they cannot be taught."[85]

In 1948 he wrote an essay originally titled "The Ethics of the Problem of Palestine" but renamed by the Jewish *Chicago Star* "The Case for the Jews." In this article, Du Bois supported the formation of a Jewish state, and in doing so, he would adopt many of the aesthetic and orientalist claims about Palestine as the Zionists. "Palestine," wrote Du Bois, "is a land largely of plateaus, mountains, and deserts, sparsely inhabited, and could easily maintain millions more people than the two million it has today. Among the million Arabs there is widespread ignorance, poverty and disease and fanatic belief in the Mohammedan religion, which makes these people suspicious of other peoples and other religions."

While the indigenous Arabs were backward, Du Bois found the Zionists to be "young and forward-thinking Jews bringing a new civilization into an old land and building up that land out of ignorance, disease, and poverty into such it had fallen; and by democratic methods erecting a new and peculiarly fateful modern state." Here Du Bois recapitulates the logic of orientalism, which views Western imperial intervention in "the Orient" as civilizing, benevolent, and uplifting. In this formulation Western intervention in the Orient benefits not only the colonizer, but also the colonized. According to Du Bois, "What the Jews have already done is for the advantage, not simply of the Jews, but of the Arabs."[86]

Du Bois's position was echoed throughout the mainstream African American public sphere. The black U.S. public sphere's discussion of Israel has been documented by Weisbord and Kazarian, as well as by Sundquist. That African American society was overwhelmingly supportive of the creation of Israel makes it all the more important to recover Bunche's (disavowed) radical writings as well as his support for binationalism. While Bunche was ostensibly part of the mainstream African American public sphere, he was nevertheless moved by a set of conjunctures different from those of Du Bois or other civil rights supporters of Israel's creation. In advocating for a binational possibility, Bunche tapped into a global political struggle beyond the confines of U.S. and Western racial nationalism.

Nakba

And yet the "radical potential" of binationalism must be tempered by the consequences, even of binationalism, on indigenous Palestinians. The international solution to the Jewish minority problem in Europe had dire consequences for Palestinians. For Palestinian Arabs, the creation of Israel would mean becoming exiles at the hands of exiles.[87] At the end of the Arab-Israeli war in 1949, the United Nations Conciliation Committee estimated the number of Palestinian refugees at 711,000.[88] The refugees fled their homes for fear of pending war, amidst ongoing attacks on their homes, or due to overt threats on the part of Israeli militias. Approximately half of the refugees were directly expelled by the Israeli army through deliberate programs to depopulate Arab villages.[89] Plans to depopulate, or ethnically cleanse, Palestinian Arab villages are now well documented by revisionist Israeli historians who represent a variety of political positions.[90] These studies estimate that thirty Arab villages were depopulated by March 1948 alone and that many more villages were targeted in deliberate programs of ethnic transfer and cleansing. By 1951 the United Nations Relief and Works Agency, the international body now in charge of caring for the refugees, had registered 876,000 refugees.[91]

The plight of the refugees and their right to return to their homelands became the fundamental issue of Palestinian activism. Refugee camps were constructed of tents or impermanent structures because the refugees and the United Nations believed that the refugee problem would be temporary. The General Assembly of the UN passed Resolution 194 on December 11, 1948. Resolution 194, which is not binding on international law, contained Article 11, which granted refugees the "right of return": "Resolves that the refugees wishing to return to their homes and live at peace with their neighbours should be permitted to do so at the earliest practicable date, and that compensation should be paid for the property of those choosing not to return and for loss of or damage to property which, under principles of international law or in equity, should be made good by the Governments or authorities responsible."[92] The failures of the United Nations and the international community to guarantee the right of return meant that the creation of Israel was especially tragic for Palestinians who lost land and have been expelled form their homelands since 1948. To Palestinians, Israeli independence would be seen as a catastrophe, or *nakba*. The magnitude of land dispossession was captured in 1948 by Constantine Zurayq, a professor of history at the American University of Beirut, who wrote in his book, *Ma'na al-Nakba* (*The Meaning of the Disaster*), "The tragic aspect of the Nakba is related to the fact that it is not a regular misfortune or a temporal evil, but a Disaster in the very essence of the word, one of the most difficult that Arabs have ever known over their long history."[93]

Conclusion

In 1947 Andrei Gromyko, the Soviet representative to the United Nations, maintained an anti-imperialist stance on the question of Palestine as he stressed the importance of an "independent democratic Arab-Jewish State." Yet even at this moment, Gromyko realized that the imperial world was changing and that an independent Israeli state would be a key asset to whichever postwar superpower claimed it as an ally. The Soviet position quickly shifted throughout 1947 from a quasi binationalism to outright support for Israeli statehood.[94] At the moment Israel declared independence, the two great superpowers, the United States and the Soviet Union, competed to be the first to recognize the new state (the U.S. won a close race). The Soviet recognition of Israel elicited a fierce reaction from the Palestinian Communists, who felt betrayed. Ultimately, however, with the formation of a bipolar world in the making, the Soviet Union embraced partition and sought to bring the new Jewish state into the Soviet orbit. Within this context, Palestinian Communists also began to endorse partition and recognition of the self-declared State of Israel. The PCP, after Israeli "independence," fully supported the Israeli national project and its self-determination, while giving muted support to a Palestinian national home next to Israel. It now viewed the Jewish state as part of the struggle against worldwide anti-imperialism.

By October 1948 the NLL and other Communist organizations in the Arab world followed the Soviet Union's support for Israel as a key state in the anti-imperialist movement. The NLL denounced Arab military attacks on Israel and accepted the partition of Palestine. The Iraqi, Lebanese, and Syrian Communist parties and the NLL issued a joint communiqué condemning the Arab invasion of Palestine: "The Palestine war was a direct result of the fierce struggle between England and the United States, who caused the war in order to exploit it to settle accounts between them. . . . The Palestine war revealed finally and completely the betrayal of the reactionary rulers in the Arab states and their complete submission to foreign imperialism."[95] As Joel Beinin has noted, the Communist denouncement of Arab attacks on Israel failed to implicate the Zionist movement, as the Communist position had in the early 1940s. Moreover, the NLL had nothing to say in support of Palestinian refugees.[96] The Marxist and Communist support for partition became the wedge that divided the Jewish and Arab-Palestinian political parties. The Communist parties increasingly framed the partition of Palestine as the only legitimate anti-imperialist politics.

By 1950, Bunche presented lectures about his efforts in Palestine for the United Nations in which he did not convey his support for binationalism. In a series of lectures he delivered at the University of Chicago titled "Man, Democracy, and Peace—Foundations for Peace: Human Rights and

Fundamental Freedoms," Bunche seemed to fully embrace the UN partition plan as the only practical course of action. He framed the Palestine question as one shaped by "fanatically nationalistic" Arab and Jewish groups.[97]

A year after receiving the Nobel Prize (1950), Bunche delivered his lecture "Review and Appraisal of Israeli-Arab Relations" to the National War College.[98] Bunche argued that during the mandate, amicable relationships between Jews and Arabs made the possibilities of a binational program promising. But this possibility was shattered by the conversion of Jewish Zionism into a fiercely nationalist movement, as well as the ascendency of the Holocaust, which made it seem impossible for Jews to settle in Europe. "But with the conversion of the Jewish homeland into the idea of a formal Jewish state, with the tremendous emphasis on immigration to Palestine that became necessary perhaps after the persecutions by Hitler, this clash was greatly accentuated."[99] There was also the problem of the Balfour declaration, which set the terms of the British mandate's evolution toward the formation of a Jewish state. "This partition decision which was reached after the commission had visited Palestine and had visited the refugees in Europe was certainly never regarded by anyone in the United Nations as an ideal decision but as possibly the only thing that could be done in the circumstances."[100]

The Afro-Arab world that had been forged at the intersection of earlier twentieth-century Arab rebellions and pan-Africanism was transformed in the 1940s due to multiple national and global changes and debates, including international debate concerning the creation of Israel, the rise of national liberation globally that emphasized liberation movements within the borders of the nation-state, and Cold War bipolarity that introduced a wedge between the Arab Islamic world and the "West" of which African Americans were precarious members. The Afro-Arab world, in the crucible of the Cold War, was no longer overlapping but was, instead, characterized by new conjunctures and contingencies.

Shortly after World War II a new international conflict, a bipolar Cold War between the Soviet Union and the United States, placed newly formed nations into a dangerous milieu; they became proxies for the great superpowers to exert regional influence. Some nations responded to the Cold War by refusing to participate and by creating different international frameworks built around what Vijay Prashad has called "national internationalism," a term used to note the ways that decolonizing nations in the so-called third world were nationalist while also seeking participation or solidarity with nations in similar positions vis-à-vis the Cold War.[101]

This was the nonaligned movement, which was first mapped in the 1936 League against Imperialism in Brussels and was given full articulation in the 1955 conference in Bandung, Indonesia. The nonaligned movement would construct a political imaginary rooted in national liberation and sovereignty, but also in a shared political imaginary that constituted the peoples and nations beyond the borders of the Cold War hegemons. In the next chapter I examine how the politics of nonalignment coupled with transformations in the black power movement and expansion of Israeli territory would constitute new conditions of possibility for the formation of Black Panther Palestine.

CHAPTER FOUR

The Black Panthers and the PLO

THE POLITICS OF INTERCOMMUNALISM

We cannot be nationalists, when our country is not a nation, but an empire. . . .
We have the historical obligation to take the concept of internationalism to its final
conclusion—the destruction of statehood itself.—Huey Newton

The [U.S.] Black Panther Party fit Mizrahim just like Zionism fit America.
—Reuven Abergil

In his 1975 novel, . . . *And Bid Him Sing*, David Graham Du Bois, the step-son of W. E. B. Du Bois and son of Shirley Graham Du Bois, focuses on the Afro-Arab politics that emerged within 1960s Cairo, a city in which he lived for twelve years.[1] The novel centers on a community of African American expats in Egypt, some of whom are former Nation of Islam members, while others are drawn to Egypt due to its location at the intersection of the Afro-Arab world. The novel is set within the historical context of Malcolm X's famous 1964 visit to Cairo and address to the Organization of African Unity, as well as within the tumultuous history—especially for Egypt—of the Six-Day War in June 1967.[2] Readers encounter Egypt as a cosmopolitan third world capital where African American Muslims, like one of the novel's protagonists, Suliman Ibn Rashid, reads antiracist poetry to Cairo café audiences comprised of "young black students from West and East Africa, young African diplomats and freedom fighters from southern Africa, some Pakistanis and Indian students from South Africa. They included some Palestinians and some Egyptians."[3]

Du Bois had arrived in Cairo in 1960, working as an English instructor at Cairo University, just when the city had become the fulcrum of Afro-Arab politics, largely due to Gamal Abdel Nasser's prominent role in the 1955 Bandung conference and his contributions to the formation of the United

Arab Republic (UAR)—a pan-Arab constellation of Arab states—and the Organization of African Unity.[4] Both of these organizations worked to foster continental, internationalist politics routed across national formations. Du Bois embraced Egypt, where in 1961 he would become an editor for the English-language *Egyptian Gazette*, a newspaper he contributed to for the next twelve years.[5] While working for the *Gazette*, Du Bois published Malcolm X's address to the Organization of African Unity conference that, importantly, signaled Malcolm's break from the Nation of Islam as he moved away from black nationalism to advocacy of global human rights.[6]

Du Bois moved to the United States in 1971, and in 1973 Huey Newton recruited him to become editor of the *Black Panther Intercommunal News Agency*. In this capacity Du Bois would publish a serialized version of . . . *And Bid Him Sing*, while inserting his analysis of Afro-Arab politics and the question of Palestine into the newspaper. Du Bois would help Newton draft a Panther policy statement on the Middle East crisis, contributing to Newton's ideas a nuanced understanding of Arab politics and the complexities of Islam.[7] There is little doubt that Du Bois's experience in Cairo and his focus on Afro-Arab politics inspired him to connect the question of Palestine to the black freedom movement. He had witnessed the 1967 June war, in which Egypt was quickly defeated by Israeli power, and was interested in the sorts of comparative racial politics that animated black politics in the United States and Arab politics in Egypt.

In Chapter 3 we saw how 1930s Popular Front black American radicalism overlapped with the Palestinian Communist Party's binationalist politics. In a much different context, yet in very similar ways, the post-1967 era inspired the reconstitution of Popular Front anti-imperialism; in the 1970s, this conjuncture took place around the liberation geography of intercommunalism, which was the Panthers' understanding of how local communities were sutured together by global processes of imperialism and racial capitalism.

In this chapter I illustrate the ways that the tumultuous politics of 1967 and 1968, in the United States and across the Arab world, constituted new conditions of possibility for Afro-Arab political imaginaries. Nasserism, the Cold War, the global politics of decolonization, the catastrophes of imperial warfare, and the narrowing of black freedom struggles in the U.S. to the confines of national inclusion and racial liberalism all influenced the possibilities for Afro-Arab politics. Yet the contradictions exposed by the end of the 1960s also revealed new political imaginaries that were most forcefully articulated by the U.S. Black Panther Party as "intercommunalism."

Intercommunalism, as I will explain, was a political imaginary that recognized the shared conditions of racial capitalism and possibilities for anti-imperialism among local communities across the world. As a political imaginary, intercommunalism was the practice of geographically linking colonial locations globally and fostering a politics of comparison and solidarity. In this way, I argue, intercommunalism was part of a genealogy of black radical politics that includes previous formations discussed in this book, including diasporic politics, pan-Africanism, and to a lesser extent, binationalism. This chapter illustrates how the Panthers' intercommunal political imaginary formed a community linking the U.S., the black freedom movement, the Palestinian nationalist movement, and the struggle among black Arab Jews within Israel who formed the Israeli Black Panther Party.[8] The growing Palestinian national movement, represented by Al-Fatah, the U.S. Black Panther Party, and the Israeli Black Panther Party, were linked by an Afro-Arab geography rooted in intercommunal understanding of racial capitalism and imperialism.[9] Although there are many globally significant moments that shaped the revolutions of 1968, this chapter focuses on three political developments that helped foster a political geography of liberation. First, I discuss the formation of the Palestine Liberation Organization in the wake of the Israeli occupation of the West Bank and Gaza. Next, the chapter moves to a discussion of the formation of the Black Panther Party and its focus on the question of Palestine via its radical politics of intercommunalism. And finally, the chapter proceeds to a discussion of how the Black Panthers' intercommunalism reverberated in unexpected locations—among Arab Jews in Israel who formed the Israeli Black Panther Party.

The PLO and the Six-Day War

An understudied coordinate in the geography of black liberation politics has been Palestine and the impact the emergence of the PLO had on the U.S. black freedom movement. There are many possible reasons for this lacuna; the question of Palestine remains, as Edward Said once argued, "America's last taboo."[10] Yet in the post-1968 era the question of Palestine animated a global politics of leftist solidarity, just as questions of Jewish diasporic politics helped animate early-twentieth-century black American politics. The Palestinian movement following the '67 war took the struggle for Palestinian anticolonialism international in an attempt to link the Palestinian struggle to the anti-imperialist politics of Southeast Asia and Africa. As Paul Chamberlin has argued, the PLO, whose founding I will address in a moment, committed to what he calls a "global offensive" against Israeli imperialism. Chamberlin argues that "while the Cold War superpowers worked to maintain and extend their influence in every region of the world, small states and guerilla groups sought to exploit a proliferating array of transnational connections that criss crossed the globe."[11] The PLO capitalized on an international network of anti-imperialist activists in order to expand the terrain of its anti-imperialist agenda.

U.S. black nationalists were similarly interested in the global anti-imperialist struggle, and some found themselves involved in political activism surrounding anticolonial struggles globally. Moreover, the PLO would come to see in black radical politics—especially in the Black Panther Party—a partner in its struggle for national liberation. It is therefore important to chart the geopolitical contexts and conjunctures that brought the U.S. Black Panthers and the PLO into a shared geography of liberation.

The Palestinian national movement had always been dispersed across the globe due to the dissolution of Palestine in the wake of the 1948 war and then the further dislocation caused by the 1967 war. In the aftermath of the 1948 war, Egypt held political sovereignty over the Gaza Strip, which included a population of approximately 479,574 Palestinian refugees; 671,285 Palestinian refugees lived in the West Bank, a territory controlled by Jordan. Approximately 583,593 Palestinian refugees were dispersed outside the borders of Israel/Palestine, where they lived in UN-administered refugee camps.[12] The dispersal of Palestinians meant that a social movement for Palestinian liberation would necessarily confront not only the national and colonial policies of Israel but also the policies of regional Arab states and the United Nations. Hence, the struggle for Palestinian liberation would, from the outset, become not a simple "national liberation" struggle but a pan-Palestinian struggle for rights in Israel, in the West Bank and Gaza, and in regional countries.[13] The PLO was thus, from the outset, conditioned to imagine a political community that was dispersed globally.

The founders of Fatah, the central political force within the PLO, were themselves trained throughout the Arab world, having faced hardships as Palestinians in Cairo, Damascus, Gaza, and the Persian Gulf region.[14] The PLO was officially formed in 1964 at the Arab League Cairo Summit convened by Gamal Abdel Nasser. The PLO's initial statement articulated its liberation agenda, "the right of the Palestinian Arab people to its sacred homeland Palestine and affirming the inevitability of the battle to liberate the usurped part from it, and its determination to bring out its effective revolutionary entity and the mobilization of the capabilities and potentialities and its material, military and spiritual forces."[15] The platform of Fatah, as it formed in 1964, included the following five points:

1. The common goal of liberating Palestine,
2. The need for armed struggle to attain this goal,
3. Reliance on Palestinian self-organization,
4. Co-operation with friendly Arab forces, and
5. Co-operation with friendly international forces.[16]

The first leaders of Fatah believed that Palestinian nationalism needed to precede pan-Arabism; hence, the organization prioritized establishing bonds of Palestinians across the Palestinian diaspora, rather than focusing on regional and pan-Arab politics. At its founding conference the PLO defined itself as an "entity" that represents the liberation goals of the Palestinian people. The PLO would become the "sole recognized representative" of the Palestinian people in regional and international meetings.

In June 1967, Israel launched the Six-Day War, resoundingly defeating Arab forces in Lebanon, Syria, Jordan, and Egypt. Fought June 5–10, 1967, the Six-Day War (or an-Naksah, "the setback") began with Israel's surprise attack against Egyptian airfields. Regional Arab states had been preparing for an attack on Israel, but Israeli spies learned of these plans and Israel struck first. By the end of the conflict, Israel had seized the Golan Heights (which had been held by Syria), the Sinai Peninsula (which had been held by Egypt), and the West Bank, including East Jerusalem (which had been held by Jordan). Overall, Israel's territory grew by a factor of three, with about 1 million Arabs under Israeli occupation. The Sinai would eventually be returned to Egypt during the 1978 Camp David Accords, but the Gaza Strip remains under Israeli occupation, although in the post-Oslo era this occupation is organized differently than in the pre-Oslo period (see Chapter 5).[17] While this war had many regional implications, it perhaps had the greatest impact on Palestinians living in the West Bank and Gaza, who came under Israeli colonial occupation forces.

Fatah responded to the 1967 events by turning to armed rebellion and the formation of guerilla groups. Yasser Arafat became the leader of the PLO in 1969 and directed the organization toward direct-armed rebellion against Israel, launching attacks from regional Arab states where PLO leaders hid. In 1970 Jordanian forces turned against the PLO and launched an attack known as Black September. Black September dispersed PLO organizations to Beirut and Damascus, with the PLO eventually setting up its headquarters in Beirut.[18]

In 1973 the Palestinian National Congress submitted to the United Nations the PLO's ten-point program. The program called for "all means" necessary, including and foremost armed rebellion, to liberate Palestine; it called for the formation of a democratic Palestinian state within which Jews could live as equals; and it called for solidarity with global socialist and anti-imperialist groups: "The Liberation Organization will strive to strengthen its solidarity with the socialist countries, and with the forces of liberation and progress throughout the world, with the aim of frustrating all the schemes of Zionism, reaction and imperialism."[19]

In the late 1960s and early 1970s the PLO moved its bases to Southern Lebanon, where it launched guerilla operations against Northern Israel's Galilee. By 1975 Palestinian guerillas in Lebanon and Christian militias (likely acting as proxies for Israel) turned their weapons against each other, initiating the Lebanese civil war, a conflict that was about sectarian division in Lebanon as well as unstable regional conflicts involving Israel and Syria, both of whom would occupy Lebanon for decades.[20] By 1982 the PLO was forced out of Lebanon by a six-month Israeli occupation of Lebanon, which included the massacre of Palestinians in the Sabra and Shatila refugee camps at the combined hands of Israeli soldiers and Lebanese Christian Phalangists. The PLO relocated to Tunis, where its headquarters came under Israeli attack in 1985.

The Palestine Question and the Black Freedom Movement

In the wake of the Six-Day War, the question of Palestine became a charged political matter within the black freedom struggle. It was a topic that threatened to challenge leftist political coalitions within the United States (especially between Jews and blacks) as well as a topic that split the black freedom movement along ideological lines.[21] The Palestine question revealed the fissures between a mainstream civil rights agenda that focused on winning full inclusion within the legal and geopolitical boundaries of the U.S. nation-state and a new generation of anti-imperialist, black nationalist activists who sought political solidarity beyond the nation and in the realm of international and "intercommunal" politics.[22] Moreover, the latter group had been influenced by the internationalist vision developed by groups like the Nation of Islam, which had, with the help of Malcolm X, linked the Middle East and black America in its conception of an "Afro-Asiatic race." Malcolm X's historic 1964 trip to Mecca and Egypt, which signaled his break with the Nation of Islam, importantly linked the politics of pan-Arabism and pan-Africanism.[23]

By 1967, therefore, the black freedom movement included many, and often contradictory, radical impulses. The NAACP and the Urban League viewed full inclusion and equality within the U.S. as the appropriate horizon of black demands. For this group, Israel was a model of liberal multiculturalism and the possibilities of the liberal nation to address the problem of racial minorities. At the same time, the black freedom movement included a younger radical component that saw the nation-state (in the U.S. and in Israel) as an instrument of imperialism and racial capitalism. For this group, the revolutionary struggle for Palestinian decolonization—and not the "liberal" inclusiveness of Israel—was most influential.

The transition from a nation-bound civil rights movement to an internationalist and anti-imperialist movement can be read in the context of black organizational responses to the Six-Day War and the question of Palestine. While much of this chapter will focus on the politics of the Black Panther Party, it should be mentioned that the Student Non-Violent Coordinating Committee (SNCC), under the leadership of Stokely Carmichael, was the first civil rights organization to articulate a break from the mainstream black freedom movement on the question of Palestine. In its June–July 1967 *SNCC Newsletter* the organization ran a two-page centerpiece article in which it sought to educate readers on the Middle East conflict, paying particular attention to the role of U.S. imperialism in shaping Israeli aggression.[24] "Third World Round-up: The Palestine Problem: Test Your Knowledge" featured thirty-two points that SNCC felt provided context for the 1967 war. SNCC sought to link Israeli aggression in Palestine to U.S. support for imperial projects globally. In addition, SNCC argued that early financial supporters of the Zionist movement had been complicit in extracting African raw materials at the expense of African sovereignty. SNCC asked readers whether they knew

That the US Government has constantly supported Israel and Zionism by sending military and financial aid to this illegal state ever since it was forced upon the Arabs in 1948?

That the Zionist terror gangs (Haganah, Irgun, and Stern gangs) deliberately slaughtered and mutilated women, children and men, thereby causing the unarmed Arabs to panic, flee and leave their homes in the hands of the Zionist-Israeli forces?

That the famous European Jews, the Rothschild's, who have long controlled the wealth of many European nations, were involved in the original conspiracy with the British to create the "State of Israel" and are still among Israel's chief supporters? *That the Rothschilds also control much of Africa's mineral wealth?*[25]

SNCC's anti-Israel article contained provocative photographs that challenged the normative pro-Israeli understanding in the U.S. media. It featured images of early Zionist terrorist groups, of Arab bodies killed by Israel in 1956, and of a hand with a Star of David and a U.S. dollar sign on it holding a hangman's rope around the necks of Gamal Abdel Nasser, late president of Egypt, and Muhammad Ali, former black heavyweight boxing champion and a noted Black Muslim.[26]

The Six-Day War and the SNCC article reverberated throughout the black freedom movement. In response to SNCC's actions, Martin Luther King Jr. signed a paid advertisement in the *New York Times* in June 1967 that called on President Lyndon Johnson to honor American commitments to ensure Israel's security.[27] Furthermore, in the wake of a "New Politics Convention" in Chicago, in which a group of activists collected signatures for a resolution condemning Israeli aggression in the West Bank and Gaza, King published a rebuttal in the *New York Times*. In this letter, sent to Morris Abram, president of the American Jewish Committee, King noted that his Southern Christian Leadership Conference "has repeatedly stated that the Middle East problem embodies the related questions of security and development. Israel's right to exist as a state in security is incontestable."[28]

Members of the A. Philip Randolph Institute, including Randolph himself, responding to the increasing number of pro-Palestinian statements by black intellectuals, formed a new organization, the Black Americans in Support of Israel Committee, with Randolph himself and Bayard Rustin as leaders. BASIC published in the *New York Times* an "Appeal by Black Americans for United States Support to Israel" signed by multiple black notables.[29] The advertisement described Israel as "the most democratic country in the Middle East" and called on the United States to guarantee Israel's security.

Roy Wilkins, executive director of the NAACP and a signatory to BASIC's "Appeal by Black Americans," criticized SNCC for its anti-Israel position.[30] At the biennial conference of the Jewish Labor Committee, Wilkins compared the alleged anti-Semitism of SNCC to that of George Lincoln Rockwell, the leader of the American Nazi Party.[31] Wilkins published his strongest support for Israel in the *Philadelphia Afro-American* in the immediate aftermath of the Six-Day War. Wilkins argued that "peace with justice and honour will come only with the recognition of the fact of Israel as a nation" and that Israel was a "bastion of democracy" that had "made a land to bloom."[32]

Despite the harsh rebuke SNCC received from mainstream civil rights organizations, in the wake of its outspoken criticism of Israel, a growing number of African Americans began to publicly criticize Israel and, more importantly, to begin to see in Palestinians' anticolonial political activism a shared project of anti-imperialism. For example, in response to the growing battle within the *New York Times* over the question of black American support for Israel, a group of influential black intellectuals and radicals signed an advertisement sponsored by the Committee of Black Americans for the Truth about the Middle East. Fifty-six African American activists, including James and Grace Boggs, the Reverend Albert E. Cleage, and Robert F. Williams, the exiled NAACP leader from Monroe, County, North Carolina, signed "An Appeal by Black Americans against United States Support of the Zionist Government of Israel."[33] The appeal criticized Zionism as an imperialist proxy for U.S. empire in Southeast Asia and in Africa. In particular, the advertisement suggested that Israel supported colonial powers in struggles for African decolonization and had established diplomatic relations with South Africa, thereby providing material support for apartheid. The advertisement concluded with an appeal for divestment from Israel and support for the Palestinian cause.

SNCC and the Committee of Black Americans for the Truth about the Middle East articulated a global political struggle against imperialism and racial capitalism that linked Palestinian resistance to struggles over black freedom in the United States, and this—far more than a "falling out" with American Jews—explains the shift. In this way, Palestine became an important geography in the making of a third world international movement.[34] No U.S.-based group was more directly responsible for creating a geography of liberation linking Palestine and urban black America, and in developing an ideological position on third world solidarity, than the Black Panther Party.

The Politics of Intercommunalism

The Black Panthers' political philosophy drew on Maoism and Marxist Leninism as it articulated a global revolutionary struggle—similar to what Chamberlin identifies as the PLO's global offensive—committed to armed self-defense and anti-imperialism.[35] Because they took a global view of anti-imperialist politics, the Panthers rejected the political framework of black nationalism, which they argued was too dependent on the logic of nationalism and liberal governance. Black nationalists, they argued, merely sought to reproduce forms of capitalism that they derisively labeled black capitalism. Equally problematic for the Panthers was that the mainstream civil rights movement failed to identify the United States as an imperial power and therefore sought inclusion in the empire rather than a global politics of anti-imperialism.

As an alternative to black nationalism and civil rights, the Panthers embraced what they called "revolutionary nationalism," which was a nationalism of liberation—against forms of racial capitalism and empire—rather than a nationalism of racism and capitalism. In staking this claim, the Panthers sought to disavow the U.S. nation while lending support to third world national liberation projects. As Newton would write, the Panthers sought "to reconcile support for revolutionary nationalism abroad, while disclaiming all forms of nationalism within the U.S. context as necessarily bound up with American oppression."[36]

Revolutionary nationalists conceived of black Americans as a colonized people who were victimized by racial capitalism and imperialism. In this way, they reconstituted the Communist Party's 1920s Black Belt thesis, which had viewed blacks as an internal colony in the United States requiring anti-imperial politics in order to become liberated. As Eldridge Cleaver, the Panthers' minister of information, would argue, "There is a White Mother Country and a Black Colony, there is Viet Nam and there is Puerto Rico, and Cuba, and other situations."[37] In this way, Cleaver produced a geography of a black country that could enter the field of international relations, despite not having the attributes of a state.

Because they viewed African Americans as constituting a black colony within the United States, the Panthers believed black liberation could emerge only through political actions aimed at decolonization. Black freedom could come only by undermining the ruling circles of the world and joining with the people of the world as internationalists. But because internationalism referred to relations between nations, the Black Panther Party realized it needed to imagine political identities beyond the nation (because the U.S. nation had become an empire). Thus the Black Panther Party theorized "intercommunalism" as a political imaginary that posited the U.S. black colony as merely one example of a community suffering from the violence of U.S. imperialism. As Nikhil Singh has argued, the Panthers focused on the ghetto as spatially different from the rest of the nation, due to the intense police violence and underdevelopment in black communities. According to Singh, "Reappropriating ghettoized spaces from the pathologizing discourse of social science, Black liberation politics instead figured the ghetto as a place of 'irredeemable spatial difference' within the nation-state, irrecuperable to unifying temporal narratives of national belonging and citizenship."[38] In this way, the Panthers saw black urban communities and the ghetto as colonized spaces that could be productively viewed in relation to similar colonies contending with U.S. empire, whether in Oakland, California, or in South Vietnam. "We see very little different in what happens to a community here in North America and what happens to a community in Vietnam. We see very little difference in what happens, even culturally to a Chinese community in San Francisco and a Chinese community in Hong Kong. We see very little difference in what happens to a Black community in Harlem and a Black community in South Africa, a Black community in Angola and Mozambique."[39] As Alyosha Goldstein points out, Newton and the Panthers "suggested an interdependent radical localism and self-determination not derived from the hegemony of the nation-state that was then so central to the postwar liberal world order."[40]

Hence the Panthers embraced a geography of liberation that directed revolutionary politics away from the nation-bound horizon of the mainstream civil rights movement and toward the global sphere of anti-imperialism and decolonization. As Eldridge Cleaver would put it, "In our struggle for national liberation, we are now in the phase of community liberation, to free our black communities from the imperialistic control exercised over them by the racists exploiting cliques within white communities, to free our people locked up as they are in Urban Dungeons, from the imperialism of the white Suburbs."[41] This geographic imaginary brought distant geopolitical entities into a shared horizon, so that Oakland and Angola were linked as similarly victimized by military repression and racial capitalism.

Black Panther Palestine

Although much has been written about the global dimensions of the Panthers' political imaginary, surprisingly little has been written about how the Palestine question served as a generative location for Panther intercommunalism.[42] And yet throughout the relatively brief history of the Black Panther movement the question of Palestine and solidarity with the PLO were prominent features of the Black Panthers' official newspaper, *Black Panther*, and helped the Panthers to articulate an Afro-Arab political imaginary.

The Panthers' political philosophy was most clearly articulated in the *Black Panther Intercommunal News Agency*; from 1968 to 1980 the newspaper distributed the political philosophy of the Panthers globally while also bringing the global struggle against imperialism to its U.S. readers. The *Black Panther* knit together a global map of communities struggling under racial capitalism and imperialism, including Mozambique, Zimbabwe, Angola, Chile, Puerto Rico, South Africa, Cuba, Namibia, Eritrea, and Palestine. Most important for our purposes, the *Black Panther* was one of the most reliable sources of news in the U.S. on the Israeli occupation of the West Bank, with regular stories on expanding Israeli settlements in the occupied West Bank and new forms of occupation. But most critically, the newspaper was also a venue for Al-Fatah and the Popular Front for the Liberation of Palestine (PFLP) to publish editorials about their struggle for U.S. audiences. Indeed, as we will see momentarily, both PLO leader Yasser Arafat and PFLP leader George Habash published editorials in *Black Panther*.[43]

The Panthers' view of the Israel/Palestine conflict evolved from 1968 to 1980 from one of strong anti-Zionism and support for the PLO to a more nuanced analysis that included criticism of Arab nationalism and its racial exclusions. This transformation occurred as a result of changing dynamics in the Arab world as well as through the education Panther leaders received while traveling throughout the Middle East in 1980. Because the political philosophy of intercommunalism relied on developing a cartography that linked disparate communities, the Panthers viewed Israeli colonialism as the same as U.S. imperialism, if not a direct extension of the U.S. empire. In this view, Palestinians and U.S. blacks contended with the same enemies: U.S.-inspired imperial violence and racial capitalism. Thus as they wrote about Israel, they transported much of their domestic analysis of state violence—which named police violence and white racism "the pigs"—to the Palestinian struggle. "The Israeli Government," the *Black Panther* published in November 1968, "is an imperialist, expansionist power in Palestine. The government is at fault, not all Jews. There are many non-Jews who support what Israel is doing. Pig Johnson is one of them. The term, Israel, is like saying racist United States, and it has the same policy as the U.S. Government has in the Middle East."[44] The *Black Panther* was clearest about the links between U.S. empire and state violence and Israeli state violence when it published "Palestine Guerillas vs. Israeli Pigs," which translated its urban black struggle and state-sponsored violence—characterized by "pigs"—in the United States into a global analysis of state violence that implicated Israel.[45]

As early as the second volume of *Black Panther*, the question of Palestine became a touchstone around which the Panthers theorized the work of global black revolutionary politics. The newspaper implored readers to critically examine claims that Palestinian guerillas were terrorists, drawing an analogy to the many black radical activists who had been imprisoned in the United States for political reasons. For example, the *Black Panther* argued that Palestinian guerillas, often imprisoned in Israeli jails, were no different from Black Panthers like Huey Newton who were similarly framed as violent and dangerous, as well as imprisoned. According to the *Panther* editorial, "No Arab can claim that a PALESTINIAN GUERRILLA, or ONE simple [*sic*] ACCUSED of BEING ONE, who is caught by the RACIST ISRAE-LIS can get a fair trail in THEIR COURTS. And let us keep in mind the GREAT SIMILARITY between the conditions under which the BLACK PEOPLE live in the U.S. and those under which the PALESTINIAN ARABS live in Israel."[46] The Panthers developed three related claims about the question of Palestine. First, they argued that Zionism was an extension of U.S. imperialism and racial capitalism. Hence acts of Israeli colonialism were, for the Panthers, extensions of U.S. imperialism, since Israel was an extension of the United States. Second, the Panthers argued that Israeli diplomatic support for South Africa demonstrated that Israel supported apartheid and, by extension, that Zionism was a racist discourse. And finally, the group argued that the PLO was struggling against the same imperial powers as black radicals in the United States and therefore the Black Panther Party and the PLO could be united in an intercommunal horizon of revolutionary nationalism.

The Panthers' analysis of Zionism emerged most clearly in discussions surrounding the 1975 adoption by the United Nations Social, Humanitarian, and Cultural Committee of a resolution linking Zionism to racism.[47] The *Black Panther* newspaper covered the proceedings of the UN's deliberations, and it featured editorials in support of the linkage of Zionism to racism. For example, in November 1975 the paper published an editorial by Farouk Kaddoumi, head of the PLO's political department, in support of "Palestinian Independence and Sovereignty." Kaddoumi argued that Zionism was a philosophy that assumed the racial superiority and manifest destiny of Jews over all others, and in this way was a racial discourse that presumed Jewish racial superiority.[48]

The Panthers expanded Kaddoumi's argument by claiming that Zionism was a European discourse of imperialism and not an organic movement of national liberation among European Jews. The merits of this argument are not the primary concern of my analysis here; rather, what interests me are the ways that the Panthers approached the question of Palestine through the optic of anti-imperialism, with a particularly sharp focus on the role of the U.S. empire in affecting the plight of Palestinians and the actions of Zionists. Hence, the Panther analysis frequently transported an analysis of U.S. domestic race relations to the question of Palestine in order to construct a useful analog, which could then serve the Panthers' politics of revolutionary intercommunialism. It was important to the Panthers that the question of Palestine be framed not as a Jewish/Arab conflict but as a question of imperialism and racial capitalism. Hence the Panthers would go so far as to argue that Zionism was bad for Jews as well as Arabs, because it encouraged Jews to embrace a false consciousness in which they allied with Western imperialism over deeper and more humane intercommunal bonds with working-class Palestinian Arabs.

In the wake of the UN's discussion of Zionism and racism, the *Black Panther* republished an article that had been distributed by the *Canada-Palestine Solidarity Association*. The article, "Zionism: Enemy of the Jews," laid out a case for Zionism as a form of racism and false consciousness that thwarted intraclass solidarity among working-class Jews and Muslims in Palestine. "Zionist racism practiced by the White, educated and more affluent European Jew in Israel against his colored, much poorer, uneducated, Sephardic (Oriental) 'Brother' is an aspect of Israeli life today few Americans are aware of."[49] By the publication of this article, the Panthers were aware of increasing racial division and conflict within Israel and had developed an analysis of Zionism that was attuned to this conflict. As I will discuss in a moment, Israeli racial conflicts had, by the early 1970s, exploded in a social protest movement among Arab Jews who called themselves the Israeli Black Panthers. The Panther analysis, therefore, spoke to a growing division within Israel along lines of race and class.

Zionism was false consciousness, the article continued, because it directed working-class Arab-Jewish alienation against Palestinians, rather than against the European, Ashkenazi Jews who embraced European imperialism and racial capitalism. "Zionism [by embracing its Westernness] thus incorporated the very essence of the disease which had plagued European Jews. It accepted the class system of Western Europe and the concept of laissez-faire capitalism."[50]

Additional evidence for the Panthers' argument that Zionism was merely a form of Western imperialism and racial capitalism was the material support the Israeli government offered the apartheid government of South Africa during the mid-1970s. During the 1960s, when Israel sought to gain the support of and enter trade agreements with newly independent African states, it took a critical stance against South African apartheid. In October 1961, for example, Israel voted in the UN General Assembly to censure the South African representative's speech in favor of apartheid. After the 1973 Yom Kippur war, however, most African states broke diplomatic ties with Israel, despite Israeli efforts to provide aid to newly independent African states and to the Organization of African States.[51]

By 1975 Israeli opposition to the South African government subsided, as the Jewish state entered the Israeli–South Africa agreement, signaling a new diplomatic tie between Israel and South Africa, one of the few African states willing to enter political, diplomatic, and economic relationships with Israel. The agreement was a secret defense cooperation agreement that enabled South Africa to work around international arms embargoes against the apartheid regime.[52] In April 1976 Israeli prime minister Yitzhak Rabin invited South African prime minister John Vorster for a state visit.[53] The same year, the nonaligned movement called for an oil embargo against Israel (and France) due to its arms trading with South Africa. Israel's diplomatic and military support for South Africa would continue until 1987, when the Israeli cabinet finally denounced South Africa's apartheid policies.[54]

The antiapartheid movement had been a touchstone around which black civil rights and black revolutionary social movements had organized. One could argue that, more than any other factor, mainstream African American support for the State of Israel was challenged by Israel's support for South Africa during most of the 1970s and 1980s. The Black Panthers made Israel's support for South Africa a central component of their analysis of the Middle East conflict, forcefully arguing that Zionism and apartheid were twin evils of imperialism and racism. In November 1975 the *Black Panther* newspaper published a brief summary of George Tomeh's *Israel and South Africa: The Unholy Alliance*, which detailed the history of Israel's diplomatic relationship with the apartheid government.[55] Tomeh was a Syrian diplomat, as well as a Lebanese college president, who advocated Palestinian causes and had served as a representative to the Organization of Petroleum-Exporting Countries.

The Panthers' analysis of the question of Palestine was not only informed by criticism of Zionism and Israel's diplomatic relationship with South Africa; it was also positively shaped by the material and ideological connections forged in the crucible of pan-Arab and pan-African politics, especially as they developed in Egypt throughout the second half of the 1960s. A formative moment in the making of post-1968 Afro-Arab political imaginaries was the Afro-Arab summit convened March 7–9, 1977, in Cairo. The meeting was a joint project of the Organization of African States and the Arab League, both of which represented nonaligned states.[56] Hosted by Egypt's Anwar Sadat, the meeting was attended by representatives from sixty African and Arab countries. The conference addressed many regional and international themes, foregrounding an anti-imperialist project that linked Zionist policies toward Palestinians and apartheid policies against black South Africans. The summit presented to the General Assembly of the United Nations a series of recommendations, including the need for Afro-Arab states to resist imperialism, in its many forms, throughout their region. "The African and Arab Heads of State and Government reaffirm the need to strengthen their peoples' united front in their struggle for national liberation and condemn imperialism, colonialism, neo-colonialism, zionism, apartheid and all other forms of discrimination and racial and religious segregation, especially under the forms in which they appear in Southern Africa, Palestine and the other occupied Arab and African territories." The summit also drafted "A Statement defining the Palestinian and African liberation movements as 'joint Afro-Arab causes' and called for support to the Arab frontline states in the Middle East and the five frontline states in southern Africa."[57] The *Black Panther* covered the summit and published an editorial by Yasser Arafat, who attended the conference as the Palestinian representative. Echoing Tomeh, he denounced "'the unholy alliance between South Africa, Rhodesia and Israel' and declared to the African delegates, 'our struggle is inseparable from your struggle.'"[58]

Intercommunalism was a multidirectional politics, in that it encouraged the articulation of global solidarity from within as well as without the United States. Thus, Palestinian intellectuals in Fatah and the PFLP capitalized on the Panthers' interest in the Israel/South Africa matrix of relations in order to garner black American support for the PLO.[59] Palestinian revolutionaries apparently shared the Panthers' analysis of the common bonds linking urban black communities and Palestinian refugees, frequently submitting articles to the *Black Panther*. In 1969, for example, the PFLP published a letter in *Black Panther* in which it articulated solidarity with the Black Panther Party. The PFLP viewed the United States as complicit with Israeli occupation of the West Bank because "the technically advanced USA supplies Israel the modern tools of destruction to be used against us." The PFLP addressed the *Black Panther* reader directly: "[The PFLP] after getting to know what you aim for and fight for, announced that it supports you morally. It is the liberation that we fight for. We are all in the same boat, facing the same ENEMY. LONG LIVE THE REVOLUTION AGAINST IMPERIALISM."[60]

Eldridge Cleaver, who had been forced into exile, chose Algeria as his home. Algeria was not only the location of a successful African struggle for decolonization but also the home of the PLO and its charismatic leader,

Yasser Arafat. While in Algeria, Cleaver met with members of Al-Fatah, including Arafat. In a published address to the members of the PLO, Cleaver "related how the United States was the Zionist regime that usurped the land of the Palestinian people as a puppet and pawn."[61] In response to Cleaver and the support from the Black Panther Party, Arafat published a letter of solidarity in *Black Panther* in which he linked the Palestinian cause to the global movement against imperialism. "The Palestine Liberation Movement considers itself a part of the peoples' struggle against international imperialism. We are fighting the same enemy whether it is in Latin America, Vietnam, or Palestine. The mask may differ but the face remains the same."[62]

The Panthers published two position papers on the Middle East conflict, one in 1974 and another in the 1980s. The second position paper was published after Huey Newton had traveled across the Middle East, where he met with Arafat in the PLO offices in Beirut. In their 1974 "Position Paper on the Middle East," the Black Panthers argued that the question of Palestine was foremost a question of human rights and not primarily about land, territory, or sovereignty. The main culprit of the Israel/Palestine question, the Panthers argued, was nationalism. The Panthers challenged Israel's national "chauvinism," arguing that "the very existence of nations is reactionary in this stage of human development, and a major cause of modern wars." Given the power of imperial nations to control other nations globally, "the very idea of national sovereignty can be a dangerous illusion."[63] In the case of Israel/Palestine, Israeli dominance depended on the support of the U.S. Congress and its military appropriations to Israel. Moreover, Palestinian resistance rested on the support, both financial and military, from oil-rich and oppressive Arab regimes.

Yet Newton was also critical of Arab nationalism, given how the wealth of Arab states was diverted away from Arab peasants and toward the needs of global empires. "For the vast majority of Arab peoples, in Saudi Arabia, in Libya, in Iran, in Kuwait and the Gulf oil sheikdoms, the struggle for self-determination is first of all a revolutionary struggle against their own oppressive states and ruling classes, partners in plunder with the oil imperialists of the West." For Palestinians, then, statehood could be a transitional stage in the advancement toward human rights. Palestinians and Jews, Newton argued, deserve the "right to the protective powers of a state."[64]

For Jews and Palestinians, according to the Panthers, only the revolutionary overthrow of imperialism could lead to human rights; the issue of territory was a secondary concern. For Israelis, this meant a struggle against U.S. imperialism and Zionist colonization efforts, particularly in the West Bank. For Palestinians and other Arabs, anti-imperialism meant overthrowing the oil barons who funnel the people's wealth to foreign armies and nations. According to Newton, to Arab dictators the Israeli question was a diversionary tool that enabled their continued oppression within their nations.

Newton signaled a break with Arab nationalists, who he believed had sided with imperialist powers (such as Nasser's post-1967 coalition with Jordan).[65] Moreover, Newton argued that slavery was an enduring legacy of Arab states that needed to be addressed as integral to anticolonial politics. "The oppression of Arabs in the Arab states is far worse than it is in Israel. There is still slavery in some Arab countries. There is oppression of women worse than in any other region of the world and there are primitive and barbarous punishments of poor people, which reflect a low esteem for human dignity and rights."[66]

Newton's position paper was shared with David Graham Du Bois, who corrected some problematic errors in Newton's draft. For example, he showed that Newton's phrase about Israel—"what was once a desert and arid land [had bloomed]"—"feeds the racist lie that until the Jews came to Palestine the land was non-productive and totally undeveloped." Moreover, Du Bois corrected Newton's mistaken inclusion of Iranians in the category "Arab." Du Bois also challenged Newton's use of the term "Israel's war of liberation." Du Bois asked, "Can we call the war that was fought in Palestine by armies of the yet to be created state of Israel a 'war of liberation'? Weren't, in fact, the Palestinians . . . fighting the war of liberation?"[67]

The Panther position on the question of Palestine was refined in the aftermath of Huey Newton's 1980 trip to Lebanon, Syria, the occupied West Bank, and Israel. During this trip, Newton toured refugee camps and met with Yasser Arafat in the Southern Lebanese camp of Rashadiya, near Tyre. Upon returning to the United States, Newton related his experiences as well as his political position on the Middle East. As they had done in their 1974 position paper on the Middle East, the Panthers drew unmistakable connections between the politics of Palestinian liberation and black American liberation. Newton admired the PLO's social welfare capacity as well as its armed revolution. Hence, in his *Black Panther* article Newton focused on the success of the PLO's Red Crescent Society and other Palestinian social welfare services that provided amenities, such as education and food, that host Arab states could not, or would not, provide.[68]

Although Newton was less critical of regional Arab states in 1980 than he was in his 1974 position paper on the Middle East, he maintained a focus

Huey Newton (*center*) outside unnamed Palestinian refugee camp in Lebanon with unknown Palestinian youth, likely members of the PLO, 1980 (M865, series 5, box 8, fol. 15, photo 43, Dr. Huey P. Newton Foundation Inc. collection, M0864, courtesy of Department of Special Collections and University Archives, Stanford University Libraries, Stanford, Calif. Permission granted by the Dr. Huey P. Newton Foundation Inc.)

on the United States as the imperial benefactor of Israeli aggression against the Palestinians. In making this strong claim, Newton argued that Palestinians and the *lumpenproletariat* blacks in America were linked as communities struggling to survive under U.S. imperialism. Thus the Panther newspaper argued that "U.S. military and economic support of the Israeli government has increased significantly in recent years—support the PLO charges has been the primary reason for the escalation of the Middle East war." The struggle for peace in the Middle East, therefore, would entail an anti-imperialist struggle against the United States, and not merely a struggle against Israeli colonialism.[69]

In charting a path toward "peace in the Middle East," in 1980 Newton advocated a two-state solution. This was likely the result of the 1976 shift within Fatah away from a single democratic state toward a two-state solution. According to the Panther newspaper, "Huey believes that the PLO would accept the following solutions to end the Israeli-Palestinian conflict: (1) creation of a non-religious state in which Palestinians and Israelis would live together or (2) creation of an autonomous and sovereign state for the Palestinians." Yet due to the severity of the conflict, Newton believed that the second option was the only viable solution.[70]

In one of its final published issues, the *Black Panther* once again provided a forum for Fatah's leader, Yasser Arafat, who by 1980 was a strong supporter of the two-state solution. The newspaper published Arafat's appeal in front of the United Nations:

> When we speak of our common hopes for the Palestine of tomorrow we include all Jews now living in Palestine who choose to live with us there in peace and without discrimination. . . . I call upon Jews to turn away from the illusory promises made to them by Zionist ideology and Israeli leadership. Those offer Jews perpetual bloodshed, endless bloodshed. . . . We invite them to emerge from their moral isolation into a more open realm of free choice. . . . We do not wish the shedding of one drop of either Arab or Jewish blood; neither do we delight in the continuation of killing which would end once a just peace, based on our people's rights, hopes and aspirations is finally established.[71]

It is all too easy to locate Jewish criticism of the PLO and the Black Panthers between 1968 and 1990. Many Jewish groups took the Panthers to task as an anti-Semitic organization. What gets lost in this criticism, however, is how the Black Panthers intercommunal politics reverberated in unexpected contexts. Throughout the period that the Black Panther Party formulated an anti-imperialist argument about Israel, and formed solidarity with Palestinians, its intercommunal politics were influencing a group of Israeli Jews for whom the Panthers' analysis of racial capitalism was especially relevant.

Israeli Black Panthers

When U.S. domestic politics involving the black power movement are framed in terms of "black/Jewish relations," or when the question of Palestine is framed as an Arab/Jewish conflict, the complexities of everyday life get subsumed under the weight of modernist racial categories and geographies. What gets lost in these framings of domestic and international issues are the facts of black Jews in the United States and Israel/Palestine as well as the facts of Arab Jews in the United States and Israel/Palestine. While it is beyond the scope of this chapter to discuss the history of black Jews and Arab Jews, I do want to focus on the complex position of Arab Jews in post-1967 Israel as both a racialized and semicolonized group within Israel.[72] The Arab Jews of Israel occupy a complex position as both colonizers and, in a way, the colonized. Arab Jews often fall victim to formations of Israeli racial capitalism while they also function as colonizers over indigenous Palestinians. My purpose in this section is not to romanticize Mizrahi Jews as outside the problem of Israeli settler colonialism; rather, it is to understand how the U.S. Black Panther movement, which had been inspired by the PLO, served as a useful analog for Arab Jews in Israel to analyze and resist the conditions of imperialism and racial capitalism in Israel during the first half of the 1970s. Moreover, I intend to show that for a brief moment, the Israeli Panthers articulated the possibility of a radically different political order in Israel/Palestine, one that privileged intercommunalism over nationalism.

Sephardic Jews were a majority of the Jewish population in late-nineteenth-century Palestine during the first European Zionist settlement, and as such, they negotiated with Ottoman leaders and set policy within Palestine's Jewish community. Yet, as early as the 1890s, when European, Ashkenazi Jews began to emigrate to Palestine, previously absent racial distinctions began to emerge, as the Ashkenazi newcomers often arrived with relatively more wealth and the desire to hire non-Ashkenazi labor. Yemenite Jews were recruited to Palestine as early as the 1890s in order to serve as migrant labor for Ashkenazi Jews, and this would establish a pattern of racialized labor within Palestinian Jewish communities. According to the Ashkenazi Zionist party, HaPoel HaTzair, importing Yemenite workers to Palestine would be financially beneficial while also enabling Ashkenazis to assume leadership positions requiring greater mental skills. "An Ashkenazi worker would not withstand the menial jobs, and we should put the Yemenites there, whose needs are smaller. I cannot accept that position that we can just call out for Ashkenazi laborers from Russia, simply because our call will not help. . . . The Mizrahi element can be used a lot, as their material requirements are not too large."[73] From 1908 to 1926 Yemenite Jews were not allowed to own land in Jewish settlements, although they were recruited to Palestine to serve as labor and to bolster Jewish demographics.[74]

Throughout the period of the British mandate in Palestine, the largest share of Jewish immigration quotas were granted to European Jews. During this period, Mizrahi Jews were limited to 10 percent of the total population of Jewish immigrants to Palestine. Moreover, non-Ashkenazi Jews were offered second-class social services; Sephardi and Mizrahi Jews were barred from attending Zionist Ashkenazi schools, which were mostly funded by world Jewish organizations.[75]

After Israeli independence, political leaders in Israel and throughout the European Jewish diaspora discussed the need both to recruit Jews from

Arab countries—in order to build demographic strength in Israel and as a supply of cheap labor—and to de-Arabize Mizrahi and Sephardi Jews who were orientalized as less fit for the Jewish project of nation building. Recruiting Jews from Arab countries, however, was not always an easy sell; in many Arab countries Jews were content to stay put. The *British Jewish Chronicle* wrote in 1949, "The Chief Rabbi and Iraqi Jews do not like Zionism, since it has caused difficulties for them. They prefer to stay in Iraq and live under the patronage of Islam and its tolerance. They are attached to their houses and traditions, and to the graves of their prophets in Iraq. They have no desire to leave their country and live in refugee camps in Israel. They believe that people there are not too friendly towards oriental Jews."[76] Lebanese Jews, a small population in 1948, chose to remain in Lebanon until the outbreak of the 1975 Lebanese civil war; after World War II the Jewish population of Lebanon saw modest increases.[77]

Yet for a variety of reasons that go beyond the scope of this chapter, Arab Jews did migrate to Palestine in the wake of the Arab-Israeli war, but they arrived in a new nation-state that defined itself as non-Arab. Hence, newly arriving Arab Jews found themselves entering a new national context in which they were racialized and slotted into a capitalist economy as racialized laborers. The head of the Middle Eastern Jews Department in the Jewish Agency, Yaakov Zrubavel, claimed, "These may not be the Jews whose arrival we desire, but we cannot tell them, 'Don't come.'"[78] Although they were recruited to the Jewish state, the Mizrahi Jews were initially excluded from political power, as European Zionists felt that Arab culture was antithetical to the modernist project of Israel. David Ben Gurion, Israel's first prime minister, argued, "Those [Jews] from Morocco had no education. Their customs are those of Arabs. . . . The culture of Morocco I would not like to have here. And I don't see what contribution present [Jewish] Persians have to make. . . . We do not want Israelis to become Arabs. We are in duty bound to fight against the spirit of the Levant, which corrupts individuals and societies, and preserve the authentic Jewish values as they crystallised in the [European] Diaspora."[79]

Journalist Arye Gelblum, writing for the Israeli newspaper *Ha'aretz* in 1949, characterized the Ashkenazi mainstream attitude about Arab Jews in Israel when he documented his visit to immigrant camps to meet North African Jewish migrants.

This is a people whose primitivity sets a record, their level of education borders on total ignorance, and yet worse is their lack of ability to absorb anything spiritual. . . . They are entirely given to the play of savage primitive instincts. . . . Have we considered what would happen to the state if this would be its population? For the day will come when the Aliyah of Jews from the Arab countries will join them! What character will the state of Israel have and what shall be its level with such populations?[80]

In 1951 Zalman Shazar, a member of the Jewish Agency executive and the future president of Israel, warned about Mizrahi immigration, "It will cost us dearly. This is unfathomable. . . . An Aliyah has come to us who never knew the taste of a high school, and they are unused to so much education, to so much learning. Will the yishuv in Israel survive without more Europeans and Anglo-Saxons, Jews like us? . . . I think this is the current function of Zionism: To bring Jews, not necessarily the Jews of the Orient, into the circle of Aliyah."[81] The Israeli government eventually curtailed Mizrahi immigration in the late 1960s. Beginning in the 1970s, immigrant quotas were based on biopolitical concerns about fitness for citizenship and orientalist concerns about the future of the Israeli state as a bastion of Western enlightenment. Nahum Goldman, chair of the Jewish Agency executive, said that "a Jew from Eastern Europe is worth twice the value of a Jew from Kurdistan. . . . A hundred thousand Mizrahi Jews should be returned to their countries."[82]

Between 1948 and 1950 during their largest migration, Mizrahi Jews were structurally discriminated against in housing, employment, and education. Mizrahi children were undereducated. Mizrahi families were precluded from prime government housing stock. Ashkenazi communities turned to Mizrahi labor for inexpensive laborers. During the first three years after the establishment of the state, about half of the 664,000 immigrants to Israel were Mizrahi. Most Mizrahi were sent to the frontier of the state (the upper Galilee and the Negev), where there were fewer job opportunities and greater risk of conflict with dispossessed Arabs. In this way, the Mizrahi were forced to enter the Israeli national project by serving as literal and symbolic frontiersmen for the expanding state.[83]

One consequence of the June 1967 war was the growth of the security industry in Israel that disproportionately benefited Ashkenazi businesses. Yet the war also led to the ascendance of Mizrahi class and culture consciousness. Economic liberalization during the 1960s disproportionately affected Mizrahi workers, who were dependent on social welfare. About 80 percent of welfare recipients during the 1960s were Mizrahim.[84] German repatriation to victims of the Holocaust boosted the revenue of 20 percent of the Ashkenazi population. The state was only required to educate

Mizrahi children until the age of fifteen. In 1970, 55 percent of Mizrahi children received no education.[85]

Within Israel, the Six-Day War was represented as the victory of European modernity over the backward Orient. The Mizrahi in Israel were thus precariously positioned as Arab and Israeli and therefore found themselves looking at the Israeli economic boom from the outside. At the same time, Palestinian Arabs in the West Bank and in Gaza constituted a new underclass that marginally elevated the social position of the Mizrahi. Thus the 1967 war illuminated both Mizrahi economic exclusion and their national inclusion.

The Israeli Black Panthers emerged among a group of ten Mizrahi youth who lived in the Mousrara neighborhood of Jerusalem. Mousrara, located near the border of Jordanian-controlled East Jerusalem, had been a frontier neighborhood until 1967. On March 3, 1971, these ten Mizrahi youth organized a public protest against substandard living conditions in their neighborhood and were arrested for their activities. Mizrahi activists published a flyer demanding their colleagues' release: "What right does the minister of politics have to deny members of his community the ability to demonstrate for rights they have been deprived of for twenty-three years?"[86] The Mizrahi activists signed their flyer "Mousrara-Harlem" in order to draw a material and ideological connection between the ghettos in which black Americans lived and those in which black Israelis lived. The flyer read,

> We, a group of screwed-up youths, address all those who have had
>   enough:
> Enough with no work.
> Enough sleeping ten in a room.
> Enough looking at the projects constructed for the olim.
> Enough taking jail and brutality every other day.
> Enough with government broken promises.
> We've had enough disenfranchisement.
> We've had enough discrimination.
> How long will they give to us and we will keep silent.
> Alone we won't do anything—Together we will make it.
> Demonstrating for our right to be like all other citizens in this state.
> The demonstration will be held on Wednesday, at 3:30 pm, in Jaffa Street
>   outside City Hall.[87]

On April 13, 1971, the Mizrahi protesters, now self-appointed Israeli Black Panthers, met with Israeli prime minister Golda Meir. In this meeting, Meir took the Panthers to task for affiliating with a U.S. organization that she felt was anti-Semitic. Moreover, she questioned whether the Panthers were duly loyal to the State of Israel. At this stage in their development, the young Israeli Panthers had yet to develop a sophisticated political philosophy, with the exception of committing to a program of opposing police brutality and increasing access to social services. Hence, the Panthers assured Meir that they were loyal to the nation and merely wanted to be included. In this way, the Israeli Panthers were unlike their U.S. counterparts, who had forcefully argued against national inclusion as a revolutionary strategy. Yet over time, as the Israeli Panthers became more sophisticated and as they entered into solidarity with members of the PLO and the U.S. Black Panther Party, their political analysis sharpened into a sustained critique of racial capitalism.

On May 18, 1971, the Israeli Panthers organized a mass demonstration that included 5,000–7,000 protesters and that became known as "the night of the Panterim." The police responded harshly, and seven hours of clashes ensued amidst Panther claims that Israel was a police state.

If the name "Black Panthers" was initially a provocation and not inspired by a sense of deep solidarity with the black freedom struggle in the United States, this would change as the Israeli Panthers' politics expanded. The Israeli Panthers began to identify class disparities in increasingly racialized language, referring to the Israeli rich as "kings" and the poor as "slaves." In a flyer distributed on August 28, 1971, during a protest at Zion Square, the Panthers expressed their racialized understanding of class conditions in Israel. "Suppose you are a menial black laborer, native of Iraq, Yemen, or Morocco, and a father of many children. One can guess, more or less, your history. Upon arrival in Israel—you were dumped in a transit camp. You were paid exploitation wages, and worse: the fruits of your labor were eaten by them—site managers, factory owners, the bosses."[88]

In January 1972 the World Zionist Congress convened in Jerusalem, and the Panthers protested; this marked the Panthers' first break with Zionism, which they argued was a colonial discourse reserved for Ashkenazi Jews. Over time the break with Zionism signaled the Israeli Panthers' increasing solidarity with Palestinians as Arabs and as victims of European imperialism. The Panthers would eventually attempt to link the oppression of the Mizrahim to that of the Palestinians. Kohavi Shemesh, one of the founders of the Panthers, remembers,

> The Panthers were ahead of Israeli society by a whole generation, and ahead of the Left as well. We had connections with the PLO as early as 1972. We met with PLO leaders and recognized them as legitimate

leaders of the Palestinian people. We had talks, and we understood their need for independence and to eliminate the occupation, and we agreed that the problems of the Misrahim and of the Arabs are intertwined. There will be no equality and no chance for the Mizrahim as long as there's an occupation and a national struggle, and on the other hand, the national struggle will not be over so long as the Mizrahim are at the bottom of the ladder, and are practically an anti-Arab level.[89]

The Israeli Black Panthers' memory of their radicalism is more radical than their actual history. The transition from a politics of inclusion and civil rights to an anticolonial politics constituted by support for Palestinian decolonization was never complete. And yet, as the founding members of the Panthers recall their movement, they draw firm connections to the U.S. Panther cause and the politics of revolutionary intercommunalism. Charlie Biton, one of the founders of the Israeli Panthers, argues that the name "Israeli Black Panthers" was not an arbitrary choice meant to illicit Israeli reaction. Biton disagreed with Golda Meir about the presumed anti-Semitism of the U.S. Panthers, arguing that they merely opposed racial capitalists, including Jewish ones. "The Panthers in the U.S. are not against the Jews as Jews," Biton explained, "but as exploiting employers. They are the masters, and that's why the fight is against them."[90] Biton had met Angela Davis and named his firstborn after her.

In 2007 I interviewed one of the founders of the Israeli Black Panthers, Reuven Abergil. Abergil is an organic intellectual who has been a key figure in the Mizrahi struggle to reconstitute a pan-Arab and Jewish identity. Moreover, Abergil is an important figure in the forging of an Afro-Arab political imaginary that expands our horizon to include those Jews who get written out of Afro-Arab politics. In the late 1960s Abergil was a Moroccan Jewish street kid, a citizen of Israel, whose family had been recruited to the Jewish state in order to bolster Jewish population demographics. Yet he was informally excluded from Israeli society and called "black."

By 1970 Mizrahi Jews were called "black Jews," and when more recent Eastern European Jewish migrants, many of whom were not Jewish, complained about having to live next to "black Jews," Mizrahi Jews began to draw alternative maps of their belonging in the world. Although Zionism had been a draw for some Arab Jews, their exclusion from Israeli society led them to reconsider their political affiliations.

Thrown in prison for petty theft, Abergil had a prison conversion after reading a newspaper report on the Black Panther Party in the United States. Abergil was taken by the Black Panthers' decolonial politics and articulation of a genealogy uniting the Afro-Asian world. Along with other imprisoned Arab Jews, Abergil formed a group within prison called the Israeli Black Panthers. The Israeli Black Panthers met with exiled PLO leader Yasser Arafat as well as with U.S. Black Panther leaders like Angela Davis in Paris. Ultimately the Israeli Black Panthers recognized how Israeli colonialism, a formation similar to U.S. setter colonialism in North America, created colonial differences, especially on a Jewish/Arab axis. Abergil knew that Arab Jews comprised a majority of the Israeli population and that they had more in common with Palestinian Arabs than with European Jews. Hence he produced a new imaginary of his belonging that linked the Arab Islamic world, North Africa, and the Jewish diaspora, a recognition of what Ella Shohat has recently called a "taboo memory."[91]

Although many scholars have argued that the Israeli Black Panthers chose their name primarily for its shock factor in Israel, Abergil remembers a different history of his political movement. In his memory of the Israeli Black Panthers, the group's connection to the U.S. Black Panther movement is more intentional. As he described this history of the Panthers to me, Abergil underscored the underlying racist logic of Israeli citizenship and nationalism. "Jews from Morocco didn't choose to come to Israel," Abergil insisted; they were coerced through Zionist tactics to sew insecurity for Jews in Arab lands. Once in Israel, Abergil argued, the Moroccan Jews, and by extension all of the Sephardim, were relegated to a second-class citizenship. Moroccan Jews were given inadequate housing, often on the frontiers of the state where political and military conflict was most pronounced. Mizrahi Jews entered an educational system that taught Moroccans that "the Orient" was backward and that only the European is truly modern. Mizrahi Jews were, put simply, racialized in Israel as black; thus when Abergil and his colleagues sought to mobilize in the early 1970s, they looked to social movements responding to similar racist and colonial contexts.[92]

Although Israeli prime minister Golda Meir believed that the U.S. Black Panther Party was "anti-Semitic," Abergil understood that the "social structure" facing blacks in America and "blacks" in Israel were similar. Thus "we didn't choose the 'red brigade' or 'Che Guavara' as the symbols of our movement," because it was the anti-imperialist and antiracist politics of the U.S. Black Panther Party that most spoke to Abergil's social conditions. Abergil pointed out that Israel "was working like America" with regard to race, in the ways that both nations created a black caste of underemployed laborers who were pathologized as incapable of national inclusion. If the "culture of poverty" thesis shaped dominant American responses to black inequality, in Israel there was a similar discourse about the Mizrahim as "bad apples" who could not shed the "spirit of the Levant," as David Ben Gurion had referred to Oriental Jews.[93]

Abergil locates the origins of the Black Panther Party in Israel in the years after the 1967 Six-Day War. This was an era in which there was growing protest of the occupation of Palestinian lands, as well as growing public racial discourse about Arab citizens and subjects of Israeli rule. Although there were a growing number of leftist organizations that criticized the occupation, none spoke to the particular concerns of Israel's own racial underclass. Hence Abergil and his colleagues founded the Israeli Black Panthers: "The Black Panther Party [in the U.S.] fit Mizrahim just like Zionism fit America." Yet despite the seeming analog that the Black Panther Party provided to some Mizrahim, Abergil notes that many of his friends needed to be convinced of racism in Israel. The nationalist discourse of "the ingathering of world Jewry" assumed that Israel would absorb all Jews regardless of their nationality. Yet just as the universalist logic of the U.S. state included exclusive legal and racial practices, the Israeli state was similarly wary of some of the national origins and racial backgrounds of some Jews, including those from the Arab world. Many Mizrahi, according to Abergil, had accepted their racialization as "a God-given structure," since Israel had been based on a logic of manifest destiny and chosenness. But Abergil explained to his Mizrahi brothers and sisters that while Russian immigrants to Israel were greeted at the airport, Ethiopian and Sephardi Jews are not. Moreover, while Israeli society idolizes Ashkenazi Israeli soldiers, the state "doesn't even look for missing Mizrahi soldiers."

As with the U.S. Panthers, a keen sense of dissonance emerged for the Mizrahi around the issues of national service in the Israeli military. Echoing the famous refusal of Muhammad Ali to fight in the U.S. military in Vietnam, Abergil points out the irony that Mizrahi soldiers are asked to protect kibbutzim (from which they were largely excluded) and to harvest the kibbutz produce (for which they did not share profits) and then asked to join the army against Palestinian Arabs. The contradictions posed by having to defend a nation from which he was excluded revealed the exclusions of Israeli nationalism.

Abergil documented numerous ways that Israeli society had created a binary racial logic in which blackness and whiteness were mapped onto the Mizrahi/Ashkenazi binary. He argues that Israeli immigration policy, especially the recruitment of Russian Jews, is organized to whiten the Israeli population. Although Israel also recruited Oriental Jews, it was through racist programs like "operation red carpet" that they were brought to Israel. While Israel presented itself as a model of European modernity, "a city on a hill," it also created a racial caste system in order to provide cheap labor for the growing state. As Abergil argues, Israel needed black Jews to serve as "working hands" who often earned only 10 percent of Ashkenazi income. Moreover, in order to curtail the size of Oriental Jewish families, argues Abergil, the state dispersed Mizrahi families throughout the country, often in frontier housing that made social interactions with other Mizrahi families difficult.

Abergil and the Israeli Black Panthers began to reconfigure their belongings in Israel and began to see commonalities not only with black anticolonialists in the U.S. but also with the national liberation struggle of the Palestinians, even though Mizrahi Jews were, to Palestinians in Israel and in the West Bank and Gaza, the oppressor. Moreover, the Israeli state recognized the possibilities of pan-Arab solidarity reuniting Mizrahim with other Arabs. Hence the Israeli state intentionally positioned Mizrahim in the colonial borderlands, where the Mizrahim would serve in positions of dominance to Arab Palestinians. Moreover, Mizrahim were accorded certain "psychological wages"—better housing, access to better schools, and a sense of inclusion in the state—that made their material conditions better than those of Palestinians. Abergil notes that many Mizrahim embraced the status in the police, in the military, and in the prison guards because, "like all slaves that want to please their masters," these Mizrahim know that their economic and political situations will be worse if they are associated with Palestinians.

Members of the Israeli Black Panthers, Abergil recalls, met with the U.S. Black Panther Party in 1975. The group that met with Angela Davis (but not with Huey Newton) was led by Sa'adia Maciano and Charlie Biton. Moreover, in 1974 the Israeli Black Panthers met with the Palestinian leadership in Europe. In 1982 Charlie Biton and Victor Alouch met in Geneva with the PLO and Yasser Arafat. The difficulties Mirzrahim had in Israel, Abergil argues, were not with Palestinians but with the Ashkenazi.

Today, as Abergil reconstructs his memory of the Israeli Black Panthers, the movement seems more subversive than perhaps it actually was. The Israeli Panthers' primary goals were for Mizrahi civil rights within Israel and not to fundamentally address the colonial question of Palestinian human rights. Recognizing his break from the Zionist project, Abergil is today part of a movement to repatriate Israeli Arab Jews to Arab "homelands" as a counterdiscourse of the right of return. According to Abergil, "Sixty years ago, following the deportation of the Palestinians from their land, Jews from Arab and Muslim countries were brought to Palestine with the full cooperation of Zionists and leaders from North America and Europe. The Jews from Arab and Muslim countries were slated to act as spare parts in place of the Palestinian deportees following the ethnic cleansing of Palestinian Arabs."[94] Using the language of Palestinian postcolonialism, Abergil advocates the "right of return," not just for the Palestinian refugee, but also for the Arab Jew.

> I hereby turn to the heads of the Arab and Muslim countries. . . . I wish to propose a similar law that would provide for a "right of return" of Jews from Arab and Muslim countries back to their homelands, financed by the property of our ancestors that was left behind in these countries, in order to facilitate settling in after 60 years of imposed exile, and to encourage support for this idea amongst other leaders and peoples. . . . If the gates will open in Arab and Muslim countries for the Jews to return home, the 40% of the Zionist Europeans will lose the "demographic security" we provided them, in addition to the "black laborers" who served them, and they will have to learn to act as a minority amongst the Arab majority, or return to their own homeland, as most of them have a second passport anyways.[95]

Conclusion

By the 1980s, the Black Panther movement in the United States had come to an end. The Federal Bureau of Investigation's Counterintelligence Program had severely undermined the Panthers' ability to function. Police assassinations of prominent Panthers, infiltrations of Panther offices, and erratic behavior among some of its leaders dealt a severe blow to the Panther movement.[96] Huey Newton was murdered in 1989 at the hands of former Panther members. Eldridge Cleaver, who had broken away from the Panthers, had become a born-again Christian and a committed Zionist in the 1980s.[97]

The Palestinian national movement also underwent dramatic changes in the late 1970s and 1980s. Yasser Arafat abandoned the politics of anti-imperialism and in 1976 embraced the international framework of "two-states" in Israel/Palestine. The PLO embrace of the so-called two-state solution took place without popular support from the Palestinian people. While it gave Arafat greater access to international aid and diplomacy, it damaged the ability of ordinary Palestinians to demand the right of return of the refugees. Arafat's politics would become less connected to the Palestinian street when he agreed to the so-called Oslo Peace Accords in 1993.[98]

The Israeli Black Panthers' radicalism was relatively short lived. By the late 1970s the Black Panthers had dissolved, and Mizrahi activists began organizing on behalf of Mizrahi land rights and civil rights within the State of Israel. The state responded to these demands by allowing Mizrahi activists land in West Bank settlements. Thus what was ostensibly a black radical movement for pan-Arab solidarity within the land of Palestine was transformed into a civil rights movement within the State of Israel.

The 1980s and beyond enshrined a new political era of neoconservativism globally. In the next chapter I discuss how post-1980s neoconservative and neoliberal policies once again reset the terrain of Afro-Arab political imaginaries. Within the context of neoliberal governance, as exemplified in the Oslo Peace Process and the restructuring of welfare in the United States, a new Afro-Arab political imaginary would emerge within the beats and breaks of globalized hip hop.

CHAPTER FIVE

Neoliberalism, Security, and the Afro-Arab International

I was born a black woman, and now, I am become a Palestinian
—June Jordan, Moving toward Home

I represent a narrative of exclusion, denial, racism and national victimization,
but I also come with a message of hope, redemption, and historical vindication
embodied in the spirit and the will of a people that has refused to succumb
to all forces of oppression, violence, cruelty, and injustice.
—Hanan Ashrawi, Durban, South Africa

In 1996 the African American poet June Jordan traveled to Lebanon, where she witnessed sixteen days of Israeli bombardment in Operation Grapes of Wrath. The 1996 war included more than 1,100 Israeli air raids that dropped 25,000 shells.[1] Jordan, who had been active in Palestinian solidarity movements since the 1980s, was concerned that Lebanon had been erased from Western consciousness in ways that seemed to legitimate exceptional violence against it. Western media, Jordan believed, had willfully erased Lebanon from the map of the Middle East conflict, and the invisibility of Palestinians (including those in Lebanon) reminded Jordan of similar erasures faced by African Americans in the United States. "If Israel and the United States agree to 'disappear' Lebanon," Jordan wrote in *The Progressive*, "then whenever Israel follows up its various invasions of that tiny place with outright annexation, nobody will notice because Lebanon will have become nowhere."[2] In order to bring international attention to the extension of Israeli militarism to Lebanon, Jordan turned to a personal analogy. "My life requires perpetual revolt against a double standard that puts me on the Easily Invisible side of the ledger, the Don't Matter and No Count side of things, the Be Good/Keep Quiet Say 'Thank You' side of the equation. And Lebanon is on the wrong side, just like me, Lebanon is not white. Lebanon is not overwhelmingly Christian or Jewish or European.... I went to Lebanon because I believe that Arab peoples and Arab Americans occupy the lowest, the most reviled spot in the racist mind of America."[3] Jordan's solidarity with Arab and Arab American people was based on her recognition of the conjunctures between racial projects in the U.S. and in Israel/Palestine. She forged a political consciousness in which the recognition of shared social conditions could become the building blocks of a transnational solidarity movement.

Jordan's writing about Operation Grapes of Wrath followed her reporting on the 1995 Israeli bombing of the UN refugee camp at Qana. The bombardment was videotaped and distributed across global media. In her writing about Qana, Jordan linked the violence of security and policing in urban America to the destruction of lives under Israeli occupation: "Here was the Rodney King video of the Middle East. At least, here was incontrovertible evidence of Israeli lies and Israeli savagery that no one could now refute."[4] Yet the video did not provide the evidence Jordan hoped would focus public attention on the plight of the Lebanese and Palestinians in Lebanon. "The video is the Rodney King video of the Middle East, but Arab life is less than and lower than African-American life, and so nothing happened."[5] Jordan's rhetoric links the destruction of Arab and black american lives at the hands of police and military violence.

Yet Jordan's acts of solidarity with Arabs and Arab Americans emerged in a different context than the one that shaped the 1970s third world leftist solidarity movements forged by the Black Panther Party and the PLO. In Chapter 4 I identified a global Afro-Arab political imaginary built around an analysis of imperialism and racial capitalism. The Black Panthers' intercommunal analysis provided the scaffolding for a transnational politics uniting Afro-Arab concerns in the 1960s and 1970s, and it emerged during the "global offensive" of third world internationalism. The 1970s third world liberationist politics took place within specific historical conjunctures produced by the bipolar Cold War era. Within this crucible, the logic of nonalignment helped forge a global, anti-imperialist, "third way" beyond the U.S. and Soviet frameworks.

By the late 1980s, however, the geopolitical context for the third world left was radically transformed by the ascendance of neoconservative politics in the United States, the 1989 fall of the Soviet Union, the incorporation of the PLO into the international framework of the "peace process," and the new rules of global neoliberalism. In the post-1989 era the United States became a unipolar hegemon with the capacity to orchestrate an American

era. U.S. policy after the Cold War rested on integrating "unruly" and insecure states into a global capitalist network of states capable of "proper" ac-
cumulation and consumption. This meant encouraging—via international
financial organizations largely controlled by the United States—top-down
and coercive reforms across the Middle East that privatized economies,
encouraged democracy (of a certain type), and prized security in order
to control the consequences of structural adjustments, including mass
poverty, inequality, and insecurity. At the same time, domestic wars on
crime, drugs, and then terror placed urban communities within the United
States within an increasingly militarized crucible. Global integration in the
unipolar American era, I will argue, knit together an assemblage of governance strategies both domestically and internationally that shared similar
rationalities and logics, including counterintelligence strategies and mass
incarceration.

Within the unipolar American era, the domestic and international politics of welfare reform, drug wars, and wars on crime and terror were linked
as densely overlapping racial projects that materially connected Israel/
Palestine to the spaces of urban black America. The rise of new security
agreements between the United States and Israel coupled with the transfer of tactics, knowledge, and forms of policing across the U.S. and Palestine worked in conjunction with advanced logics of liberal governance to
produce American-led globalization that collapsed geographic space and
time. In this chapter I describe the post–Cold War American era in terms
of two related processes that linked the U.S. to Israel/Palestine: First is the
overlapping process of privatization and racialization that characterized
the neoliberalizing of the Israel/Palestine peace process evidenced in the
Oslo Accords in conjunction with the transformation in welfare within the
United States. Second, I discuss what Laleh Khalili calls the "horizontal circuit" of colonial security strategies across Israel/Palestine and the United
States that materially linked wars on crime, drugs, and terror globally.

Confronted with the unipolar American era, in which communities
within the United States were being re-racialized, the geographies of liberation were transformed by new conjunctures. In this chapter I argue
that the transnationalizing of economies under U.S. tutelage at home and
abroad, coupled with the global "war on terror" that knit together global
and domestic security strategies, established the conditions of possibility
for an Afro-Arab political imaginary I will call the Afro-Arab international.
I use the term "Afro-Arab international" to describe a political imaginary
based on confronting the American era of neoliberal reforms based in
privatization and security. The Afro-Arab international was not rooted in

guerilla warfare or mass protest—both strategies had been contained by counterrevolutionary and counterinsurgent forces—but in United Nations conferences and in the cultural politics of hip hop and slam poetry that flew under the radar of legitimate social movements. I describe the Afro-Arab international as it was initially formed in the 2001 UN World Conference against Racism, Racial Discrimination, Xenophobia, and Related Intolerance in Durban, South Africa, where Zionism was linked to racism; in the transnational solidarity that emerged in the wake of Hurricane Katrina; and in the more contemporary politics of Arab diasporic hip hop and slam poetry.

In many ways, the contemporary era's dense conjunctures make this chapter's topic the most difficult to analyze. The clarity of the past is often elusive in the present. In this chapter I am therefore attempting to analyze the present, with the full recognition that the present may not yet be fully available for analysis.

The Unipolar American Era's Neoliberal Turn

The 1990s ushered in a new era of geopolitics, as the bipolar world was transformed by the 1989 fall of the Soviet Union and the ascendancy of the United States as the sole global superpower. Within the context of a unipolar American era, liberalism underwent transformation as a consequence of the rise of neoconservative movements in the United States as well as in some European countries. In *The Twilight of Equality?* Lisa Duggan argues that neoliberalism emerged most powerfully in the 1990s as President Bill Clinton sought to develop a "third way" politics located between the neoconservatism of Ronald Reagan and the "old liberalism" of the social welfare state.[6] Third way politics was a combination of neoconservative mandates for policies that benefited businesses, the market, and free trade with what remained of older social welfare and civil rights programs. The new liberalism—neoliberalism—emphasized smaller government modeled on corporate structures and rules.

According to David Harvey, neoliberalism is characterized by the conversion of social life into market economies that can be governed as a business would.

> Neoliberalism is in the first instance a theory of political economic practices that proposes that human well-being can best be advanced by liberating individual entrepreneurial freedoms and skills within an institutional framework characterized by strong private property rights, free

markets and free trade. The role of the state is to create and preserve an institutional framework appropriate to such practices. . . . Furthermore, if markets do not exist (in areas such as land, water, education, health care, social security, or environmental pollution) then they must be created, by state action if necessary.[7]

Governing society as a market has meant turning over many of the functions of the public sphere to the private sector. In the realm of domestic politics, neoliberalism demands small government, increased emphasis on law and order (as well as incarceration of surplus populations), a privatized economy, and the importance of individual "responsibility."

In the international sphere, neoliberalism has altered the terms of liberal engagement in the world. Neoliberal governance emphasizes the importance of financial and trade incentives as a means to coerce state behaviors that benefit Western economic interests. World bodies like the International Monetary Fund, the World Trade Organization, and the World Bank offer "conditioned loans" to developing nations as a means to coerce privatization among needy nations.[8] Neoliberal governance also stresses the importance of responsibility as a prerequisite of foreign aid, and the terms of responsibility often mean that leaders of poorer nations have to guarantee to world lending agencies that anticapitalist and nationalist behaviors within their country will be suppressed.[9]

During the 1990s, neoliberal politics transformed U.S. domestic and international policies in significant ways. Domestically, Bill Clinton's third way politics ushered in an era of welfare reform that emphasized personal responsibility as a requirement for government support. In an attempt to forge a third way politics between neoconservatism and New Deal era social liberalism, in 1996 Clinton reformed welfare in ways that privatized the social safety net and that stressed personal responsibility on the part of welfare recipients. The Personal Responsibility and Work Opportunity Reconciliation Act fulfilled Clinton's promise to end "welfare as we know it."[10]

Welfare had been under intense attack throughout the 1980s as neoconservatives argued that governmental programs aimed at providing a social safety net created dependency and laziness among recipients.[11] The neoconservative attack on welfare created popularized images of undeserving poor people who "gamed the system" in order not to work. Often presented as black "welfare queens" or illegal immigrants, the poor were represented as a group unwilling to work because of government largesse.[12] Clinton's legislation ended the federal entitlement for welfare, ended the Aid to Families with Dependent Children program, set time limits on the number of years the poor could receive welfare, and granted states increased authority to set welfare policy. According to Judith Goode and Jeff Maskovsky, the act signaled "a mode of governance, economy and politics in which the poor are not so much vilified as they are marginalized or erased by the institutional and ideological aspects of work, social welfare and politics that dominate under neoliberalism."[13]

Under the new regime, poor people left the welfare rolls to assume low-wage jobs in the private sector (if they were among the lucky ones able to find work). Under this new framework, social services such as health care were transferred to private insurance companies rather than federal programs, and aid to children was entirely eliminated. According to a 2000 study of Welfare to Work commissioned by several government agencies, the 1996 law increased poor people's reliance on earnings (as opposed to welfare), "but family incomes were largely unchanged. As a result, the programs lifted few families above the poverty line."[14] As the report demonstrated, welfare reform shifted the burden of care for the poor to private entities but was not intended to alleviate poverty itself.

Neoliberalism similarly drove the U.S. engagement with the Middle East. Clinton's approach to Israel/Palestine was based on a desire to mediate conditions of stability in order to coerce neoliberal adjustments.[15] In order to explicate the ways that neoliberal domestic and international policies established conditions for an Afro-Arab political imaginary, I turn now to a discussion of the 1993 Oslo Peace Process in order to demonstrate its overlapping concerns with domestic welfare reform.

Oslo Neoliberalism

On August 20, 1993, Israeli negotiators and members of the PLO agreed to a Declaration of Principles on Interim Self-Government Arrangements, which became known as the Oslo Accords or the Oslo Peace Process. Hailed in the press as a meaningful stage in negotiating a final peace between Israel/Palestine, the declaration of principles enshrined the logic of "limited self-government" as a framework for partial dis-occupation of the territories occupied during the June 1967 war. On September 13, 1993, Yasser Arafat and Yitzhak Rabin signed the Oslo Accords on the White House lawn in front of Bill Clinton. The Oslo Accords were read in the United States as the successful formation of a "pax-Americana" in the Middle East that would garner new legitimacy in the region for the post–Cold War world.[16]

The Oslo process enabled Israel and the United States to implement neoliberal governance as a substitute for overt colonial occupation. Under

Oslo, a nonelected Palestinian National Authority (PNA) would be installed as the governing authority in small portions of the West Bank. The PNA would only have the authority to encourage social responsibility among the Palestinian population. It would police areas under its jurisdiction and supervise education and culture, health and social welfare, taxation, and tourism in the West Bank and Gaza. In exchange, Israel would withdraw military powers from limited areas of the West Bank and Gaza while maintaining control of water, electricity, and all security and borders. Israel and the PNA would also agree to bilateral recognition, ending a decades-long Palestinian stance against normalization with Israel. The eventual borders of a Palestinian state, the fate of Israeli settlers in the West Bank, the status of Jerusalem, the Palestinian refugees' rights of return, and water rights were to be decided after a five-year interim, provided the PNA could demonstrate responsible governance—which, translated, meant that the PNA could undermine Palestinian popular rebellion. These decisions, called "final-status arrangements" were to be decided at an undetermined future date, which has not been set as of this writing.

Arafat, exiled in Tunis, entered the Oslo process with diminished stature within the Arab world. The fall of the Soviet Union meant the decline of aid to the PLO. Moreover, Arafat had been an outspoken supporter of Saddam Hussein during the first Persian Gulf War of 1990–91. This marginalized the PLO leader within parts of the Arab world, especially in the Gulf states that had been important donors. Recognizing Israel and negotiating on behalf of the Palestinians was a significant maneuver to maintain control of the PLO as well as to regain stature within the international community (Arafat would share the 1994 Nobel Peace Prize with Yitzhak Rabin and Shimon Peres). Importantly, the PFLP and many Palestinian organizations in the diaspora rejected entirely the Olso process, recognizing that it was a power grab by Arafat as well as the fact that the status of the refugees, the most important issue for a majority of Palestinians, was ignored, if not undermined, by Arafat's negotiations. In the wake of Oslo, Mahmoud Darwish and Shafiq al-Hout, members of the PLO executive committee, resigned in protest.[17]

Oslo partitioned the West Bank into areas of Palestinian and Jewish settlement and authority. These areas, designated A, B, and C, were introduced in the ongoing negotiations over the Oslo process and were not part of the original 1993 declaration of principles. In the West Bank, only 2 to 3 percent of the land was transferred to full PNA control (area A). Towns located in area A are noncontiguous and are de facto enclaves in a sea of Israeli control. Twenty-six percent of the West Bank falls under area B, a

Map of Oslo Areas A, B, and C, 1995

zone of limited PNA sovereignty in which the PNA has only civil and police powers while Israel maintains internal security. In area B, Israel continued to confiscate Palestinian land and to enforce severe policing and imprisonment of Palestinians. The remaining 70 percent of the West Bank was designated area C; this is a contiguous mass that surrounds areas A and B in their entirety. Area C, comprising the water-rich and border areas of the West Bank, is fully under Israeli authority. Oslo did not restrict the expansion of settlements in area C, and Israel has been free to develop bypass roads connecting a vast network of outposts and settlements. These bypass roads have enabled Israel to expand greater Jerusalem into the West Bank and to make West Bank settlement into what Ehud Olmert would describe as "a permanent part of Israel."[18]

Oslo can be read as a form of neocolonial governance that enabled Palestinians to "self-govern" their own occupation and the dispossession of their land while also enabling Israel to receive an infusion of Western aid. As Joel Beinin has noted, from 1968 to 1985 Israeli military expenditures ranged from 21.7 to 32.8 percent of GDP (as compared with 3 to 6 percent in the developed capitalist world).[19] As a result of heavy investment in the military and lack of investment in other sectors of society, inflation grew dramatically and Israel found itself in economic crisis. In 1984 the United States offered emergency aid in the amount of $1.5 billion, conditional on Israel implementing a new economic model. The new economic model hewed closely to the neoliberal structural adjustments required of Bolivia, Chile, and Mexico. As Beinin points out, the new economic model called for intensive austerity measures and privatization of public services. According to Beinin, the U.S. required Israel to implement "a 10 percent reduction in government expenditures, devaluation of the shekel, and cuts in subsidies on food and transportation."[20] As a consequence of these demands, Ashkenazi business owners in Israel began to call for the dis-occupation of the West Bank in order to spark foreign investments in Israel as well as to forfeit some of the costs of occupation. International monetary policy, the high cost of occupation, and the increasing role of Palestinian protest convinced Israeli capitalists "that pursuing a market culture of profit, pleasure and individualism required resolution of the conflict with the Palestinians and the Arab world."[21]

The road to neoliberalism had already been entered by the Israeli labor government during the 1992–96 period, during an era of transition that Yoav Paled has termed "from Zionism to capitalism."[22] During this period the labor government had committed to privatization of key portions of the economy related to social safety net services, health care, and education.

In the wake of neoliberal reforms, foreign investment in Israel boosted Israel's economic growth to 5.8 percent by 1995. As Beinin points out, by the mid-1990s, "nearly one-hundred Israeli firms were listed on US stock exchanges."[23]

While partial dis-occupation and privatization garnered vast sums of international aid to Israel, similar incentives were offered, but ultimately denied, to the PNA. In exchange for policing the West Bank and maintaining Israeli security, the Palestinians were promised $2.4 billion in foreign aid during the five-year interim.[24] Yet throughout the Oslo period, only half of this aid was delivered due to bad faith as well as perceived failures on the part of the PNA to halt Palestinian protest, including attacks on Israel (the second intifada began in 2000). Moreover, Israeli control of air, sea, and land undermined attempts to grow the Palestinian economy. Beginning in March 1993 Israel implemented multiple forms of closure on the West Bank that severely impeded the ability of Palestinian workers to enter Israel. Moreover, during the Oslo years, the settler population in the West Bank grew 39 percent to 145,000.[25] Israel has built a capillarious network of by-pass roads that enabled settlements to be linked by infrastructure. In East Jerusalem, the Jewish population grew by 22,000 during this period.[26] As Hanan Ashrawi has argued, the peace process "became a punitive process manipulated by Israel to pursue its politics of expansion, ethnic cleansing, colonialism, and subjugation of the weaker side by force. . . . It is an occupiers' version of what's good for the natives."[27]

The "Horizontal Circuits" of Counterinsurgency

Although neoliberalism helps explain a broad array of economic transformations to domestic and international governance at the twilight of the twentieth century, alone it is insufficient to describe the thick and overlapping processes that linked African Americans to the question of Palestine in the new millennium. The linkages across the United States and Israel are not merely characterized by overlapping logics of financial restructuring and privatization—although those conjunctures are there—they are also constituted by the global transiting of technologies of policing and security that have spanned wars on drugs, crime, and terror, especially in the post–September 11, 2001, era. While the neoliberal reforms of Oslo and welfare reform accelerated the pace of economic inequality in the developing world and in the United States, the linkages between the two geographies were further solidified through the bilateral transit of policing and security strategies deployed in Palestine. From Israeli practices of urban combat, surveillance, and partitioning to the use of U.S. Apache helicopters and armored transport, Palestine has been a laboratory for a bilateral U.S./Israeli security industry that has shaped Israel's approach to the "problem" of Palestinians *and* the U.S.'s approach to the "problem" of the urban black poor. Throughout the 1990s and 2000s, Palestinians and African Americans were both, in different ways, rendered as surplus populations beyond economic inclusion and therefore were viewed as potential threats—insurgencies—that had to be contained via counterinsurgency measures characterized by heightened security and military techniques as well as mass incarceration.[28]

Although the "war on drugs" has a history dating back to early-twentieth-century prohibition laws, President Richard Nixon gave it its modern name in 1970. By 1988 the federal government appointed a "drug czar" to coordinate national and state antidrug-enforcement strategies. Beginning in 1989, the war on drugs in the United States was increasingly cast in terms of the language of insurgencies and counterinsurgencies. The 1989 National Defense Authorization Act named drugs a national security threat and authorized the Department of Defense to coordinate state and community tactics in the war on drugs. Under the department's broad authority in the war on drugs, local and state police mechanisms increasingly deployed tactics and weapons more commonly used in overseas warfare. The coordinated efforts of the Department of Defense and state and local policing included using reconnaissance and observation teams to report illegal drug use and trafficking, aerial surveillance, coast guard patrols, aerial spraying of herbicides on potential drug crops, aerial thermal imaging, and more. According to Major Reyes Z. Cole of the California National Guard, "Counterdrug and counterinsurgency operations strive for the same end state, rely heavily on the use of counterinsurgency doctrine to be effective, and are examples of fourth-generation warfare-low intensity asymmetric warfare conducted by groups (rather than by nations or states) who seek major reallocations of power or the overthrow of social systems."[29] At the same time that the war on drugs and the war on gangs were increasingly understood as military counterinsurgency measures requiring military hardware in urban cities, within the U.S. new sentencing requirements—called mandatory minimums—were developed for certain classes of gang- and drug-related crimes. Drug lords and gang members would be referred to as "street terrorists." In 1988 the California Street Terrorism Enforcement and Prevention Act (California Penal Code 186.20 et Seq.) established a separate legal category of gang-related crimes and criminalized gang crimes distinct from other traditional crimes.[30] Throughout the 1980s

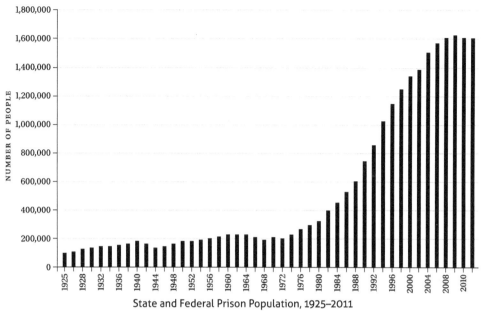

State and Federal Prison Population, 1925–2011
Source: Bureau of Justice Statistics *Prisoner Series*

the number of arrests for drug-related crimes increased 126 percent.[31] The drug war led to a precipitous rise in incarcerations. The United States has the highest rate of incarceration in the world (748 inmates per 100,000 citizens), and according to a 2010 Human Rights Watch report on prisons in the U.S., "Black non-Hispanic males are incarcerated at a rate more than six times that of white non-Hispanic males and 2.6 times that of Hispanic males. One in 10 black males aged 25–29 were in prison or jail in 2009; for Hispanic males the figure was 1 in 25; for white males only 1 in 64."[32] The disproportionate number of African Americans incarcerated in U.S. prisons is largely due to the drug war and mandatory minimum sentencing laws. In 2011, 48 percent of all federal prisoners had been convicted on drug offenses.[33] According to Human Rights Watch's global report, "Blacks constitute 33.6 percent of drug arrests, 44 percent of persons convicted of drug felonies in state court, and 37 percent of people sent to state prison on drug charges, even though they constitute only 13 percent of the US population and blacks and whites engage in drug offenses at equivalent rates."[34] In 2003, the Bureau of Justice estimated the lifetime likelihood of imprisonment for black men at 1 in 3, as opposed to 1 in 17 for whites.[35]

In the 1990s and beyond, as the United States turned to wars on drugs and then on terror, Israel became both a pupil of and a mentor to U.S. antiterrorism and urban domestic crime-fighting efforts. Israeli counterinsurgency measures, perfected and practiced in the West Bank and Gaza in the wake of two intifadas, served as a laboratory for U.S. engagements in Iraq, Afghanistan, and increasingly, U.S. urban cities. Hence, as Laleh Khalili has argued, Palestine is an important global nexus of imperial interests in population control and counterinsurgency. "The violence of Israeli counterinsurgency against Palestinians cannot be understood without locating it in a broader global space, where imperial control through military intervention continues apace, and in a more historical context, where the violent technologies of domination travel across time and space, making Palestine an archetypal laboratory and a crucial node of global counterinsurgencies."[36] Khalili traces the transit of colonial power across space and time by examining how colonial military tactics help to shape policing tactics in the colonial metropolis. The relationship between militarization in the colonies and policing in the metropolis is not historically unique. The French Empire regularly used Algeria as a proving ground for forms of population control that ultimately returned to the French metropolis.[37] The United States similarly used the Philippines as a means to experiment with new modalities of policing.[38] In the contemporary moment, however, the conjuncture between Israeli and U.S. security regimes is somewhat anomalous, as it signifies a multidirectional transfer of security technologies across nation-states rather than between a colony and a metropolis. In this way, Palestine is something of a proxy colony, via Israel, for the U.S. wars at home and abroad. Hence, Israeli experiments in counterinsurgency have served as experiments for the United States in Iraq, Afghanistan, and the urban U.S.

In the wake of September 11, 2001, as the U.S. began wars on terror that included invasions of Iraq and Afghanistan—the United States increasingly turned to Israel as a laboratory for testing new technologies of counterinsurgency. The U.S./Israel security relationship constituted what Khalili has called a "horizontal circuit" in which "colonial policing or 'security' practices have been transmitted across time from one location to another, with Palestine as either a point of origin or an intermediary node of transmission." As Mike Davis has written, "This tactical 'Israelization' of U.S. combat doctrine has been accompanied by what might be called a 'Sharonizing' of the Pentagon's worldview."[39]

In 2002 the U.S. military visited the West Bank Palestinian city of Jenin in order to observe and practice Israeli counterinsurgency tactics in densely populated urban cities. Drawing on the Israeli example in Jenin, the U.S. began to model similar forms of urban warfare in its siege of Iraq. Most importantly, this strategy meant constructing walls to partition areas of U.S.

control, as well as to contain insurgent activities. Consequently, as Steve Niva has argued, "Iraq has become increasingly caged within an archipelago of isolated ethnic enclaves surrounded by walls and razor wire and reinforced by aerial occupation."[40] Commenting on the Israeli/U.S. security linkages in 2003, investigative journalist Seymour Hersh argued,

> One step the Pentagon took was to send active and secret help in the war against the Iraqi insurgency from Israel, America's closest ally in the Middle East. According to American and Israeli military and intelligence officials, Israeli commandos and intelligence units have been working closely with their American counterparts at the Special Forces training base at Fort Bragg, North Carolina, and in Israel to help them prepare for operations in Iraq. Israeli commandos are expected to serve as ad-hoc advisers—again in secret—when full-field operations begin.[41]

Thomas H. Henriksen, a senior fellow at the Hoover Institute and the U.S. Joint Special Operations University, lamented the inability of the United States armed forces to successfully emulate the Israeli counterinsurgency model in the U.S. occupation of Iraq and Afghanistan, two "combat theaters" that Henriksen views as analogous to the occupied Palestinian territories. "In its grinding counterinsurgency operations and its counterterrorist sweeps, Israel's missions could furnish abundant lessons and even warnings for American strategists willing to observe and profit from them."[42] Most striking, perhaps, is that the horizontal circuit not only assisted the U.S. abroad in wars against Iraq and Afghanistan, but that it has also penetrated the United States, as the U.S. "homeland" has become a space that is increasingly understood as a foreign battleground in the war on terror.[43]

In 2005 the *Washington Post* reported that Israeli experts had visited the United States to train urban police forces in the use of new forms of surveillance, urban policing, and bomb detection strategies. U.S. Capitol Police Chief Terrance W. Gainer suggested that "Israel is the Harvard of antiterrorism."[44] The U.S.-based Jewish Institute for National Security Affairs established the Law Enforcement Exchange Program (LEEP), a joint initiative of the Israeli National Police, the Israeli Ministry of International Security, and the Israel Security Agency (Shin Bet), "to support and strengthen American law enforcement counter terrorism practices." LEEP educates U.S. law enforcement specialists in areas of joint Israeli/U.S. concerns, such as surveillance of terrorists and border security. LEEP attracts law enforcement agents in many agencies, including drug enforcement. Anthony Placido, chief of intelligence for the Drug Enforcement Agency, participated in LEEP and linked the drug war to terrorism. "It is impossible to fight trans-national crime which is terrorism unilaterally. It is partnerships, the bounds that are being forged here, it is the cooperation around the globe that will ultimately allow us to prevail." Police Chief Joe Polisar, from the Garden Grove, California, police department and a LEEP participant, suggested, "American Law Enforcement and American Public Saftey [sic] is starving for this kind of information, the experience the Israelis can bring."[45]

The linkages between Israeli and U.S. counterinsurgency technologies translate to a domestic U.S. infrastructure of policing and prisons that increasingly looks like, and is rationalized through, a global war on terror. Throughout the 1990s, urban policing increasingly turned to militarized strategies employing heavy equipment such as helicopters and armored SWAT teams. The combined power of high-tech surveillance, heavily armored police forces, and rapidly expanding incarceration rates transformed law enforcement in U.S. cities into a quasi occupying army. The geographies of occupied Palestine and occupied urban communities of color appeared much closer throughout the post-1990 era due to the horizontal circuit of securitization across the United States and Israel. In *Cities under Siege*, Stephen Graham argues,

> The U.S. military's focus on operations within the domestic urban sphere is also being dramatically strengthened by the so-called War on Terror, which designates cities—whether US or foreign—and their key infrastructures as "battlespaces." Viewed through such a lenses, the Los Angeles riots of 1992; the various attempts to securitize urban cores during major sports events or political summits; the military response to Hurricane Katrina in New Orleans in 2005; the challenges of "homeland security" in US cities—all become "low intensity" urban military operations comparable to conducting counter-insurgency warfare in an Iraqi city.[46]

Durban and the New Geographies of Liberation

While the September 2001 terrorist attacks on the U.S. marked a new stage in the development of the security circuit between Israel and the United States, it was also the moment when a new political imaginary emerged among Palestinians and African Americans contending with mass incarceration and military force. I turn now to the ways that African Americans and Palestinians responded to neoliberal and military regimes by producing a decolonial political imaginary that linked the geographies of urban America and Palestine. June Jordan's recognition of similarity between African

Americans and Arabs constituted one form of this political imaginary; the sameness is, I argue, constituted by Jordan's recognition of a shared structure of feeling uniting African Americans and Arabs. The Afro-Arab international was constituted by the profound impact of militarization and neoliberal governance on urban black and Palestinian communities. Although there were important and significant differences between the plight of stateless refugees living under occupation and of African American citizens of the United States facing mass incarceration, there were affective similarities across both communities that led to a new politics of Afro-Arab solidarity.

An unintended consequence of the conjuncture of neoliberal policies and the global security industry in the United States and Israel/Palestine was the creation of the conditions of possibility for a radically new and unanticipated Afro-Arab political imaginary that coalesced at the 2001 UN World Conference against Racism, Racial Discrimination, Xenophobia, and Related Intolerance in Durban, South Africa, and in the cultural politics of Palestinian and African American hip hop and poetry. The Durban conference's demand for reparations and its recognition of Israeli colonialism, along with the aesthetic politics of Palestinian hip hop and spoken-word poetry, illustrate the desire for an Afro-Arab political imaginary that redraws the geographies of the millennial world order.

From August 31 to September 8, 2001, in the days before al-Qaeda's attack on the World Trade Center in New York, the United Nations convened an international conference to address the impact of racism and related forms of discrimination on people across the world. The third World Conference against Racism, Racial Discrimination, Xenophobia, and Related Intolerance was hosted in the Indian Sea coast city of Durban, South Africa, and attracted more than 2,000 representatives from 163 governments.[47] Alongside the UN conference was an affiliated, although unofficial, forum for nongovernmental organizations that attracted around 7,000 participants.[48]

The UN, since World War II, has been a venue for African American petitions seeking recognition and reparations for the atrocity of slavery.[49] In this way, the UN is a complex entity that articulates an international order often favorable to the wealthiest hegemons in the West while also providing a forum for the most vulnerable and least powerful nations and communities. Hence, the UN has been viewed as a viable body for groups like the Nation of Islam and the Black Panthers to demand legal redress for forms of racial and colonial power. The UN conference on racism illustrates the tensions of the organization.

The goals of the intergovernmental conference were to encourage governments to identify, remedy, and eliminate racism and xenophobia against a broad group of constituents, including global migrants and asylum seekers, racial minorities, refugees, women, and sexual minorities. The conference agenda was established during a yearlong process of regional preparatory conferences (held in Strasbourg, Santiago, Dakar, Tehran, Warsaw, Kathmandu, Cairo, and Quito). The preparatory meetings were intended to elaborate on the central concerns of the conference as a means to agree on an agenda and eventual action. During the preparatory meeting process, two issues emerged that would ultimately derail the Durban conference. African representatives at the meetings insisted that reparations for slavery be made a central topic of the Durban conference. Asian representatives from the Middle East sought to link Zionism to the discussion of racism and, in doing so, to identify Israel as a colonial presence in Palestine.

The African preparatory conferences recommended proposals to the conference's Programme of Action that included a framework for international compensation for victims of the slave trade, including the formation of a UN fund for reparations. The report from the Asian preparatory conferences included recommendations that language be included in the Programme of Action that would reject "the concept of regional fortresses, bolstered by political and economic accords amongst some developed countries, that generate a climate in which foreigners are readily discriminated against."[50] Moreover, the Asian delegations recommended language on Palestine that "affirmed that a foreign occupation founded on settlements, its laws based on racial discrimination . . . constitutes . . . a crime against humanity, a form of genocide and a serious threat to international peace."[51]

President George W. Bush threatened to withdraw from the conference before it began due to the language associating Zionism with racism. U.S. representatives argued that this issue singled out Israel and had the effect of "diminishing the historically unique tragedy of the Holocaust in Europe."[52] Yet what was even more problematic for the U.S. delegation was the conference's position on slavery and reparations. The United States was willing to embrace the conference's calls for "regret of historical injustices, such as slavery and the slave trade," yet it was unwilling to consider reparations for anything but contemporary forms of racism.[53] The United States also rejected the conference's linking of slavery to a "crime against humanity," because it feared that such language would make the United States a target of lawsuits from descendants of slaves.[54]

Although the U.S. delegation to the UN was unwilling to participate in the racism conference, some elected officials within the U.S. government endorsed the call for reparations. During the conference, in a public event in Durban's city hall, Durban officials hosted members of the Congressional

Black Caucus (CBC), including representatives Cynthia McKinney, Sheila Jackson Lee, Eddy Bernice Johnson, Barbara Lee, and Ambassador Diane Watson, who offered support to the reparations movement.[55] Representative John Conyers (D-Mich.), the outgoing chair of the CBC, used the UN conference as an opportunity to reintroduce a discussion about bill HR 40, calling for a study on reparations (Conyers had proposed the bill in 1980).

The final report on the conference omitted any reference to Zionism and reparations and hewed fairly closely to U.S. State Department positions on Israel/Palestine and on how to commemorate and recognize slavery. The final conference report included the following:

13. We acknowledge that slavery and the slave trade, including the transatlantic slave trade, were appalling tragedies in the history of humanity not only because of their abhorrent barbarism but also in terms of their magnitude, organized nature and especially their negation of the essence of the victims, and further acknowledge that slavery and the slave trade are a crime against humanity and should always have been so, especially the transatlantic slave trade and are among the major sources and manifestations of racism, racial discrimination, xenophobia and related intolerance, and that Africans and people of African descent, Asians and people of Asian descent and indigenous peoples were victims of these acts and continue to be victims of their consequences;

. . . .

63. We are concerned about the plight of the Palestinian people under foreign occupation. We recognize the inalienable right of the Palestinian people to self-determination and to the establishment of an independent State and we recognize the right to security for all States in the region, including Israel, and call upon all States to support the peace process and bring it to an early conclusion.[56]

In the end, few of the representatives at the UN conference were pleased with the outcome. Israeli and U.S. delegations condemned the statements on reparations and Palestine, even though the diluted versions that were ultimately adopted supported U.S. statements on this issue. Moreover, Arab delegates were disappointed that stronger language condemning Israeli colonialism was excluded, while language on the Holocaust seemed to be inserted to appease the U.S. and Israeli delegations (who had already abandoned the conference). Farouk Al-Shara, the representative of the

Syrian Arab Republic, stated, "Syria wished for clearer wording, especially on the Middle East." Al-Shara was concerned that the conference's ultimate statement that included the sentence "We recall that the Holocaust must never be forgotten" was overly ideological and implicated the entire world in a European atrocity. "The Holocaust was a horrible thing, regardless of where it happened," the Syrian delegate argued.

> But we must remind our European friends who are very sensitive about the Holocaust that the Holocaust happened in Europe, and was committed mostly by Europeans. . . . Let's be morally courageous enough to tell the truth: what do they mean by, "We recall that the Holocaust must never be forgotten"? It should not be forgotten by the people who made it, who created it, who did it. We were not party to it, and that is why we do not accept this general term here. We would like it to be very concise and very specific and not to be applied to every nation on earth.[57]

Although Durban was boycotted by U.S. and Israeli officials, it was the Arab and African delegates who left the conference disappointed due to the ways that the final conference report capitulated on questions of reparations and Israeli colonialism.

The possibilities of Durban were also limited by the fact that three days after the conference, before final recommendations were published, members of al-Qaeda attacked the World Trade Center in New York City and the Pentagon in Washington, D.C., on September 11, 2001. The political and cultural fallout of 9/11 is far too large a topic for this chapter. What is relevant is that 9/11 pushed the Durban conference out of public consciousness as the world's singular global hegemon turned to a global war on terror that ratcheted up the racialization and incarceration of Arab and Muslim peoples in the United States. The war on terror—which appeals to exceptional times in order to diminish civil and political rights for Arab and Muslim Americans—created a consciousness among some Arab Americans that they occupied the social position previously held by African Americans in the United States; they had become the "new blacks" in America.[58] In the following section I turn to the ways that before and after 9/11 a transnational aesthetic politics that transposed blackness and Palestinianness emerged within the cultural terrain of Katrina politics, poetry, and hip hop.

The Afro-Arab International

In 2005 Hurricane Katrina exposed the combined violence of neoliberal governance and heightened domestic counterinsurgency. A primarily

African American metropolis was devastated not only by a natural disaster but also by the unnatural processes of neoliberal privatization. The flood exposed the inadequacy of public care for certain classes of people, including the poor and African Americans. Moreover, the military response to homelessness—which appeared to be an occupation deploying counterinsurgency tactics—underscored how excluded the black underclass in the United States had become. The full story of Katrina is well beyond the scope of this chapter.[59] What interests me are the transnational insights and solidarity that emerged in the storm's wake. Among the first donations to the city of New Orleans came from Palestinian refugees from the Amari refugee camp near Ramallah, who raised $10,000 for Katrina's victims. Jihad Tomeleh, one of the organizers of the fund-raising drive, notes, "Palestinian refugees who have lived more than fifty years displaced from our homes are very sensitive to the Katrina victims."[60] At the ceremony to donate the funds, Rafik Husseini, an aide to Palestinian leader Mahmoud Abbas, referred to what happened in New Orleans as a *nakba*.

About the donation Abbas said, "On behalf of the Palestinian people and, in particular, the refugee communities of the West Bank and Gaza Strip, I wish to express our deepest sympathy with the survivors of Hurricane Katrina. With our humble donation, we feel it is important to show our concern since Palestinians know all too well the pain and hardship caused by being a refugee. We pray that they will soon be able to return to their homes."[61] For its part, the U.S. consulate in Jerusalem sought to depoliticize the donation by publicizing it not as a signal of international solidarity among refugees but instead as a donation from one poor group to another. Jake Walles, the U.S. consul general in Jerusalem, said the donation was especially significant "because we know it came from poor people."[62]

Palestinian refugees saw the necessity of comparison and solidarity, sharing the inadequacy of the U.S. government's feeble attempts to aid the victims of Katrina, most of whom were black. While the Palestinian refugee and the displaced person from Katrina have different relationships to state violence and colonial governmentality, they share the experiences of being forced to leave their homes, having to live in a foreign home as outsiders, and having little or no support from their political representatives. The Palestinians' recognition of their similarities to Katrina victims produces a political imaginary that reveals how Palestinian refugees fall victim to colonial violence and racism, and how much places like New Orleans constitute socialized "third world" refugee sites.

On June 14, 2008, three years after Hurricane Katrina devastated the region, a diverse range of people from New Orleans crowded into a local arts studio for a unique hip-hop concert. Featuring poetry and music about structural racism in New Orleans in the wake of Hurricane Katrina and the enduring Israeli occupation of the West Bank and Gaza, "liberation hip hop" marked an important moment of activism for Palestinian American, Palestinian, and African American grassroots activists. The event featured readings of Palestinian poet Mahmood Darwish's writing as well as presentations by community activists in New Orleans. After the poetry reading, the hip hop began. New Orleans Palestinian hip-hoppers Shaheed and Arabian Outlaw took to the stage to rap about structural inequalities in New Orleans and Palestine. New Orleans–based African American artists Truth Universal and Sess 4-5 took the stage next to rap about African American self-determination and the struggle against housing discrimination in New Orleans. The concert concluded with a performance by Mohammed Al-Farrah, of the first Gazan hip-hop group, Palestinian Rapperz.

Although African American and Palestinian activists do not always draw comparisons between U.S. welfare reform and the Oslo Peace Process or between the legacy of slavery and the racial politics of Zionism, or point out the similarities of mass incarceration of surplus populations across Palestine and the United States, they do engage in cultural politics that articulate a shared structure of feeling, in which the everyday realities of police brutality, drug wars, racialization, and state violence in urban black communities in the United States and in Arab cities in Israel/Palestine are compared. Palestinian and African American claims that blackness and Palestinianness are interchangeable rests on a politics of translation, in which Arab Americans locate themselves in a long history of antiblack racialization in the United States and black Americans see the Israeli occupation as an extension of U.S. racial capitalism. Translational politics such as these identify shared conditions produced by globalization and incarceration while also paying homage to a previous generation's political imaginaries. In the following analysis I am interested in the aesthetics of post-1990s black and Palestinian cultural formations that translate Palestinian and black political imaginaries in order to constitute a geography of liberation. In spoken-word poetry and in Palestinian rap, disparate localities like Lod, Israel, and Compton, California, are brought into a shared horizon—just as they were in the Durban conference—in ways that reveal the violence of neoliberal globalization and the "war on terror."[63]

Raymond Williams defined a structure of feeling as an emergent cultural formation that defines a particular historical moment. A structure of feeling describes an unconscious political sentiment that is not yet publicly articulated but that can be sensed or "felt" among a certain culture.

Williams used the term in *The Long Revolution* in order to understand how working-class communities developed class consciousness through their engagement with art and culture.[64] Culture provided a critical nexus, Williams argued, for the formation of a working-class political consciousness, yet prior to its public articulation a structure of feeling defined working-class political consciousness. I use the term "structure of feeling" to describe the ways that Afro-Arab political imaginaries in the 1990s and 2000s were articulated through cultural engagement, in poetry and in hip hop. These cultural forms signify an emergent cultural formation, a structure of feeling, not yet articulated as a social movement but as an important component of political consciousness nevertheless.

Since its emergence in the late 1970s, hip hop has been an effective medium for articulating global imaginaries linking distant geographies. Hip hop's global imaginary is partly a function of its medium; it is a syncretic cultural form produced through sampling transnational musical archives as well as splicing different genres and beats in the "breaks" of songs and rhythms. Scholars of black American hip hop locate its origins in globalized Brooklyn, New York, where Jamaican toasting combined with local vernaculars to produce a new aesthetic. Hip hop is a mode of translocal and transnational communication that is constituted by a pastiche of local sounds and beats produced over globalized corporate and commercial networks. In hip hop the local is always and already formed by transnational sonic migrations, and because of this, hip hop is uniquely capable of articulating solidarities and extranational belongings, while also being grounded in specific localities.[65]

Hip hop is also a postindustrial cultural form that creates cultural politics that respond to the dismantling of U.S. urban black communities under the forces of the globalized economy. The forms of hip-hop culture—break dancing, graffiti, disc jockeying, and rap—are low-cost arts, often performed with the refuse of industrialization like vacant buildings. In this way, hip hop is grounded in a particular historical conjuncture that unites the U.S. dismantling of social welfare projects and the neoliberalization of economies, leading to "globalization."[66]

While the history of hip hop has been well documented, my interest is in the ways Palestinian hip hop and spoken-word "slam" poetry, which are relatively new contributions to Palestinian postcolonial aesthetics, engage a genealogy of Afro-Arab politics. Palestinian hip hop and spoken-word poetry link questions of Palestinian refugees—their exilic politics and right of return—to the colonial geographies of the United States, in which places of structural racial violence, like Compton and New Orleans, are significant coordinates. This geographic linkage is not merely a simplistic politics of comparison but is, I contend, an attempt to reconfigure the geographies of modernity in ways that forge Afro-Arab political imaginaries.

The broken geographies of modernity—characterized by uneven development and dispossession—are the subject of Palestinian hip hop, which is created transnationally in Palestine and in places like Brooklyn and the Bay Area of California. There are Palestinian hip-hop artists in the West Bank (Ramallah Underground), in Israel (Da Arabian MC, or DAM), in Gaza (Palestinian Rapperz), and in multiple other sites throughout the Arab world, Europe, and the globe. Palestinian hip hop reflects the global coordinates of the Palestinian diaspora and therefore emerges from multiple loci of enunciation and local contexts.[67] Palestinian hip hop produced in Oakland, California, is both local and global, reflecting the contexts of urban Oakland and the estrangement from, and existential threats to, Palestine.[68] The first Palestinian rap group emerged from an urban ghetto within Israel.

Lod, the Israeli name for the former Palestinian city of Al-Lydd, is an Israeli city just fifteen kilometers from Tel Aviv. Like many of the colonial geographies of Israel/Palestine, Lod/Al-Lydd is a contested city in which Palestinians recall an indigenous Arab history of the city Al-Lydd, while Jewish Israelis insist on the modern Hebrew title, Lod. Understanding the colonial present that constitutes Al-Lydd/Lod requires remembering the violent transformation of Al-Lydd into the Israeli city of Lod. On July 11, 1948, the Jewish army entered Al-Lydd and killed 426 Arab men, women, and children, 176 of whom were killed inside the town's mosque. Following the massacre, Arab residents of Al-Lydd were terrorized and fled. Of the 19,000 Arabs who used to call Al-Lydd home, only 1,052 were permitted to return at the end of the Arab-Israeli war. Yitzhak Rabin, who participated in the massacre, wrote in his diary about the psychological toll it had on Israeli soldiers who had not embraced the idea of ethnic cleansing. "Great Suffering was inflicted upon the men taking part in the eviction action. [They] included youth-movement graduates who had been inculcated with values such as international brotherhood and humaneness. The eviction action went beyond the concepts they were used to. There were some fellows who refused to take part. . . . Prolonged propaganda activities were required after the action . . . to explain why we were obliged to undertake such a harsh and cruel action."[69] The Arabs who remained in Al-Lydd following the Arab-Israeli war became Arab citizens of Israel and were segregated in densely packed, low-income housing. In 2010, the population of Al-Lydd (now transformed into the Israeli city of Lod) was approximately

69,000; 25 percent of this population is Arab citizens of Israel. Lod is today one of the few remaining mixed Muslim-Jewish cities in Israel, although this is slowly changing as the Arab population is regularly subject to evictions and home demolitions. The Lod municipality will not give Palestinians building permits to renovate their homes, while Jewish enclaves are given generous grants to build Jewish-only apartments.[70] Lod's Arab population is segregated in slum housing on the periphery of the city. In these areas, crime and murder rates are the highest in all of Israel. Moreover, an active and dangerous drug trade runs through Lod.

Lod has become an urban ghetto where Israeli defense forces target Palestinian residents in their "war on drugs," while the state attempts to eviscerate the historical memory of the 1948 village. Yet around 1998 a new anthem pulsed through Lod's crowded streets as the bass-filled beats of DAM, Palestine's first hip-hop group, played through home stereos. Hip hop has always been a means of unsanctioned political journalism as well as an aesthetic politics that articulates often-unarticulated structures of feeling. Chuck D of the highly influential U.S. group Public Enemy once called hip hop, the "CNN for urban youth." In the spirit of Chuck D's statement, we might argue that DAM is black America's Al Jazeera counterpart.[71]

DAM reproduces many of the aesthetic and political sensibilities of U.S. urban rap, including a focus on structural violence, poverty, and drug warfare. Tamer Nafar, one of DAM's MCs, released a debut single in 1998 titled "Stop Selling Drugs," which mimicked U.S. rap's interest in the war on drugs but was firmly located in Lod's context. The title imitated the concerns of Lod's U.S. counterpart's illicit drug trade and police control and violence. Nafar raps about the structural violence Palestinians in Lod face and, in so doing, attempts to confront the neoliberal discourse of the Israeli state that attributes violence and crime in Arab districts within Israel to deficient comportment on the part of Arabs. As DAM grew in 2000 to a three-member group, it felt a deep sense of affinity with the political sensibilities of black urban Americans. As Tamer Nafar told an interviewer,

[During the 2000 intifada] there was an article about two kids who killed an officer and they blamed Tupac's lyrics. "Pump ya fists like this / Holla if you hear me" . . . I think, was the name of the song. . . . It made the first impression that they are talking something that I'm feeling, or that I'm seeing, or what I'm experiencing. It all started from 2pac. . . . When you see a Black man who's being chased by the police, we get chased by the police, here. If I didn't experience it, then my cousin did. If he didn't, then my friend did. If he didn't, then my neighbor did. When you see he's talking about people in prison. Most of our friends are in prison. When he's taking about drug dealing . . . When he talks about slavery, you can compare it to the occupation.[72]

In 2001, following the start of the second intifada, DAM released the popular single "Meen Erhabi?—Who's the Terrorist?" The song was popularized in the West, in part, through a music video produced by Palestinian American filmmaker Jackie Salloum, who created the documentary *Sling Shot Hip-Hop* (2008). Salloum's DAM video makes explicit the translocal connections between the U.S. urban ghetto and Lod, Israel, as the footage reproduces U.S. hip-hop aesthetics and a particular narrative of police and state violence that could be as much about the Los Angeles riots and the beating of Rodney King as everyday colonial violence in Lod.[73] "Who's the Terrorist?" resists the racialization of Arabs in Israel and the West by focusing attention on the structural racism Palestinians face in Israel. According to the song, it is Israel's policies of ethnic cleansing, and not the enduring resistance to erasure on the part of Palestinians, that represent terrorism. "Who's the Terrorist?" reveals that the violence of the state is regularly normalized while subaltern resistance is viewed as dangerous and threatening.

> Who's a terrorist? You've taken everything I own while I'm living in my
>   homeland
> You're killing us like you've killed our ancestors . . .
> You're the Witness, the Lawyer, and the Judge!

DAM's website demonstrates its global understanding of resistance, listing as its influences Tupac Shakur, Malcolm X, Fairuz, Edward Said, The Notorious BIG, Nas, and KRS One. These identifications with pan-African and indigenous anticolonial intellectuals are not arbitrary but illustrate the shared structures of feeling produced out of colonial modernity. As Tamer Nafar articulates, "Growing up in [Lod], Israel my reality is hip-hop. I listened to the lyrics and felt they were describing me, my situation. You can exchange the word 'nigger' for 'Palestinian.' [Lod] is a ghetto, the biggest crime and drug center in the Middle East. When I heard Tupac sing, 'It's a White Man's World,' I decided to take hip-hop seriously."[74]

Although Suheir Hammad, lives in Brooklyn, New York, far from Lod, she is the descendant of Palestinians from Al-Lydd and a colleague of DAM's. A Palestinian American poet and, recently, an actress, Hammad published her first book of poetry in 1996, and in 2002 she became a regular presence on Russell Simmons Def Poetry Slam.[75] Like DAM, Hammad's aesthetics combine African American and Palestinian cultural forms, like black urban hip hop and Palestinian poetry, yet her work is also in dialogue with a tradition of Afro-Arab political imaginaries that Hammad locates in the poetics and politics of the African American poet June Jordan. In the introductory essay to her 1996 book, *Born Palestinian, Born Black*, she writes, "The last stanza of June Jordan's 'Moving Towards Home' changed my life. I remember feeling validated by her statement."[76]

Moving toward Home (1989) is a collection of poems Jordan wrote in response to the 1982 Israeli invasion of Southern Lebanon. Jordan was interested in the Palestinian solidarity movement that had formed out of the intercommunal analysis of groups like the Black Panther Party, as they forged an anti-imperialist third world left (see Chapter 4). In the poem to which Hammad refers, Jordan identified the Afro-Arab international by transposing blackness with Palestinianness.

> I was born a black woman
> and now
> I am become a Palestinian
> against the relentless laughter of evil
> there is less and less living room
> and where are my loved ones?[77]

In *Born Black, Born Palestinian*, Hammad develops Jordan's trajectory by linking her own belongings as a Palestinian in Jordan, Beirut, and Brooklyn to blackness. For Hammad blackness describes a double-consciousness that links Arab and African American political imaginaries. "There are," Hammad writes, "many usages of the word 'Black,'" and in her poem, Hammad names a variety of usages that suggest the range of antiblack stereotypes as well as positive black diasporic images. Blackness is, for Hammad, multivocal, naming a range of ideas from "Black September" to "the Arabic expression 'to blacken your face.'" Although blackness is regularly associated with darkness and subservience in both Western and Arab contexts, Hammad's poem demonstrates that black is also

> like the genius of Stevie, Zora and Abdel-Haleem
> relative purity
> like the face of God
> the face of your grandmother.[78]

For Jordan and Hammad, shifting between blackness and Palestinianness produces a political consciousness that brings urban black America and occupied Palestine into imaginative contact. For Jordan, this translational politics shaped her physical encounter with the Middle East. In describing what she saw in the Lebanese refugee camps she visited in 1996, Jordan said, "I hadn't seen anything like them since the Harlem riots."[79]

In similar ways, Suheir Hammad develops a political aesthetic based on uniting heterogeneous geographies that confront similar neoliberal and colonial forms of violence. In her poem "On Refuge and Language," which was recited on Democracy Now and published in Joy James's 2007 collection, *What Lies Beneath: Katrina, Race, and the State of the Nation*, Hammad dwells on the homelessness of Katrina victims in order to engage a comparative exercise in which black victims of Katrina are posed as Palestinian refugees. This comparison was likely inspired by the regular usage, within U.S. media, of the word "refugee" to describe the people of New Orleans made homeless by the flood. The poem focuses on the inability of the words "refuge" and "refugee" to adequately convey the state of homelessness and dispossession faced by both groups. In the word "refuge" Hammad finds a public attempt to contain the narrative of displacement into a narrative of homecoming, of becoming, of sanctuary.[80]

It is through her comparison of the African American poor to the Palestinian refugee that Hammad illustrates the incomparability of New Orleans's desires for refuge and the refugee's desire for homeland. Hammad writes that "refugees are not Americans" in order to demonstrate that despite their homelessness, African Americans are still Americans with rights of citizenship, while Palestinian refugees have no similar legal status. Yet the failure of the comparison becomes productive of a different epistemology that reveals the structural limits of citizenship and the state to provide "refuge" for black residents of New Orleans and Palestinian refugees, respectively. "Refugees are not Americans" is also a statement about how African Americans are afforded only second-class belonging in the U.S. Hammad links the presumed foreignness of the Palestinian refugee to the alien presences of African American "refugees" in the U.S.

> What do we pledge allegiance to?
> A government that leaves its old
> To die of thirst surrounded by water
> Is a foreign government.[81]

Here Hammad plays with the notion of foreignness, illustrating how the U.S. state's inadequate attempt to comfort the black citizens of New Orleans placed the U.S. state as foreign to New Orleans citizens. Yet she also illustrates how, despite the promise of citizenship, the liberal state is just as alienating and violent as are those states the U.S. regularly views as backward and underdeveloped.

Having established differences and similarities between Palestinian refugees and Katrina survivors, Hammad refashions geographies in ways that link Palestinians to black Americans through both groups' un-refuge and homelessness. Echoing the post–World War II writing of Adorno, who argued that homes are always precarious and exiles can never be at home, in the final part of the poem Hammad illustrates a geopolitical awareness that sutures refugees together through a different kind of belonging. She writes of "Ahmad from Guinea," who makes her falafel sandwich in Brooklyn while questioning her about to whom and where she belongs. In her response to Ahmad, she answers to another foreigner/insider of the U.S. nation-state, "The rest of the world lives here too / In America."[82]

Here, the Palestinian refugee and the Katrina victim are merged, as both are "evacuated as if criminal, rescued by neighbors, shot by soldiers." While Hammad denies that there is "refuge" for victims of either Katrina or *al-nakba*, there is something that is structurally and qualitatively different that links both groups in a shared horizon: belonging. "These my people," Hammad writes about the people of New Orleans, but also about the Palestinian refugees throughout the globe to whom she is similarly different, yet alike. Hammad constructs a bond forged within the crucible of colonial modernity; in her poetry Palestinians and Katrina refugees both wander across a landscape in which they are excluded. Yet where the black New Orleans resident may find refuge, the Palestinian remains always and forever a refugee.[83]

Key to Hammad's comparison between Palestine and New Orleans is the recognition of incommensurability. Ultimately the comparison between the Katrina victim and the Palestinian refugee breaks down because black Americans have some recourse to national rights, insufficient as these may be, while Palestinian refugees remain stateless. But underneath the incommensurable realities of citizenship and statelessness lie a more profound layer of similarity—a structure of feeling—that is constituted by colonial modernity and border thinking. It is not that Palestinians and Katrina refugees are the same; it is that both the *nakba* and the flood unearth a structure of feeling, a sense that the geographies of colonial modernity are broken, as the U.S. state's "protections" of citizenship and the UN's creation of the State of Israel are both exposed as violent ruptures.

Hammad develops the linkages and breaks between black America and Palestine further in her collection *Breaking Poems* (2008) as she performs the experiences of displacement, violence, and incompleteness that constitute Palestinian refugee belongings in places like Palestine, Beirut, and Brooklyn.[84] Her title is provocative, invoking multiple simultaneous meanings. "Breaking" is multivocal for Hammad, signifying the ways that colonial modernity physically breaks Palestinian refugees as well as signifying the ways that globalization contains disjunctures and uneven development that enable a certain kind of political consciousness. In this sense, Hammad's poems are similar to the aesthetic of breaks described by Fred Moten. Moten argues that black radicalism is constituted by unarticulated sounds and feelings that refuse closure and are often produced in poetics and music. "Syncopation, performance, and the anarchic organization of phonic substance delineate an ontological field wherein black radicalism is set to work."[85] Suheir Hammad engages the "breaks" of black and Palestinian radicalism, where subjectivity and personhood confront exile and homelessness. *Breaking Poems* is a singular poem, and yet it is "broken" by Hammad's breaks—literally written as "break"—between sections, as well as by the Arabic words that literally connect the disparate English significations.

In the first part of *Breaking Poems*, Hammad dwells in the concept of "break" as a means to articulate a body torn apart through exile and homelessness. In showing the sorts of dismemberment entailed in exile, Hammad expresses a geopolitical awareness that links various sites of colonial modernity. The poem traces her body as it moves across national borders to expose a world of uneven development, violent exclusions, and "broken" bodies. These sites are Deheisheh refugee camp, Beirut, Tel Aviv, Gaza, Khan Younis, New York City, Houston, Bombay, Brooklyn, New Orleans, Baghdad, and then, finally, a deterritorialized place called "here," which is represented by Hammad's corporal body.

Through lyrical sequences in which she employs anglicized Palestinian Arabic to suture together English words, Hammad articulates the spaces, broken, within modernist geographies, where Palestinians, stateless and homeless, reside. In the process of finding a language to express what cannot be otherwise identified, spoken, or located on a map, Hammad finds a grammar that links similarly displaced bodies, including residents of New Orleans and Palestinian refugees.

Conclusion

In this chapter I have identified the ways that the combined forces of neoliberal governance and the horizontal circuit of security regimes across the United States and Israel/Palestine established new conditions of possibility within which Afro-Arab political imaginaries formed. The geographies of liberation were profoundly shaped by a new post–Cold War unipolar American era that produced uneven development as well as new political imaginaries in which the spaces of neoliberal governance were brought closer together. In this context, I argued that the 2001 UN world conference on racism, which foregrounded an analysis of slavery and of Israeli colonialism, was an important moment in the forging of an Afro-Arab political imaginary. Although questions of reparations and of Zionist racism were ultimately contained by the end of the conference—and by the events of 9/11—the conference nevertheless inspired comparisons between U.S. racial slavery and racism in Israel and, in so doing, inspired comparisons between African Americans and Palestinians.

Yet the linkages between African Americans and Palestinians were most fully articulated in the cultural politics of hip hop and poetry, where African American and Palestinian artists enunciated a political imaginary in which blackness and Palestinianness collide and merge. DAM, Suheir Hammad, and June Jordan developed an aesthetic that rests on linking racialized and pathologized urban settings in order to translate global localities. Key to this political maneuver is transposing Lod on Compton, or Gaza on New Orleans, or Beirut on Harlem. These cultural politics demonstrate that while globalization and neoliberalism have restricted the horizon of social movements in the public sphere, they have been unable to do so in the realm of cultural politics, where new geographies of liberation are being imagined.

Liberation at the Twilight
of the American Era

Gaza Strip was getting bombed, Obama didn't say shit.
—Lupe Fiasco

Geographies of Liberation has mapped part of the Afro-Arab world within the context of changing colonial and national configurations. Geopolitical changes throughout the twentieth century brought with them significant transformations in racial belongings and meanings. Within the context of global political change, the contours of the Afro-Arab world transformed. In the late nineteenth century the shape of Afro-Arab politics was informed by the overlapping histories of Jewish and African diasporic longings. In the wake of the Ottoman Empire's decline, coupled with the imposition of the European mandate governments, the Afro-Arab world was shaped by overlapping politics of pan-Islamism, pan-Africanism, and pan-Arabism. In the era of World War II and beyond, the Afro-Arab world was character-ized less by overlap than by conjunctures and contingencies that made it "feel" connected. In the crucible of the post–World War II moment and its ascendant liberal nationalism, the politics of binationalism became one coordinate of Afro-Arab conjuncture. In the post-1967 era, during a moment of global third world left political struggle, the Afro-Arab world was shaped by the anti-imperialist politics of intercommunalism. And in the so-called unipolar American era an Afro-Arab political imaginary was forged amidst global neoliberal policies and colonial policing technolo-gies linking the processes of incarceration in urban black communities and Israel/Palestine.

Liberation in this book has referred to a political consciousness rooted in a desire for political freedoms as well as the right to belong, to *feel* at home. The desire for the affective nourishment of home is a fundamental political demand that requires confronting the geographies of modernity that impose dominant understanding of belonging and exclusion. The political consciousness described in *Geographies of Liberation* has been characterized by moments in which subjects imagine new futures within contexts not of their making. In this way, late-nineteenth-century African Americans imagined a politics of diaspora by transiting between the United States, Palestine, and Africa. In the post–World War I era, Dusé Mohamed Ali conceived of the Afro-Arab world through his movement across the political terrains of pan-Islamism, pan-Africanism, and pan-Arabism. In the World War II moment, Ralph Bunche and Jewish and Arab Palestinians attempted, unsuccessfully, to imagine a political formation called binationalism that could organize political community beyond ethnoracial nationalism. In the 1970s, within a context of global anti-imperialist politics, the Black Panthers articulated an intercommunal politics that emphasized internationalism across communities. And finally, within a new unipolar American era, an Afro-Arab international formed in the breaks of neoliberal restructuring and a new security state.

The political imaginaries I describe transit between competing national formations, and in this way the geographies of liberation describe a set of highly mobile imaginaries. At the same time, however, the political imaginaries I map are not always "radical," nor are they always liberationist for all. Political imaginaries often react to hegemonic forces, and in this way they often reproduce the logic of dominant forces. Pan-Africanists' designs for Liberia, for example, engaged a liberationist and diasporic politics within the West, and yet they reproduced the processes and norms of colonialism in Africa. Similarly, early European Zionism was a liberation politics that reacted against racist forms of European modernity, and yet it was also a discourse rooted in Eastern European conceptions of homelands and Eurocentric understandings of human progress.

Moreover, transnational solidarity movements frequently emphasize moments of symmetry across global geographies, but they sometimes ignore the important uneven power relations that shape the international terrain. The mid-twentieth-century politics of binationalism in Palestine represents a liberationist moment against the wave of nationalist movements for partition. And yet the call for a joint Jewish-Arab political structure often ignored the geopolitical realities of Jewish Zionist colonization in Palestine. Similarly, the 1970s politics of the Israeli Black Panthers momentarily and radically redrew the lines of Arab-Jewish belongings while leaving unquestioned the 1948 colonial question at the heart of even the post-1967 Palestine question.

Geographies of Liberation is also about the fugitive memories of history that have become taboo in the contemporary public sphere. Black/Jewish relations, for example, are all too often bracketed by a domestic history of ethnic and urban relationships that erases the possibilities of black Jews, not to mention Arab Jews. Moreover, if we use modernist racial categories, we fall prey to nationalizing what is a very complicated international story, concerning decades of overlapping and conjunctural political imaginaries. African American engagement with Palestine and Israel, I suggest, is shaped more by a global history of nationalism and racialization than merely by U.S. interethnic rivalries.

Another taboo engaged here is the question of Palestine. *Geographies of Liberation* has linked the Palestine question to a moral horizon that includes the "Jewish question" and the "Negro question." I have made a case that Jews, blacks, and Palestinians share a similar and overlapping history of dispossession in the face of modern nationalism. Moreover, I have demonstrated multiple ways that Jewish, Arab, and black intellectuals have recognized in each other connections across time and space. The question of Palestine is imprisoned in a web of modernist racial categories. Israel/Palestine is not primarily an Arab-Jewish conflict, although U.S. media regularly present it as such. If we only see the question of Palestine through the lens of an interethnic Arab-Jewish conflict—a lens that was focused by nationalism in the modern era—we will forcefully ignore a long history of Arab-Jewish conviviality prior to the era of the United Nations, and we will forget the complex possibilities for alternative political communities beyond nationalism. The Palestine question is not, in my view, primarily a Jewish question or any question related to modernist identity politics. Instead, as I have documented throughout *Geographies of Liberation*, it is a question of modern nationalism and colonialism. Finding a just decolonial solution to the Palestine question must begin, at the very least, with an honest and rich history.

Geographies of Liberation also makes a claim for an expansive understanding of black radicalism and black studies. By placing black liberation at the center of a global history of coloniality and national development, we can see struggles for freedom as they took place in different sorts of modernist structures of power, including under colonial conditions, conditions of slavery, conditions of segregation, and conditions of incarceration. In the process of mapping new coordinates in the geographies of black liberation, we expand our understanding of the global dimensions of the black radical tradition and develop a better sense of the forms of de-colonial politics that take place within it. Moreover, placing black studies at the center of global history enables a complex view of the global assemblages of racialization that take place across uneven and unequal geopolitical conditions.

The "American era," characterized by neoliberal forms of governance—privatization, responsibility societies, and mass incarceration—is undergoing transformation as we reach its twilight. At the time of this writing, the U.S. state finds itself in the process of losing prestige in the Middle East/ North Africa, in part because of its unyielding and lonely support for Israel at a time when Israel pushes the boundaries of international law, as well as the global social movements that have emerged to challenge the unipolar American era. The so-called Arab Spring, the Occupy Wall Street movement, and the European anti-austerity movements all pose challenges to the American era and forecast a different political formation, with different political imaginaries ahead.

Afro-Arab political imaginaries are also undergoing significant change at the close of this writing. President Barak Obama has just been inaugurated for a second term. At an inaugural gala, security guards interrupted and terminated Rapper Lupe Fiasco's performance because Fiasco rapped, "Gaza Strip was getting bombed, Obama didn't say shit."[1] In Palestine, recognizing the power of the South African antiapartheid movement, activists are organizing a boycott, divestment, and sanctions movement against Israel while waiting for their "South Africa moment."[2] Off the shores of Gaza, in international waters presumed to lie beyond any one national jurisdiction, a global solidarity movement including the African American writer Alice Walker prepares to join a flotilla carrying food and building materials to the people of Gaza, who have been besieged for decades under Israeli sanctions.[3] In prisons across Palestine, young men and women incarcerated for their political beliefs refuse food and advocate prison abolitionism. And the Palestinian poet and former member of the PLO Mahmoud Darwish, who passed on in 2008, implores us to speak truth to power:

> On the day when my words were earth, I was a friend to stalks of
>   wheat. . . .
> On the day when my words were a rebellion, I was a friend to
>   earthquakes. . . .
> But when my words became honey . . . flies covered my lips![4]

Notes

INTRODUCTION

1. This position could be seen at the outset of the Egyptian uprising when U.S. vice president Joe Biden defended Hosni Mubarak as an ally and not a dictator. Biden argued that Mubarak should not step down due to popular protest. Over time, the U.S. government's position shifted, as Mubarak's fall was inevitable in the face of massive popular rebellion in Tahrir square and across Egypt. See Bridget Johnson, "Biden: Mubarak not a dictator, protests not like Eastern Europe," *The Hill* blog, January 28, 2011, at http://thehill. com/blogs/blog-briefing-room/news/140923-biden-mubarak-not-a-dictator-protests-not-like-eastern-europe (accessed August 23, 2012). Under Mubarak's rule, Egypt received U.S. foreign aid in an amount second only to Israel's. See http://www.politifact. com/truth-o-meter/statements/2011/feb/04/ross-douthat/egypt-got-more-foreign-aid-anyone-besides-israel-s/ (accessed August 26, 2012).

2. In the wake of the Cold War a consensus developed within that United States that U.S. foreign aid should be directed toward "democracy promotion" through aid to civil society organizations. George H. W. Bush offered $3 million in aid to create the Middle East Democracy Fund as a means of encouraging economic and political liberalization. From 1991 to 2001, the United States spent $250 million on democracy programs in the Middle East. After September 11, 2001, U.S. officials questioned the utility of "democracy promotion," but the U.S. continued to encourage civil society development via top-down initiatives. See Muravchik, "Exporting Democracy to the Arab World"; Carapico, "Foreign Aid for Promoting Democracy in the Arab World"; and Denoeux, "Promoting Democracy and Governance in Arab Countries."

3. Among the most significant examples of armed self-defense within the U.S. black freedom movement are the NAACP chapter of Monroe, N.C., led by Robert F. Williams in the 1950s–60s; the 1960s Deacons for Defense; and the 1970s Black Panther Party. See, for example, Tyson, *Radio Free Dixie*; Hill, *Deacons for Defense*; and Williams, *Negroes with Guns*.

4. Obama, "Remarks by the President on a New Beginning."

5. Obama's "Remarks by the President on a New Beginning" presented a teleology of Western progress that could also be seen in his important speech on race in America, "A More Perfect Union." In that speech, Obama argued that the U.S. was constantly improving its attitudes and policies toward racial minorities in ways that were leading to "a more perfect union." The speech was a rebuke to his pastor, the Reverend Jeremiah Wright, who had embarrassed Obama by naming racism as something that was constitutive of the United States and not a mere dilemma the state had to confront on its route toward perfection. For the text of Obama's speech, see Obama, "More Perfect Union."

6. Obama, "Remarks by the President on a New Beginning."

7. Ibid.

8. Among the many excellent books on the history of U.S. cultural and diplomatic engagement with the Middle East, I have been most drawn to those that discuss the cultural and affective dimensions of U.S. foreign policy. See, for example, Makdisi, *Faith Misplaced*; Little, *American Orientalism*; and McAlister, *Epic Encounters*.

9. The Foundation for Middle East Peace estimates a West Bank settler population of 328,423 as of 2011. According to their statistics, this represents a population increase of 177 percent from 1999 (when the settler population of the West Bank was 177,411). These data are based on Israeli census figures and may not account for the nonrecognized "outposts" or pre-settlements that contain settler populations unrecognized by Israel in settler demographics. Demographics are immensely important and contested in Israel/Palestine. For the purpose of showing the expansion of Israeli settlers in the West Bank, I've chosen here the most conservative figures, recognizing that there are estimates of greater settler population figures. See *Foundation for Middle East Peace Settlement Report* 21, no. 1 (2011), http://www.fmep.org/settlement_info/settlement-info-and-tables/stats-data/settlements-in-the-west-bank-1 (accessed August 24, 2012).

10. There are many excellent studies of the racialization of Arabs and Muslims in the United States after September 11, 2001. See, for example, Jamal and Naber, *Race and Arab Americans before and after 9/11*; Sheehi, *Islamophobia*; Shyrock, *Islamophobia/Islamophilia*; and Alsutany, *Arabs and Muslims in the Media*. Each of these studies argues that the U.S. justifies the suspension of civil liberties for Muslim Americans by appealing to the war on terror's "exceptional" nature. In making this case, the authors invoke Giorgio Agamben's argument that national crises can precipitate a state of exception that permits dehumanization in the name of state security in exceptional times. See, for example, Agamben, *State of Exception*.

11. For a discussion of Malcolm X's 1964 visit to Cairo, see Marable, *Malcolm X*. Also see Nkrumah, "Through African Eyes." For information on Gamel Abdel Nasser's hosting of the 1964 meeting of the Organization of African Unity, see Akinsanya, "Afro-Arab Alliance."

12. Shohat, *Taboo Memories*.

13. Said, *Reflections on Exile and Other Essays*; Adorno, *Minima Moralia*.

14. I use the term "polycultural" to connote the late Ottoman society's practice of conviviality. Polyculture signifies a difference-with-coexistence rather than difference-as-one, among a polity. See, for examples, Barkey's *Empire of Difference* and Makdisi's *Artillery of Heaven*. Polyculturalism also signifies the contingencies of cultural identity within an individual, whereas multiculturalism often reifies cultural boundaries of difference. See, for example, Kelley's "Polycultural Me"; also see Ewing's *Being and Belonging*.

15. "Citizenship and Entry into Israel Law" (Temporary Order) 5763. The law reads, "During the period in which this law shall remain in force, despite what is said in any legal provision, including article 7 of the Citizenship Law, the Minister of the Interior shall not grant the inhabitant of an area citizenship on the basis of the Citizenship law, and shall not give him a license to reside in Israel on the basis of the Entry into Israel Law, and the Area Commander shall not grant a said inhabitant, a permit to stay in Israel, on the basis with the security legislation in the area." Unofficial translation available on Knesset website: http://www.knesset.gov.il/laws/special/eng/citizenship_law.htm (accessed August 23, 2012).

16. Du Bois's writing on Israel is a topic I consider in Chapters 1 and 3. Also see Sundquist, *Strangers in the Land*; Weisbord and Kazarian, *Israel in the Black American Perspective*, 23; Blum and Young, *Souls of W. E. B. Du Bois*; and McAlister, *Epic Encounters*.

17. See, for example, Duberman, *Paul Robeson*; Weisbord and Kazarian, *Israel in the Black American Perspective*; and Sundquist, *Strangers in the Land*.

18. On BASIC, see Weisbord and Kazarian, *Israel in the Black American Perspective*; Anderson, *A. Philip Randolph*; and Levine, *Bayard Rustin and the Civil Rights Movement*.

19. Schneier, *Martin Luther King Jr. and the Jewish Community*. Schneier presents relevant data on King's public statements on Israel, including his appeal to the U.S. government to support Israel during the Six-Day War. Schneier also conveys some of the Jewish community's dismay that King wasn't more vocal in his support for Israel. Schneier's analysis is typical of a scholarly approach that confines King's writing about Israel to domestic U.S. black/Jewish relations. As black nationalists began to criticize Israel, especially in the wake of the 1967 war, King admonished them not to equate Zionism with racism, a move that King believed was anti-Semitic. Also see Blum and Young, *Souls of W. E. B. Du Bois*, and Sundquist, *Strangers in the Land*. King demonstrated some ambivalence in private about his support for Israel after 1967. In the FBI's wiretap of King's telephone conversations with his lawyer Stanley Levison, King articulates his concerns for Arab lives during the 1967 war and his criticism of Israeli occupation. See Garrow, *Martin Luther King, Jr., FBI File*.

20. The CBC has a complex history with the issue of Israel/Palestine. During the 1970s the CBC was among the only elected bodies willing to criticize Israel. Recently, however, the CBC, as a body, has muted criticism of Israel and regularly provides political defense for Israeli policies. There are notable exceptions to the dominant CBC position on Israel. Cynthia McKinney had been a vocal critic of Israel within the CBC before she lost her elected office. Representative Barbara Lee has been more willing than others in the CBC to support Palestinian causes. It is not uncommon, however, for CBC members to speak at the American Israel Political Action Committee meeting and to tour Israel on delegations funded by the committee.

21. See, for example, McAlister, *Epic Encounters*; Marable, *Malcolm X*; Feldman, "Representing Permanent War"; and Feldman, "Towards an Afro-Arab Diasporic Culture."

22. See, for example, Lerner and West, *Jews and Blacks*; Kaufman, *Broken Alliance*; and Weisbord and Kazarian, *Israel in the Black American Perspective*. A more nuanced version of this history can be found in Sundquist's encyclopedic *Strangers in the Land*.

23. We might also think of geographies of liberation in terms of Frederic Jameson's observation that the postmodern condition requires a political culture that "will necessarily have to raise spatial issues as its fundamental organizing concern." Jameson advocates "aesthetic cognitive mapping" as a means of becoming disalienated from a world increasingly constituted by multinational capital. According to Jameson, "The political form of postmodernism, if there ever is any, will have as its vocation the invention and projection of a global cognitive mapping, on a social as well as a spatial scale" (Jameson, *Postmodernism*, 54).

24. As George Lipsitz has argued, globalization demands the recognition of "new epistemologies and new ontologies" that constitute "new ways of knowing and new ways of being. New social subjects produce new archives and new imaginings" (Lipsitz, *American*

Studies in a Moment of Danger, 8). Also see, for example, Pease, *New American Exceptionalism*; Edwards and Gaonkar, *Globalizing American Studies*; Fluck, Pease, and Rowe, *Re-Framing the Transnational Turn in American Studies*; and Rowe, *Afterlives of Modernism*. These books and others were recently reviewed by Evan Rhodes in "Beyond the Exceptionalist Thesis."

25. The transnational turn has led scholars to engage a postnationalist scholarship that confronts that seeming naturalness of nation-states themselves. Michael Shapiro, for example, argues for a postnationalist scholarship that deconstructs the seeming naturalness of the nation-state—modernity's most powerful geographic imaginary—by recovering alternative cartographies that include those imaginaries subsumed or forgotten by modernity. "Thinking outside of state boundaries requires specific genealogical recoveries which denaturalize those boundaries and thereby destabilize discursive hegemonies attached to special configurations associated with the system of state sovereignty" (Shapiro, "Moral Geographies and the Ethnics of Post-Sovereignty," 481–82).

26. Mignolo, *Local Histories/Global Designs*; Quijano, "Coloniality of Power, Eurocentrism, and Latin America."

27. Some may bristle at the suggestion that slavery is a trace of colonial history, rather than the foundational moment in national and race formation. However, the development of U.S. slavery can be seen as an extension of the British colonization of Africa as well as of North America, not to mention that the importation of African slaves was in response to the desire to eliminate and replace a native and indigenous population. The British "triangular trade" of human and other property was a function of colonialism, and coloniality was the process of capturing foreign lands as well as bodies, while replacing the native within the frontier. In this way, I view slavery and colonialism as twin evils of what Cedric Robinson has termed "racial capitalism." As Robin D. G. Kelley points out in his preface to Cedric Robinson's *Black Marxism*, Robinson develops an analysis of "racial capitalism" that understands slavery and colonialism as shared projects of European modernity. Kelley shows that, for Robinson, "Capitalism and racism . . . did not break from the old order but rather evolved from it to produce a modern world system of "racial capitalism" dependent on slavery, violence, imperialism and genocide" (preface to Robinson, *Black Marxism*, xiii).

28. Quijano, "Coloniality of Power, Eurocentrism, and Latin America." Quijano maps a global world order produced in the sixteenth century through coloniality. He locates European modernity within the sixteenth-century context of the colonial Americas, and not in European projects in the "orient." Hence, for Quijano, "Western" imperial culture has its invention not in orientalism but in "Indus Occidentales." Occidentalism was the process through which a Eurocentric interdependent colonial world order was produced.

29. "The colonial difference creates the conditions for dialogic situations in which a fractured enunciation is enacted from the subaltern perspective as a response to the hegemonic discourse and perspective. Thus, border thinking is more than a hybrid enunciation. It is a fractured enunciation in dialogic situations with the territorial and hegemonic cosmology" (Mignolo, *Local Histories/Global Designs*, x).

30. "Communities of shared fate" is a beautiful articulation of transnational and transborder solidarity employed by Ramon Saldivar in *The Borderlands of Culture*. I locate the term "geographies of liberation" in a scholarly genealogy that includes Paul Gilroy's work

on black cultures of "counter-modernity," Edward Said's work on "contrapuntal modernity," Alicia Schmidt Camacho's work on the "migrant imaginary," and Ramon Saldivar's work on "meztizo modernism." These terms have been deployed in order to describe the complex aesthetic politics and subjectivities of transnational and transborder exiles who have forged new epistemologies as well as new cartographies. While they describe distinct and particular histories and political practices, they nevertheless share an interest in the cultural and imaginative work of exile and liberation. See, for example, Gilroy, *Black Atlantic*; Said, *Reflections on Exile and Other Essays*; Schmidt Camacho, *Migrant Imaginaries*; and Saldivar, *Borderlands of American Culture*.

31. Edwards, *Practice of Diaspora*.

32. According to a 2010 Pew Research Center study, the country with the largest Muslim population globally is Indonesia, and Asia/Southeast Asia hosts 62 percent of the world's Muslim population. See "Muslim-Majority Countries" in *The Future of the Global Muslim Population*, Pew Research Center, http://www.pewforum.org/The-Future-of-the-Global-Muslim-Population.aspx (retrieved December 22, 2011).

33. I am reminded here of Gershon Scholem's criticism of Hannah Arendt in the wake of the publication of her controversial book *Eichmann in Jerusalem*, in which Arendt argued that Nazi violence was not exceptional but merely an extreme example of a human capability. Scholem, like many Jewish critics of Arendt, argued that Arendt did not "love the Jewish people." For Scholem, the category "Jewish" was not merely a religious term but a racial term that united a people across geography. Arendt responded to Scholem that she indeed did not love any people—as a group—but loved individuals, many of whom are Jewish. An analysis of this debate can be found in Butler, *Parting Ways*. Also see Arendt's writing about Zionism and the Jewish question in Arendt, *Jewish Writings*. Arendt's ethical position vis-à-vis Jewishness is a topic I consider in Chapter 3.

34. Twain, *Innocents Abroad*, 505.

35. In a scathing critique of the absence of Arab North Africa in Henry Louis Gates's PBS documentary "Wonders of the African World," Ali Masrui argues that Gates perpetuates orientalism when he ignores Arab Islamic influences in Africa. As an example of this, Masrui argues that Gates's Arabic-speaking informants in the documentary series were mistranslated in ways that included inserting pro-government sentiments into the speakers' speech. See Masrui, "Black Orientalism?," 15.

36. The term "exiled by exiles" can be found in Said, "Reflections on Exile."

37. The post–World War II transition from black internationalism to a nation-bound horizon of civil rights is most thoroughly described in Singh, *Black Is a Country*.

38. Zinn, *People's History of the United States*.

39. Said, "Reflections on Exile," 144.

40. Ibid., 185.

41. Ibid., 186.

42. Chaterjee, *Nationalist Thought and the Colonial World*; Chaterjee, *Nation and Its Fragments*.

43. As I will explain in Chapter 2, Dusé Mohamed Ali's national origins are difficult to ascertain not only because of the complexities of citizenship status after World War I, but also because he may have fabricated his origins in order to improve his life prospects. He claimed to be Sudanese Egyptian, yet contemporaries note that he never spoke or

understood Arabic. He lectured as an "Islamic expert," yet he appears to not have fully studied Islam. These anomalies are explored further in Chapter 2.

CHAPTER 1

1. Jones, *Travel in Egypt and Scenes of Jerusalem*, 5.

2. On religious travel to the Holy Land, see Rogers, *Inventing the Holy Land*; Yothers, *Romance of the Holy Land in American Travel Writing*; Vogel, *To See a Promised Land*; and Obenzinger, *American Palestine*.

3. See, for example, Chireau and Deutsch, *Black Zion*, and Moses, *Creative Conflict in African American Thought*.

4. Scholarship on the pre-1948 history of African American engagement with the Middle East is relatively scant. See Obenzinger, *American Palestine*; Trafton, *Egyptland*; and Turner, *Islam in the African American Experience*.

5. I use "imperial culture" here to connote Edward Said's analysis of orientalism as part of the cultural politics of imperialism. For Said, orientalism was a structuring component of imperial culture that participated in the discursive formation of the Orient. Said likely would not have included the United States at the turn of the twentieth century within the context of Western orientalism in part because he conceived of orientalism not merely as discourse but as active imperial engagement. Yet, along with scholars such as Malini Schueller and Melani McAlister, I conceive of American orientalism as something that was formed prior to direct imperial engagement with the Middle East. See Schueller, *U.S. Orientalisms*, and McAlister, *Epic Encounters*.

6. Makdisi, *Artillery of Heaven*.

7. Ibid., 84.

8. On the history of American University of Beirut, see Anderson, *American University of Beirut*; Makdisi, *Artillery of Heaven*; and Khalaf, *Protestant Missionaries in the Levant*.

9. Bruce Greenfield describes "aesthetic authority" as the power that accrues to the travel writer with the authority to describe landscapes. The aesthetic authority positions the viewer and writer with geopolitical power to name and label. See Greenfield, *Narrating Discovery*.

10. See Pratt, *Imperial Eyes*; Spur, *Rhetoric of Empire*; and Said, *Culture and Imperialism*.

11. Shamir, "'Our Jerusalem'"; Vogel, *To See a Promised Land*.

12. Obenzinger, *American Palestine*; Ra'ad, *Hidden Histories*.

13. See Winthrop, "Model of Christian Charity."

14. Shamir, "'Our Jerusalem.'" Also see Vogel, *To See a Promised Land*, and Ariel and Kark, "Messianism, Holiness, Charisma, and Community."

15. Lubin, "We Are All Israeli"; Bain, *Bitter Waters*; Lynch, *Narrative of the United States' Expedition to the River Jordan and the Dead Sea*.

16. In *Orientalism*, Said argued that "Americans will not feel quite the same about the Orient, which for them is much more likely to be associated with the Far East (China and Japan, mainly)" (1). Said argued that Americans began to participate in the imperial discourse of orientalism only after World War II.

17. Lubin, "We Are All Israeli."

18. Rubin, "When Jerusalem Was Built in St. Louis." On the St. Louis World's Fair, see Rydell, *All the World's a Fair*, and Gilbert, *Whose Fair?*

19. Rubin, "When Jerusalem Was Built in St. Louis"; Davis, *To See a Promised Land.*

20. "Empire of Liberty" was the term used by Thomas Jefferson to distinguish between European imperialism and New World, American empire. The latter would be characterized by the spread of enlightenment and freedom rather than the violence and conquest of the former. See Wood, *Empire of Liberty.*

21. Du Bois, *Black Reconstruction in America*; Woodward, *Strange Career of Jim Crow.*

22. Posnock, *Color and Culture.* Also see Du Bois, *Dusk of Dawn*, 30, 48.

23. Quoted in Foner, "Black-Jewish Relations in the Opening Years of the Twentieth Century," 360.

24. Read, *Dreyfus Affair*; Burns, *France and the Dreyfus Affair*; Begley, *Why the Dreyfus Affair Matters.*

25. Herzl, *Der Judenstaat.*

26. Ibid., cited in Smith, *Palestine and the Arab-Israeli Conflict*, 53.

27. See, for example, Laquer, *History of Zionism*, and Stanislawski, *Zionism and the Fin de Siècle.*

28. Gilroy, *Black Atlantic.*

29. These categories are somewhat arbitrary, and they are in no way exclusive. Pan-Africanists, to take one example, could also be Christian Zionists (as in the case of William Sampson Brooks). I use these categories to show how the travel writing was shaped by a particular set of political and religious motives.

30. Dorr, *Colored Man Round the World.*

31. Ibid., 63–64.

32. Ibid., 172–73.

33. Ibid., dedication.

34. Ibid., 186.

35. Fore more on African American Christian Zionism, see Brouwer, Gifford, and Rose, *Exporting the American Gospel*, and Blum and Young, *Souls of W. E. B. Du Bois.*

36. Seaton, *Land of Promise*, 15.

37. Ibid., 48.

38. Ibid., 46.

39. Ibid., 140–43.

40. Jones, *Travel in Egypt and Scenes of Jerusalem.*

41. Ibid., 5.

42. Ibid., 71.

43. Brooks, *Footprints of a Black Man.*

44. Ibid., 123.

45. Ibid., 185.

46. Ibid., 186.

47. Another interesting text from this period is Bishop Alexander Walter's autobiography *My Life and Work*, in which he describes his Holy Land pilgrimage undertaken in 1882.

48. Bagley, *My Trip through Egypt and the Holy Land*, 187.

49. See http://www.israelipalestinianprocon.org/populationpalestine.html#sources1 (accessed September 1, 2012).

50. See, for example, Singh, *Black Is a Country*; Edwards, *Practice of Diaspora*; Von Eschen, *Race against Empire*; and Plummer, *Rising Wind*.

51. Powell, *Palestine and Saints in Caesar's Household*, vii.

52. Ibid.

53. Ibid., viii.

54. Ibid., 24. Powell also described the movement as not religious but one that was "commercial and political."

55. Ibid., 29.

56. Ibid.

57. Ibid., 16.

58. See, for example, Campos, *Ottoman Brothers*, and Shaw, *Jews of the Ottoman Empire and the Turkish Republic*.

59. Powell, *Palestine and Saints in Caesar's Household*, 91–92.

60. James Clifford argues that the term "diaspora" describes a complex range of identities that often cohere around the following concepts: "a history of dispersal, myths/memories of the homeland, alienation in the host (bad host?) country, desire for eventual return, ongoing support of the homeland, and a collective identity importantly defined by this relationship" (Clifford, "Diasporas," 305). Also see Safran, "Diasporas in Modern Societies."

61. See, for example, Mathieu, *North of the Color Line*; Barnes, *Journey of Hope*; Redkey, *Black Exodus*; and Anderson, "Black Émigrés."

62. "The African-American Mosaic: A Liberation of Congress Resource Guide for the Study of Black History and Culture," website on American Colonization Society based on library holdings, http://www.loc.gov/exhibits/african/afam002.html (accessed September 1, 2012).

63. Blyden, "Edward Jones"; Dixon, *African America and Haiti*; Harris, *Global Dimensions of the African Diaspora*; Jenkins, *Black Zion*.

64. Brewer, "Henry Highland Garnet"; Stuckey, *Slave Culture*; Lapsansky-Werner and Bacon, *Back to Africa*.

65. This is obviously not a comprehensive list of activists interested in Liberian emigration. Marcus Garvey's United Negro Improvement Association in 1919 chartered a shipping company named the Black Star Line to transport African Americans to Liberia, and Garvey himself had negotiated land deals in Liberia in preparation for black American emigration. See Cronon, *Black Moses*; Grant, *Negro with a Hat*; and Sundiata, *Brothers and Strangers*.

66. Delany, *Condition, Elevation, Emigration, and Destiny of the Colored People of the United States*; Adeleke, *Without Regard to Race*; Griffith, *African Dream*; Levine, *Martin Delany, Frederick Douglass, and the Politics of Representative Identity*.

67. Delany, *The Condition, Elevation, Emigration, and Destiny of the Colored People of the United States*, published in Brotz and Austin, *African American Social and Political Thought*, 38.

68. Ibid.

69. Ibid.

70. Ibid.

71. DellaPergola, "Demography in Israel/Palestine."

72. In *The Black Atlantic*, for example, Paul Gilroy correctly identifies Blyden's interest in Jewish politics and an analog for black politics in Africa. Yet Gilroy overlooked Blyden's engagement with Arab North Africa, his travels in the Ottoman Empire, and his advocacy of Islam as a religion for black American emigrants. A similarly limited view of Blyden is presented in Weisbord and Kazarian, *Israel in the Black American Perspective*.

73. See Lynch, *Edward Wilmot Blyden*.

74. Blyden, *From West Africa to Palestine*, 136, 141.

75. Ibid., 154.

76. Ibid., 192–93.

77. Ibid., 9.

78. Ibid., 105. Teage was one of the founding fathers of Liberian independence that penned that country's Declaration of Independence.

79. Ibid., 106.

80. Ibid., 109–10.

81. Blyden, *Jewish Question*.

82. Ibid.

83. Ibid.

84. Blyden, "Mohammedism and the Negro Race," 111.

85. Ibid., 115.

86. Kaplan, *Anarchy of Empire in the Making of U.S. Culture*, 173.

87. Harry Stecopolis makes the insightful point that Du Bois's internationalism often derived from his recognition of the coloniality of the U.S. South. In linking southern geographies to his analysis of the global color line, Du Bois, argues Stecopolis, attempted to imagine new forms of global citizenship. However, these forms were also rooted in powerful imperial rationales and logics, including dollar diplomacy. See Stecopolis, *Reconstructing the World*.

88. Du Bois, *Crisis*, March 1915.

89. See Lewis, *When Harlem Was in Vogue*, 102, and Lewis, "Parallels and Divergences."

90. On Du Bois in Liberia, see Sundiata, *Brothers and Strangers*, and Robinson, "Du Bois and Black Sovereignty."

91. Lewis, "To Turn as on a Pivot."

CHAPTER 2

1. Dusé Mohamed Ali to Balfour, August 9, 1919, Foreign Office Papers, 371/3728/114805, British Library, London.

2. On the British protectorate, see Mitchell, *Colonising Egypt*, and Powell, *Egypt, Great Britain, and the Mastery of the Sudan*.

3. Dusé Mohamed Ali to Balfour, August 9, 1919, Foreign Office Papers, 371/3728/114805, British Library, London.

4. Aubrey Herbert, M.P., to Sir William Bull, May 16, 1918, Colonial Office Papers, 554/40/21897, British Library, London.

5. Dusé Mohamed Ali to Balfour, August 9, 1919, Foreign Office Papers, 371/3728/114805, British Library, London.

6. M. Cheetham, British Residency, Ramleh, to Curzon, October 9, 1919, Foreign Office Papers, 371/3728/143799, British Library, London.

7. The definitive study of Ali's life is Duffield's dissertation, "Dusé Mohamed Ali and the Development of Pan-Africanism." Also see Ali, *Leaves from an Active Life*.

8. Ali, *Leaves from an Active Life*, n.p.

9. Ali's origins are difficult to determine. The story he presents in his autobiography contains many suspicious details. For example, he claimed to have lived the first seven years of his life in Egypt; yet he never learned Arabic, and the Egyptian authorities reported to the British authorities that they had no records of him. There is no evidence discounting his autobiography, although many of the details are impossible to believe.

10. Ali, *Leaves from an Active Life*, in *Comet*, June 12, 1937, n.p.

11. See, for example, Taylor, *Orage and the New Age*, and Orage, *Orage as Critic*.

12. Ali borrowed heavily from Cromer, *Modern Egypt*, and Blunt, *Atrocities of Justice under British Rule in Egypt*.

13. Duffield, "Dusé Mohamed Ali and the Development of Pan-Africanism"; Ali, *In the Land of the Pharaohs*.

14. Ali, *Leaves from an Active Life*, in *Comet*, October 9, 1937, n.p.

15. Spiller, *Papers on Interracial Problems*, xiii.

16. On the decline of scientific racism and the ascendance of cultural anthropology, see Barkan, *Retreat of Scientific Racism*; Baker, *Anthropology and the Racial Politics of Culture*; and Gershenhorn, *Melville J. Herskovits and the Racial Politics of Knowledge*.

17. See, for example, Gobineau, *Moral and Intellectual Diversity of Races*, and Fortier, "Gobineau and German Racism."

18. Spiller, "First Universal Races Congress."

19. Boas, "Instability of Human Types."

20. Du Bois, "Negro Race in the United States of America."

21. Ibid., 364.

22. In the early phase of Du Bois's political career, he imagined that the black freedom movement would be led by a vanguard of intellectuals. In his essay "The Talented Tenth," Du Bois argued, "The Negro race, like all races, is going to be saved by its exceptional men." Du Bois would ultimately amend this belief and embrace a more democratic, bottom-up approach to organizing black masses. See Du Bois, "Talented Tenth."

23. Lake and Reynolds, *Drawing the Global Colour Line*, 258.

24. Du Bois, "Hymn to the People." The global dimensions of Du Bois's writings on the color line were fostered by the Universal Races Congress. One can easily see how the liberal politics of cultural pluralism informed Du Bois's 1928 novel, *Dark Princess*, in which representative members of the global south convene to plot anticolonial politics. But Du Bois's revolutionary internationalism contained absences and boundaries. The Arab is silent in *Dark Princess* and speaks only in halting grunts. A similar absence informed the Universal Races Congress itself, in that Arab intellectuals were largely absent.

25. An example of the limits of cultural pluralism can be found in the case made for territorial Zionism in the Universal Races Congress. It was perfectly consistent for Israel Zangwill to make a case for territorial Zionism—Jewish colonization of Palestine—in his lecture to the Congress, "The Jewish Race." Zangwill argued, "The comedy and tragedy of Jewish existence to-day derive primarily from this absence of a territory in which the race

could live its own life." See Spiller, *Papers on Interracial Problems*. As Hilton Obenzinger has argued, Zionism and cultural pluralism were complementary ideologies because within the paradigm of cultural pluralism only race-as-national-type was recognized as race. In other words, in order for Jews to be recognized within the paradigm of cultural pluralism, a Jewish race, made legible only through territory, was required. As the congress had already largely ignored the Arab world, it was quite easy to embrace the ethical principles of racial diversity alongside the argument for territorial Zionism. On Zionism and cultural pluralism, see Obenzinger, "Naturalizing Cultural Pluralism, Americanizing Zionism."

26. On Mustafa Kamil's Egyptian nationalism, see Hourani, *Arabic Thought in the Liberal Age*, 199–212. On the Egyptian Nationalist Party, see Beinin, *Workers and Peasants in the Modern Middle East*.

27. Ali, *Leaves from an Active Life*.

28. See GhaneaBassiri, *History of Islam in America*, 205. Also see Khwajah Kamal-ud-Din, "Cross versus Crescent" and "Jesus, an Ideal Godhead and Humanity," *African Times and Orient Review*, December–January 1910, 197–98 and 217–22.

29. Ali, "Forward."

30. Described in Geiss, *Pan-African Movement*.

31. On the Negro Society for Historical Research, see Crowder, *John Edward Bruce*, and Des Verney Sinnette, *Arthur Alfonso Schomburg*.

32. Prashad, *Darker Nations*.

33. Young, *Soul Power*.

34. Garvey, "British West Indies in the Mirror of Civilization."

35. Hill, *Marcus Garvey and Universal Negro Improvement Association Papers*, 2:256.

36. Ali's connection to C. L. R. James is mentioned in Mamigonian and Racine, *Human Tradition in the Black Atlantic*.

37. Ali, "Forward."

38. Ibid.

39. Ibid.

40. Ali, "Yesterday, To-Day, and To-Morrow."

41. Haskins, "Problems of American Dependencies."

42. Raja, "Real Situation in India."

43. Peer, "Muslim Unity."

44. In the same issue of *ATOR*, Sheikh Aly El Ghainty published his article, "Panislamism." Also see Ziaudin Ahmad, B.A., "Pan-Islamism," *African Times and Orient Review*, n.s. 1, no. 14 (June 2, 1914).

45. See, for example, Hadad and Ochsenwald, *Nationalism in a Non-National State*, and Esherick, Kayali, and Van Young, *Empire to Nation*.

46. On the League of Nations and national minorities, see Fink, "Paris Peace Conference and the Question of Minority Rights"; Sharp, "Britain and the Protection of Minorities at the Paris Peace Conference"; and de Azcarate, *League of Nations and National Minorities*.

47. On the multiculturalism of the Ottoman Empire, see Barkey, *Empire of Difference*, and Makdisi, *Artillery of Heaven*.

48. Mahmood, "Religious Freedom, the Minority Question, and Geopolitics in the Middle East," 424.

49. Henig, *League of Nations*; Knock, *To End All Wars*; Walters, *History of the League of Nations*.

50. See, for example, Manela, *Wilsonian Moment*, and Ambrosius, *Wilsonianism*.

51. Anghie, "Colonialism and the Birth of International Institutions."

52. The Covenant of the League of Nations, Article 22, http://avalon.law.yale.edu/20th_century/leagcov.asp#art22 (accessed September 2, 2012).

53. Prashad, *Darker Nations*.

54. There are many excellent overviews of the history of the modern Middle East. See, for example, Pappé, *Modern Middle East*; Kamrava, *Modern Middle East*; and Lockman, *Contending Visions of the Middle East*.

55. On pan-Arabism, see, for example, Jankowski and Gershoni, *Rethinking Nationalism in the Arab Middle East*, and Doran, *Pan-Arabism before Nasser*.

56. Kastan, "Lawrence, T. E." Emphasis in original.

57. On Sykes-Picot, see Barr, *Line in the Sand*, and Pappé, *History of Modern Palestine*.

58. Tripp, *History of Iraq*; Fieldhouse, *Western Imperialism in the Middle East*; Simon and Tejirian, *Creation of Iraq*.

59. Miller, "Syrian Revolt of 1925"; Khoury, "Factionalism among Syrian Nationalists during the French Mandate."

60. Quoted in Yapp, *Making of the Modern Near East*, 290.

61. Quoted in Morris, *Righteous Victims*, 76. Also see Schneer, *Balfour Declaration*.

62. "Report by His Majesty's Government in the United Kingdom of Great Britain and Northern Ireland to the Council of the League of Nations on the Administration of Palestine and Trans-Jordan for the year 1937," December 31, 1937, website of United Nations Information System on the Question of Palestine (UNISPAL), http://unispal.un.org/UNISPAL.NSF/0/7BDD2C11C15B54C2052565D10057251E (accessed September 12, 2012).

63. Interesting to note here is how the administration of imperial governance would contribute to the drawing of nationalist belongings within the Afro-Arab world. In this sense, the "imagined community" that was the Afro-Asian world was enabled by the administrative practices of imperial rule.

64. Grant, *Negro with a Hat*.

65. On the *Negro World*, see ibid.

66. See, for example, Baker, *Modernism and the Harlem Renaissance*; Huggins, *Harlem Renaissance*; and Lewis, *When Harlem Was in Vogue*.

67. On the Communist Party's Black Belt thesis and the African Blood Brotherhood, see Biondi, *To Stand and Fight*; Kelley, *Hammer and Hoe*; and Bush, *We Are Not What We Seem*. On Cyril Briggs, see Marable and Mullings, *Let Nobody Turn Us Around*.

68. See, for example, Stoval, *Paris Noir*, and Stoval, *Black France/France Noire*.

69. Edwards, *Practice of Diaspora*; Kesteloot, *Black Writers in French*; Sharpley-Whiting, *Negritude Women*.

70. See Hill, *Marcus Garvey and the UNIA Papers*, 1:55, xcii.

71. Ali, *Leaves from an Active Life*.

72. GhaneaBassiri, *History of Islam in America*, 206–7.

73. Ibid., 212–13.

74. Ali, *Leaves from an Active Life*.

75. Ali, *Ere Roosevelt Came*.

76. Ali's *Ere Roosevelt Came* bears some resemblance to the contours of W. E. B. Du Bois's 1928 *Dark Princess*, although it is in no way as sophisticated or complex as Du Bois's text. Ali's novel mirrors *Dark Princess*'s interest in black diasporic politics, and it uses an interracial subplot to challenge scientific racial science. It would not be out of character for Ali to mimic contemporary writers, as he had with his first monograph, including those with whom he expressed strong disagreement. Despite the similarity of the two novels, however, Ali's never engages a political critique as sophisticated as Du Bois's. Whereas the protagonist of Du Bois's internationalist novel, Matthew Towns, ultimately helped lead a global anti-imperialist movement that involves his political and romantic union with Princess Kautilya of Bwodpur, India, Ali's internationalist novel concludes within the United States, with the valorization of African American airmen. See Du Bois, *Dark Princess*.

77. Khalidi, "Palestinians and 1948," 21, 35.

78. Hurewitz, *Struggle for Palestine*; Palmowski, "Arab Revolt"; Choueiri, *Arab Nationalism*; Kedourie, *In the Anglo-Arab Labyrinth*.

CHAPTER 3

1. Marx wrote,

> Now, as for myself, I do not claim to have discovered either the existence of classes in modern society or the struggle between them. Long before me, bourgeois historians had described the historical development of this struggle between the classes, as had bourgeois economists their economic anatomy. My own contribution was (1) to show that the existence of classes is merely bound up with certain historical phases in the development of production; (2) that the class struggle necessarily leads to the dictatorship of the proletariat; [and] (3) that this dictatorship, itself, constitutes no more than a transition to the abolition of all classes and to a classless society.

See Marx's letter dated March 5, 1852, in Marx and Engels, *Collected Works*, 39:62–65.

2. Bunche, "Marxism and the Negro Question."

3. On racial capitalism, see Robinson, *Black Marxism*, and Marable, *How Capitalism Underdeveloped Black America*.

4. Bunche, "Marxism and the Negro Question," 39.

5. On the 1930s Communist position on the Negro question, see Kelley, *Hammer and Hoe*; Solomon, *Cry Was Unity*; and Robinson, *Black Marxism*.

6. Bunche, "Marxism and the Negro Question," 43.

7. Ibid., 44.

8. On the impact of the 1939 Hitler-Stalin Pact on the African American left, see Mullen, *Popular Fronts*; Smethurst, *New Red Negro*; and Solomon, *Cry Was Unity*.

9. See, for example, Cooper, *Africa since 1940*, and Burke, *Decolonization and the Evolution of International Human Rights*.

10. On the meaning of binationalism, see Aloni, Žižek, and Badiou, *What Does a Jew Want?*, and Butler, *Parting Ways*.

11. Public Broadcasting Service, *Ralph Bunche: An American Odyssey*, http://www.pbs.org/ralphbunche/ (accessed September 12, 2012).

12. In this argument we can see the influence of liberal internationalism on Bunche's approach to colonialism. He accepted that colonial subjects were in need of cultural and social elevation, and he believed that advanced nations could assist in educating modernity. In this way, Bunche rejected racist arguments about the inherent poverty of the savage while embracing cultural pluralist arguments about the need for changing environmental conditions in order to elevate colonies.

13. Quoted in Urquhart, *Ralph Bunche*, 56.

14. Bunche, *World View of Race*.

15. See, for example, Lenin, *Imperialism*, and Anderson, *Lenin, Hegel, and Western Marxism*.

16. Quoted in Urquhart, *Ralph Bunche*, 62.

17. Quoted in Kirby, "Race, Class, and Politics," 37.

18. See, for example, Kirby, *Black Americans in the Roosevelt Era*; Wolters, *Negroes and the Great Depression*, 353–82; Sitkoff, *New Deal for Blacks*; Naison, *Communists in Harlem during the Depression*; and Wittner, "National Negro Congress."

19. Bunch, "Critical Analysis of Tactics and Programs of Minority Groups," 41.

20. Ibid., 54.

21. On the ways the American Communist Party employed the discourse of Americanism, see Gerstle, *Working Class Americanism*, and Roediger, *Working toward Whiteness*, 217–18.

22. Hilderbrand, *Dumbarton Oaks*.

23. Quote in Urquhart, *Ralph Bunche*, 6.

24. Beitz, *Idea of Human Rights*; Moyn, *Last Utopia*; Glendon, *World Made New*.

25. On the rise and fall of the Communist Party's Black Belt thesis, see Horne, *Black Liberation/Red Scare*, and Howe, *Afrocentrism*, 90.

26. Quoted in Henry, *Ralph Bunche*, 135.

27. On the Anglo-American Committee of Inquiry, see Nachmani, *Great Power Discord in Palestine*.

28. Anglo-American Committee of Inquiry, "Report to the United States Government and His Majesty's Government in the United Kingdom."

29. Ibid.

30. On the Zionist response to he Anglo-American Committee of Inquiry, see Tamari, "Conflict over Palestine," and Little, *American Orientalism*, 81.

31. Anglo-American Committee of Inquiry, "Report to the United States Government and His Majesty's Government in the United Kingdom."

32. See, for example, Schaeffer, *Severed States*, 34–35, and Aronson, *David Ben-Gurion and the Jewish Renaissance*, 148.

33. See Pappé, *Making of the Arab-Israeli Conflict*; Khalidi, *Iron Cage*; Rogan and Shlaim, *War for Palestine*; and Khalidi, *From Haven to Conquest*.

34. The term "taboo memory" is used by Ella Shohat to signify the recovery of historical moments that challenge what we think we know about the present. Shohat specifically uses the term in the context of her discussion of Arab Jews and their history in places like Iraq. See Shohat, *Taboo Memories*.

35. On the Jewish Poalei-Zion Left Party, see Shore, *Caviar and Ashes*, and Hashav, *Polyphony of Jewish Culture*, 159.

36. Beinin, *Was the Red Flag Flying There?*; Beinin, *Workers and Peasants in the Modern Middle East*; Budeiri, *Palestine Communist Party*; Ismael, *Communist Movement in the Arab World*; Kaufman, *Arab National Communism in the Jewish State*.

37. Ismael, *Communist Movement in the Arab World*, 59.

38. See, for example, Frankel, "Soviet Regime and Anti-Zionism," 310–54.

39. Quoted in Ismael, *Communist Movement in the Arab World*, 60.

40. Ibid., 62.

41. Quoted in Beinin, *Was the Red Flag Flying There?*, 41.

42. Ibid., 43.

43. Ibid., 44.

44. Ibid., 45.

45. United Nations Special Committee on Palestine, "Verbatim Record of the Twenty-Ninth Meeting (Public), Held at the Y.M.C.A. Building."

46. United Nations Special Committee on Palestine, "Report of the General Assembly."

47. United Nations Special Committee on Palestine, "Verbatim Record of the Twenty-Ninth Meeting (Public), Held at the Y.M.C.A. Building."

48. Cultural Zionism is the belief that the Jewish diaspora is connected via culture, rather than via the politics of territory and nationalism. Historically, cultural Zionism emerged from German Zionists like Walter Benjamin and Martin Buber. For example, see Gelber, "Concept of Diaspora and Exile in German-Jewish Literature and Art."

49. On the history of Ihud, see Drezon-Tepler, *Interest Groups and Political Change in Israel*. On Brit Shalom, see Eyal, *Disenchantment of the Orient*.

50. On Judah Magnes's biography, see Kotzin, *Judah L. Magnes*, and Brinner, *Like All Nations?*

51. United Nations Special Committee on Palestine, "Official Records of the Second Session of the General Assembly, Supplement No. 11, UNSCOP."

52. Ibid.

53. Ibid.

54. On Martin Buber's biography, see Hodes, *Martin Buber*, and Moore, *Martin Buber*.

55. On debates within Zionism over cultural and political approaches, see Pianko, *Zionism and the Roads Not Taken*, and Butler, *Parting Ways*.

56. See, for example, Buber, "Hebrew Humanism," and Schaeder, *Hebrew Humanism of Martin Buber*.

57. Buber, "Binational Approach to Zionism," 11.

58. Ibid., 9–13.

59. On the League for Jewish-Arab Rapprochement and Cooperation, see Mendes-Flohr, *Divided Passions*, 401, and Friedman, *Encounter on the Narrow Ridge*.

60. Buber, Magnes, and Simon, *Towards Union in Palestine*.

61. On Arendt's political philosophy, see Benhabib, *Reluctant Modernism of Hannah Arendt*; Hansen, *Hannah Arendt*; and Kristeva, *Hannah Arendt*.

62. Arendt, "Herzl and Lazare," 338.

63. Arendt, *Origins of Totalitarianism*, 290.

64. Quoted in Butler, *Parting Ways*, 143. Also see Piterberg, "Zion's Rebel Daughter."

65. Arendt, "Crisis of Zionism," 336.

66. Arendt, "Can the Jewish–Arab Question Be Solved?"

67. On April 9, 1948, 120 Zionist fighters attacked the Palestinian village of Deir Yassin (population around 600). Approximately 107 Palestinians were killed, including women and children. On the history of the massacre, see Pappé, *Making of the Arab-Israeli Conflict*.

68. See Arendt, *Jewish Writings*, 235, 396–97, 451.

69. Arendt, "Zionism Reconsidered," 343–45.

70. The reform Jewish movement in the United States articulated a concern that the formation of a Jewish state would lead to accusations of Jewish dual loyalties (to the United States and Israel). The reform movement was also cultural Zionist and rejected political Zionism on those grounds, too. See, for example, Kolsky, *Jews against Zionism*.

71. See, for example, Kotzin, *Judah L. Magnes*.

72. See, for example, Urquhart, *Ralph Bunche*.

73. "Text of Suggestions Presented by the United Nations Mediator on Palestine to the Two Parties on 28 June 1948," S/863, http://unispal.un.org/unispal.nsf (accessed June 17, 2012).

74. Ibid.

75. Ibid.

76. On Bernadotte's recommendation regarding the "right of return," see Adelman and Barkan, *No Return, No Refuge*, 203–4.

77. On Bernadotte's assassination, see Bell, *Assassin*, 226–27, and Heller, *Stern Gang*.

78. Urquhart, *Ralph Bunche*, 147.

79. Shertok quoted in Ben-Dror, "Ralph Bunche and the Establishment of Israel," 520.

80. Quoted in Urquhart, *Ralph Bunche*, 198.

81. Ibid.

82. Ibid.

83. Ibid.

84. Du Bois, "As the Crow Flies," 1:297.

85. Ibid., 1:355.

86. Du Bois, "Case for the Jews."

87. The term, "exiled by exiles" comes from Said, "Reflections on Exile."

88. United Nations, "First Interim Report of the United Nations Economic Survey Mission for the Middle East," November 16, 1949, A/1106. Available online at http://unispal.un.org/UNISPAL.NSF/0/3B693EFF5F4E4D4B852577D60051EF13 (accessed September 10, 2012).

89. Although they represented opposing political positions on the ethics of Palestinian removal, Benny Morris and Ilan Pappé each demonstrate the Zionist plan to depopulate Arab villages as a strategy of Israeli state-making. See Morris, *Righteous Victims*, and Pappé, *Ethnic Cleansing of Palestine*.

90. See Morris, *Righteous Victims*, and Pappé, *Ethnic Cleansing of Palestine*.

91. "Report of the Director of the United Nations Relief and Works Agency for Palestine Refugees in the Near East," General Assembly Official Records: Sixth Session Supplement No. 16 (A/1905), 1951, http://unispal.un.org/UNISPAL.NSF/0/8D26108AF518CE7E052565A6006E8948 (accessed September 10, 2012).

92. "United Nations General Assembly Resolution 194," A/RES/194 (III), December 11, 1948, http://unispal.un.org/UNISPAL.NSF/0/C758572B78D1CD0085256BCF0077E51A (accessed September 10, 2012).

93. Quoted in Ghanim, "Poetics of Disaster," 25.

94. See, for example, Behbehani, *Soviet Union and Arab Nationalism*.

95. Quoted in Beinin, *Was the Red Flag Flying There?*, 53.

96. Joel Beinin has described the formation of several Communist, anti-Zionist organizations among Jews and Arabs in Egypt. The Palestinian NLL, for example was closely aligned with the Egyptian party, New Dawn. The Iskra organization was founded in 1942 by Hillel Schwartz. In 1946, Ezra Harari formed the Jewish Anti-Zionist League, which organized Jews in Cairo to oppose Zionism. A Jewish Egyptian of Italian origins founded the Egyptian Movement for National Liberation in 1943. The Egyptian Communist parties, in order to combat imperialism and protect Egyptian sovereignty, called for a united front of Jews and Arabs in Palestine against imperialism. The Egyptian Communist parties, however, split over the question of Palestine in ways that were even more divided than their Palestinian counterparts. See ibid., 55–63.

97. Quoted in Urquhart, *Ralph Bunche*, 194.

98. Bunche, "Review and Appraisal of Israeli-Arab Relations."

99. Quoted in Urquhart, *Ralph Bunche*, 177.

100. Ibid., 197.

101. See Prashad, *Darker Nations*.

CHAPTER 4

1. Graham Du Bois, *. . . And Bid Him Sing*.

2. On Malcolm X in Cairo, see Sales, *From Civil Rights to Black Liberation*, and Marable, *Malcolm X*.

3. Graham Du Bois, *. . . And Bid Him Sing*, 103.

4. On the United Arab Republic, see Rejwan, *Nasserist Ideology*, and Podeh, *Decline of Arab Unity*. On the Organization of African Unity, see Harris, *Organization of African Unity*, and Hyden, *African Politics in Comparative Perspective*.

5. See, for example, Feldman, "Towards an Afro-Arab Diasporic Culture."

6. See, for example, Marable, *Malcolm X*, esp. 331–32.

7. Newton, "On the Middle East."

8. I use the term "black Arab Jews" because of the fact of Arab Jewish racialization in Israel. Arab Jews are regularly called "black" (or worse) within Israel. See, for example, David Theo Goldberg's chapter "Targets of Opportunity (On Racial Palestinianization)" in Goldberg, *Threat of Race*, 106–51.

9. It is crucial to point out that I am not merely celebrating the PLO, the Black Panthers, and the Israeli Black Panthers as radical organizations. Each group had important limits and sometime embraced practices that undermined their political ideals. Rather, my purpose here is to argue that these groups forged an important political imaginary out of the contradictions and political conditions presented to them. Moreover, I argue that these groups developed a liberation geography that constitutes part of a longer genealogy of Afro-Arab politics.

10. See Said, "America's Last Taboo," 45–53.

11. Chamberlin, *Global Offensive*, 3.

12. These figures are estimates and include refugees in nonrecognized (by the UN) camps. The data come from the United Nations Relief and Works Agency, the international

body that administers Palestinian refugee camps. The data are compiled by Badil Resource Center for Palestinian Residency and Refugee Rights and can be found online at http://www.palestineremembered.com/download/Badil/pal-ref-idp-world-2006.pdf (accessed September 10, 2012).

13. Schulz and Hammer, *Palestinian Diaspora*; Sayigh, "Struggle Within, Struggle Without."

14. Cobban, *Palestine Liberation Organization*, 24.

15. Palestine Liberation Organization, "Statement of Proclamation of the Organization," Jerusalem, May 28, 1964. Online on the site of the Permanent Observer Mission of Palestine to the United Nations, http://www.un.int/wcm/content/site/palestine/cache/offonce/pid/12354;jsessionid=ED2AC7E70A82F5C7CCB42BC6357FCDEC (retrieved December 5, 2006).

16. Cobban, *Palestine Liberation Organization*, 24.

17. Bailey, *Four Arab-Israeli Wars and the Peace Process*; Bowen, *Six Days*; Shlaim, *Iron Wall*.

18. On the PLO in Beirut, see Cobban, *Palestine Liberation Organization*, and Fisk, *Pity the Nation*.

19. Palestine Liberation Organization, "10-Point Program of the PLO (1974)." Online on the site of the Permanent Observer Mission of Palestine to the United Nations, http://www.un.int/wcm/content/site/palestine/cache/offonce/pid/12354;jsession id=ED2AC7E70A82F5C7CCB42BC6357FCDEC (retrieved July 9, 2012). By 1976 Arafat increasingly called for diplomacy and embraced a UN resolution to implement a two-state solution, creating a sovereign and independent Palestinian state alongside a Palestinian state.

The Popular Front for the Liberation of Palestine and other radical groups affiliated with the PLO broke with Fatah over the ten-point program because they viewed it as a Fatah takeover of the Palestinian national movement and because they saw it as too moderate. See al Madfai, *Jordan, the United States, and the Middle East Peace Process*, and Khalidi, *Iron Cage*.

20. See, for example, Traboulsi, *History of Modern Lebanon*; Salibi, *House of Many Mansions*; and Fisk, *Pity the Nation*.

21. There have been numerous books that present the "dissolution" of the black/Jewish left alliance. These studies often assume black support for Palestine signifies tension within black/Jewish alliances; however, as I have argued throughout this book, black support for Palestine is far more complex than merely a story of black/Jewish relations in the United States. See, for example, Kaufman, *Broken Alliance*, and Lerner and West, *Jews and Blacks*. A more scholarly approach to the question of black/Jewish relations in the U.S. is Sundquist, *Strangers in the Land*.

22. On racial liberalism, see Bell and Stanley, *Making Sense of American Liberalism*; Klinker and Smith, *Unsteady March*; and Singh, *Black Is a Country*.

23. On the role of the Nation of Islam in black internationalism, see McAlister, "One Black Allah," in McAlister, *Epic Encounters*; Turner, *Islam in the African American Experience*; and Marable and Aidi, *Black Routes to Islam*.

24. "Third World Round-up," *SNCC Newsletter*, June–July 1967, 4–5.

25. Ibid. Emphasis in original.

26. See Young, "American Blacks and the Arab-Israeli Conflict." Feldman, "Representing Permanent War," offers a brilliant read of SNCC's newsletter. On SNCC's politics, see Carson, *In Struggle*, and Zinn, *SNCC*.

27. *New York Times*, June 4, 1967.

28. "Anti-Semitism Held Immoral by Dr. King," *New York Times*, October 11, 1967, 59.

29. *New York Times*, June 28, 1970, 5.

30. "Prejudiced Negroes Scorned by Wilkins," *New York Times*, November 1, 1967, 18.

31. "Canard of Black Anti-Semitism," *Crisis*, December 1969.

32. Wilkins, "Israel's Time of Trial Also America's."

33. *New York Times*, November 1, 1970, sec. 4, p. 4.

34. See, for example, Young, *Soul Power*.

35. On the politics of "black Maoism" within the black freedom movement, see Robinson, *Black Marxism*; Kelley and Esch, "Black Like Mao"; and Mullen and Ho, *Afro Asia*.

36. Erikson and Newton, *In Search of Common Ground*, 133. Nikhil Singh makes a compelling case that "perhaps that best way to describe the Panthers is as 'resolute counternationalists'—men and women who believed themselves to be 'inoculated against all national anthems.'" See Singh, "Black Panthers and the 'Undeveloped Country' of the Left."

37. Eldridge Cleaver, editorial, *Black Panther: Black Community News Service* 2, no. 1 (March 16, 1968).

38. Singh, "Black Panthers and the 'Undeveloped Country' of the Left," 77.

39. Newton, "Let Us Hold High the Banner."

40. Goldstein, *Poverty in Common*, 219.

41. Cleaver, "Jails Are the First Black Concentration Camps."

42. On the global dimensions of the Panthers' politics, see Young, *Soul Power*; Joseph, *Black Power Movement*; Kelley, *Freedom Dreams*; and Bloom and Martin, *Black against Empire*.

43. See, for example, the following from *Black Panther*: "Mounir—A Heroic Palestinian," vol. 2, no. 8 (October 1968); "Palestine Guerillas," vol. 2, no. 9 (October 1968); "Support for Palestine Commandos," vol. 2, no. 11 (November 1968); "Arabs Protest U.N. Partitioning of Palestine," vol. 2, no. 19 (1969); "Arab People Determined to Fight until Victory or Death," vol. 3, no. 4 (May 1969); "Al Fath Speaks," vol. 2, no. 16 (1969); "From Al Fat'h," vol. 3, no. 19 (1969); "Al Fateh Statement towards a Democratic State in Palestine," vol. 5, no. 19 (November 7, 1970); "Revolutionary Sister, Leila Khaled," vol. 5, no. 17 (October 25, 1970); "Al Fath Does Not Intend to Push the Jews into the Sea," vol. 4, no. 16 (March 1970); "Palestine Voices of Rebellion, Yasir Arafat," vol. 4, no. 4 (December 1969); "Paper Presented by the Supporters of the Popular Front for the Liberation of Palestine," vol. 4, no. 8 (January 1970); "Fifth Anniversary of Fat'h, 1965–1970," vol. 4, no. 10 (February 1970); "Survival Strategies of Arabs in Israel," vol. 14, no. 10 (November 22, 1975); "For Palestinian Independence and Sovereignty," vol. 14, no. 10 (November 22, 1975); "Palestinian Popular Front Leader: 'This Revolution Is Our Revolution,'" vol. 16, no. 4 (December 4, 1976); "Abu Daous: 'I Am a Palestinian Revolutionary, Not a Terrorist," vol. 16, no. 11 (January 22, 1977).

44. "Mao Condemns U.S.-Israel Link," *Black Panther* 2, no. 12 (November 1968).

45. "Palestine Guerillas vs. Israeli Pigs," *Black Panther* 2, no. 16 (1969).

46. "The Role of the Arab Student in the U.S.," *Black Panther* 2, no. 5 (September 7, 1968). Emphasis in original.

47. On the 1975 UN General Assembly consideration of Zionism as racism, see Hadawi, *Bitter Harvest*, 183–86, and Schechter, *United Nations Global Conferences*, 71–72.

48. Farouk Kaddoumi, "For Palestinian Independence and Sovereignty," *Black Panther* 14, no. 10 (November 22, 1975). Also see "Like We Said, Zionism Is Racism," *Black Panther* 14, no. 6 (October 25, 1975).

49. "Zionism: Enemy of the Jews," *Black Panther* 14, nos. 10 and 14 (November 1975).

50. Ibid. Many would argue with this claim, even those who support the conclusion that Zionism may be a form of racism. Zionism was not merely a nationalist movement but also a socialist movement. It did not embrace "laissez-faire capitalism."

51. See, for example, Lulat, *United States Relations with South Africa*, and Ismael, *International Relations of the Contemporary Middle East*, 248–55.

52. Polakow-Suransky, *Unspoken Alliance*; Stevens and Elmessiri, *Israel and South Africa*; Tomeh, *Israel and South Africa*.

53. McGreal, "Brothers in Arms—Israel's Secret Pact with Pretoria."

54. "P. W. Botha Felt Israel Had Betrayed Him," *Jerusalem Post*, November 2, 2006.

55. "The Unholy Alliance: Israel and South Africa," *Black Panther* 14, no. 10 (November 22, 1975).

56. For a discussion of the summit, see Ismael, *International Relations of the Contemporary Middle East*; Haseeb, *Arabs and Africa*; and Curtis, *Middle East Reader*.

57. "Letter dated 15 March 1977 from the Deputy Prime Minister and Minister for Foreign Affairs of Egypt to the Secretary-General," United Nations General Assembly, March 17, 1977, A/32/61, http://unispal.un.org/UNISPAL.NSF/0/97F79F017B276FB085256FDB006E4C08 (accessed July 10, 2012).

58. "Unity Forged at First Afro-Arab Summit" *Black Panther* 16, no. 19 (March 19, 1977).

59. For example, "Report on Israeli Aid to South Africa," *Black Panther* 13, no. 24 (August 4, 1975); "1976—The Year of the Youth," *Black Panther* 16, no. 8 (January 1, 1977), features Occupied Palestine, Oakland Community School, Azania (South Africa).

60. "Arab People Determined to Fight until Victory or Death," *Black Panther* 3, no. 4 (May 1969). Also see "Paper Presented by the Supporters of The Popular Front for the Liberation of Palestine," *Black Panther* 4, no. 8 (January 1970), in which the PFLP writes,

> The PFLP has always been trying to expose the bourgeois misconception of revolutionary struggle by explaining to the Palestinian masses that their struggle against Zionism is an integral part of the world revolution against imperialism-capitalism, and that it is not an isolated battle against Israel. Thus the revolution cannot be victorious by being "non-political" or neutral at home or abroad as the bourgeois "revolutionary" movements are trying to do. The PFLP identifies its struggle with the heroic struggle of the Vietnamese, the Angolans, the Cubans, and Afro-Americans, and the International Revolution.

61. "Cleaver, Panthers Cheered in Algeria," *Black Panther* 3, no. 14 (July 1969).

62. "Palestine, Voices of Rebellion, Yasser Arafat, Commander of Al Fat'h," *Black Panther* 4, no. 4 (December 1969).

63. Newton, "Position Paper on the Middle East."

64. Ibid.

65. On post-1967 Arab regional alliances, see Walt, *Origins of Alliances*, and Choueiri, *Arab Nationalism*.

66. Newton, "Position Paper on the Middle East."

67. David Graham Du Bois to Huey P. Newton, Memorandum #28, May 2, 1974, "Re: Position Paper on the Middle East," Dr. Huey P. Newton Foundation Inc. collection, M0864, Department of Special Collections, Stanford University Libraries, Stanford, Calif.

68. "Toward Peace in the Middle East," *Black Panther* 20, no. 7 (July 1980): 8–9

69. Ibid.

70. Ibid.

71. Ibid.

72. On the history of black Jews, see Jacob Dorman's much anticipated *Chosen People*.

73. Quoted in Chetrit, *Intra-Jewish Ethnic Conflict in Israel*, 28.

74. Ibid.; also see Shohat, *Taboo Memories*.

75. On the material and psychological benefits offered to Ashkenazi Jewish immigrants over Mizrahi immigrants, see Shohat, "Sephardim in Israel"; Massad, "Zionism's Internal Others"; and Shama and Iris, *Immigration without Integration*.

76. Quoted in Chetrit, *Intra-Jewish Ethnic Conflict in Israel*, 32.

77. See, for example, Schulze, *Jews of Lebanon*, and Simon, Laskier, and Reguer, *Jews of the Middle East and North Africa in Modern Times*.

78. Quoted in Chetrit, *Intra-Jewish Ethnic Conflict in Israel*, 33.

79. Quoted in Allouche, "Oriental Communities in Israel."

80. Arye Galblum, *Ha'aretz*, August 19, 1948.

81. Quoted in Chetrit, *Intra-Jewish Ethnic Conflict in Israel*, 35.

82. Quoted in ibid., 36.

83. Haim Yacobi, in *Constructing a Sense of Place*, 126–29, discusses how Mizrahim are located within "development towns" within Israel. Also see Lefkowitz, *Words and Stones*, 54–55.

84. Quoted in Chetrit, *Intra-Jewish Ethnic Conflict in Israel*, 83.

85. Ibid., 46–50.

86. Ibid., 99.

87. Quoted in ibid., 100–101.

88. Quoted in ibid., 111.

89. Ibid., 121.

90. Ibid.

91. Shohat, *Taboo Memories*.

92. Reuven Abergil interview with author, October 24, 2007.

93. Ibid.

94. Reuven Abergil, "Sixty Years of the State of Israel, Sixty Year of Exile for Jews from Arab and Muslim Countries," The Alternative Information Center, Jerusalem, May 1, 2008, http://www.alternativenews.org/english/index.php/news/news/1173-sixty-years-of-the-state-of-israel-sixty-years-of-exile-for-jews-from-arab-and-muslim-countries-.html (accessed September 12, 2012).

95. Ibid.

96. On the FBI's COINTELPRO, see Blackstock, *Cointelpro*, and Churchill and Wall, *Agents of Repression*.

97. As Eric Sundquist writes, "After his conversion to evangelical Christianity . . . Cleaver became a fervent Zionist, declaring in 1976 that Arabs were 'among the most racist people on earth,' while Jews 'have done more than any other people in history to expose and condemn racism'" (Sundquist, *Strangers in the Land*, 351).

98. On Arafat's shifting politics in the era of Oslo, see Jones, *Cosmopolitan Mediation?*, 114–16, and Nofal, "Yasir Arafat."

CHAPTER 5

1. On Operation Grapes of Wrath, see Amnesty International, "Israel/Lebanon"; Human Rights Watch, "Operation Grapes of Wrath"; and Fisk, *Pity the Nation*.

2. Jordan, "Eyewitness in Lebanon."

3. Ibid.

4. Rodney King was an African American construction worker who was pulled over by the Los Angeles Police on March 3, 1991, following a high-speed car chase. A bystander videotaped the police beating King following the end of the chase. The videotape circulated on national and global media, leading to popular interest in the prosecution of the four offending police officers. When the officers were acquitted by an all-white jury in a Los Angeles suburb, residents of Los Angeles's black communities protested and rioted in what became known as the LA riots of 1992. Fifty-two people died during the riots. The King case exposed a long history of police violence in urban black communities while also illustrating how the facts of videotape evidence—which seemed conclusive—could be made suspect in court. See, for example, Gooding-Williams, *Reading Rodney King/Reading Urban Uprising*, and Jacobs, *Race, Media, and the Crisis of Civil Society*.

5. Jordan, "Eyewitness in Lebanon."

6. Duggan, *Twilight of Equality?* Also see Peck, *Constructions of Neoliberalism*, and Melamed, "Spirit of Neoliberalism."

7. Harvey, *Brief History of Neoliberalism*, 2. Also see Duggan, *Twilight of Equality?*, and Prashad, *Poorer Nations*.

8. On conditional lending practices to developing countries, see Vreeland, *International Monetary Fund*; Clemens, *Dynamics of International Relations*; and Rudra, "Globalization and the Decline of the Welfare State in Less-Developed Countries."

9. International mandates for structural adjustments among developing nations are often precipitated by manufactured crises that seem to require neoliberal intervention. This is a process that Naomi Klein has termed "disaster capitalism." See Klein, *Shock Doctrine*.

10. H.R.3734—Personal Responsibility and Work Opportunity Reconciliation Act of 1996, http://thomas.loc.gov/cgi-bin/query/z?c104:H.R.3734.ENR (accessed September 12, 2012).

11. On the attack on welfare, see Scram, *Welfare Discipline*; Smith, *Welfare Reform and Sexual Regulation*; and Chappell, *War on Welfare*.

12. On the racialization and criminalization of welfare recipients, see Gustafson, *Cheating Welfare*; Hancock, *Politics of Disgust*; and Hays, *Flat Broke with Children*.

13. Goode and Maskovsky, *New Poverty Studies*, 10.

14. Manpower Demonstration Resource Corporation, "Welfare-to-Work Approaches: Two-Year Impacts for Eleven Programs, Executive Summary," June 2000, http://aspe.hhs.gov/hsp/NEWWS/11-prog-es00/index.htm (accessed September 12, 2012).

15. On the Clinton administration's Middle East policies in general, see Peretz, "U.S. Middle East Policy in the 1990s," and Bierman, "Role of the United States as an Initiator and Intermediary in the Arab-Israeli-Palestinian Peace Process."

16. On the creation of the pax-Americana in the context of Oslo, see Beinin, "Oslo Process and the Limits of a Pax Americana"; Beinin, "Palestine and Israel"; and Paul, *Discourse of Palestinian-Israeli Relations*.

17. The PFLP's response to the PLO-brokered Oslo agreement is described in Usher, *Palestine in Crisis*, 50–52, and Robinson, *Building a Palestinian State*.

18. Quote in Rabbani, "Palestinian Authority, Israeli Rule," 79.

19. Beinin, "Oslo Process and the Limits of a Pax Americana," 23.

20. Ibid.

21. Ibid., 24.

22. Paled, "From Zionism to Capitalism."

23. Beinin, "Oslo Process and the Limits of a Pax Americana," 34.

24. See, for example, Murphy, "Buying Poverty."

25. Beinin, "Oslo Process and the Limits of a Pax Americana," 29.

26. Ibid.

27. Ashrawi, "Racism, Racial Discrimination, Xenophobia, and Related Intolerances," 102.

28. On surplus populations, see Gilmore, *Golden Gulag*; Davis, *Are Prisons Obsolete?*; and Wacquant, *Prisons of Poverty*.

29. Major Reyes Z. Cole, "Drug Wars, Counterinsurgency, and the National Guard," *The U.S. Army Profession Writing Collection*, November–December 2005, http://www.army.mil/professionalWriting/volumes/volume4/march_2006/3_06_1.html (accessed February 3, 2013).

30. See, for example, Connors et al., *Urban Street Gang Enforcement*. Also see Gilmore, *Golden Gulag*; Alexander, *New Jim Crow*; and Wacquant, *Punishing the Poor*.

31. McVey, *1989 NCCD Prison Population Forecast*.

32. http://www.hrw.org/en/world-report-2011/united-states (accessed July 1, 2013).

33. "The Sentencing Project" website, http://sentencingproject.org/doc/publications/inc_Trends_in_Corrections_Fact_sheet.pdf (accessed February 3, 2013).

34. http://www.hrw.org/en/world-report-2011/united-states (accessed July 1, 2013).

35. "The Sentencing Project" website, http://sentencingproject.org/doc/publications/inc_Trends_in_Corrections_Fact_sheet.pdf (accessed February 3, 2013).

36. Khalili, "Location of Palestine in Global Counterinsurgencies," 416.

37. See, for example, Cooper and Stoler, *Tensions of Empire*; Hall and Rose, *At Home with the Empire*; and Rabinow, *French Modern*.

38. See, for example, Go and Foster, *American Colonial State in the Philippines*; Kaplan, *Anarchy of Empire in the Making of U.S. Culture*; and Kramer, "Empires, Exceptions, and Anglo-Saxons."

39. Khalili, "Location of Palestine in Global Counterinsurgencies," 416; Davis, "Pentagon as Global Slumlord."

40. Niva, "Walling off Iraq," 67.

41. Hersh cited in ibid., 71–72.

42. Henriksen, "Security Lessons from the Israeli Trenches," 19.

43. See, for example, Amy Kaplan's discussion of the word "homeland" following September 11, 2001. "A relation exists between securing the homeland against the encroachment of foreign terrorists and enforcing national power abroad. The homeland may contract borders around a fixed space of nation and nativity, but it simultaneously also expands the capacity of the United States to move unilaterally across the borders of other nations" (Kaplan, "Homeland Insecurities," 87).

44. Sari Horwitz, "Israeli Experts Teach Police on Terrorism," *Washington Post*, June 12, 2005, http://www.washingtonpost.com/wp-dyn/content/article/2005/06/11/AR2005061100648.html (accessed January 31, 2012).

45. "Empowering Law Enforcement Protecting America," The Jewish Institute for National Security Affairs, http://www.jinsa.org/files/LEEPbookletforweb.pdf (accessed January 21, 2013).

46. Graham, *Cities under Siege*, 20.

47. Previous UN racism conferences were held in 1978 and 1983 in Geneva. The U.S. government did not attend either previous conference.

48. See, for example, Henry, *Long Overdue*, and Winant, *New Politics of Race*.

49. See, for example, Biondi, "Rise of the Reparations Movement," in Martin and Yaquinto, *Redress for Historical Injustices in the United States*, and Goldstein, *Poverty in Common*, 236–43.

50. Quoted in Banton, *International Politics of Race*, 148.

51. Ibid.

52. Quoted in Schechter, *United Nations Global Conferences*, 178.

53. Quoted in ibid.

54. On reparations lawsuits, see Biondi, "Rise of the Reparations Movement," in *Radical History Review*, and Ogletree, "Litigating the Legacy of Slavery."

55. CBC support for reparations did not extend to support for the "Zionism as racism" argument. Representative Sheila Jackson Lee supported the U.S. delegation's claim that the Zionism issue was anti-Semitic. "The berating of the Jewish people and . . . the equating of Zionism with racism fills the conference with unnecessary hatred." See Chris Tomlinson, "Non-Governmental Groups Vote Resolution at Durban Conference: U.N. Forum Equates Zionism and Racism," *Pittsburgh Post-Gazette*, September 3, 2001, A-4.

56. "Declaration of the World Conference against Racism, Racial Discrimination, Xenophobia and Related Intolerance," http://www.un.org/WCAR/durban.pdf (accessed September 12, 2012).

57. Banton, *International Politics of Race*, 165.

58. The claim that Arab Americans are the "new blacks" in the United States is described in Bayoumi, *How Does It Feel to Be a Problem?*, and Jamal and Naber, *Race and Arab Americans before and after 9/11*.

59. See, for example, Squires and Hartman, *There Is No Such Thing as a Natural Disaster*; James and the South End Press Collective, *What Lies Beneath*; and Dyson, *Come Hell or High Water*.

60. Lubin, "We Are All Israeli," 687.

61. Quoted in ibid.

62. Quoted in ibid.

63. Analyzing hip-hop imaginaries linking Palestinians and African Americans requires confronting entrenched scholarly frameworks for understanding the terms of cultural politics and geopolitical awareness. First, from the perspective of understanding the Palestinian struggle for existence, one might question the utility of popular culture and cultural studies to the existential crisis faced by many Palestinians. As Rebecca Stein and Ted Swedenburg point out in their essay, "Popular Culture, Relational History, and the Question of Power in Palestine and Israel," in the area of scholarship on Israel/Palestine, Birmingham cultural studies has had to confront structural Marxist approaches that view culture as superstructural, as well as nationalist frameworks that view popular culture merely as globalized consumer culture. Perhaps most challenging, Palestinians' persistent existential struggle for survival makes a study of Palestinian popular culture seem apolitical, at best. As Stein and Swedenburg point out, "The violence and catastrophe that so frequently characterize the landscape of Palestine and Israel give added weight to analytical tendencies to read culture as outside and/or strictly determined by the realm of the political—and thus of subsidiary importance to the radical scholarly agenda" (Stein and Swedenburg, *Palestine, Israel, and the Politics of Popular Culture*, 7).

64. Williams, *Long Revolution*. Also see Higgins, *Raymond Williams*.

65. There are many excellent histories of hip hop. Among them are Rose, *Black Noise*; Chang, *Can't Stop, Won't Stop*; Kelley, *Race Rebels*; and Forman and Neal, *Hip-Hop Studies Reader*.

66. See, for example, Rose, "Style Nobody Can Deal With."

67. It is difficult to ascertain accurate data on the Palestinian diasporic population due to the often hidden nature of Palestinian identity in "host" countries. According to the Palestinian Central Bureau of Statistics, there are approximately 3.2 million Palestinians in the West Bank and Gaza, approximately 900,000 in Israel, 2.2 million in Jordan, 400,000 in Lebanon, 400,000 in Syria, and 460,000 in the United States. See "Palestine in Figures," The Palestinian National Authority, 2009, http://www.pcbs.gov.ps/Portals/_PCBS/Downloads/book1661.pdf (accessed September 12, 2012).

68. There is a growing scholarship on Palestinian hip hop. See, for example, Alim, *Roc the Mic Right*; Sabry, *Arab Cultural Studies*; and Maira, "'We Ain't Missing.'"

69. Quoted in "Welcome to Al-Lydd," www.Palestineremembered.com, http://www.palestineremembered.com/al-Ramla/al-Lydd/ (accessed September 13, 2012).

70. See, for example, "Israeli apartheid in Lod (original Palestinian name Lydd)" Aljazeera, December 12, 2010, hosted on the website, PULSE Media, http://pulsemedia.org/2010/12/12/israeli-apartheid-in-lod-palestinian-name-lydda/.

71. Chuck D's "CNN" quote can be found in Chuck D. and Yusuf Jah, *Fight the Power*, 256.

72. Harry Allen, "When DAM Breaks, the Sound of Palestinian Freedom Gets Unleashed," Media Assassin website, April 30, 2010, http://harryallen.info/?p=7453 (accessed September 12, 2012).

73. See DAM's website www.dampalestine.com. Jackie Salloum's website can be found at jsalloum.com.

74. www.dampalestine.com. A similar sonic geography unites rappers throughout the West Bank and Gaza and in refugee camps in Lebanon and Syria, as well as Palestinian

refugees living throughout Europe and the United States. Among the most interesting collaboration is that of Gaza-based hip-hop group Palestinian Rapperz, who produce music transnationally with contributors in Khan Younis and Paris.

75. Hammad appeared in Annemarie Jacir's 2008 drama *Salt of This Sea*.

76. Hammad, *Born Palestinian, Born Black*, xi.

77. Jordan, *Moving toward Home*.

78. Hammad, *Born Palestinian, Born Black*, x.

79. "In Memory of June Jordan," June Jordan interview with David Barsamian, produced by David Barsamian, September 2000, Boulder, Colo., http://www.radio4all.net/index.php/program/4859 (accessed September 12, 2012).

80. James and the South End Press Collective, *What Lies Beneath*; Feldman, "Contrapuntalism and Rupture."

81. Hammad, "On Refuge and Language."

82. Ibid.; Adorno, *Minima Moralia*.

83. Hammad, "On Refuge and Language."

84. Hammad, *Breaking Poems*.

85. Moten, *In the Break*, 85.

CONCLUSION

1. http://www.huffingtonpost.com/2013/01/21/lupe-fiasco-inauguration-concern_n_2518319.html.

2. See, for example, Mullen, "Global Intifada."

3. Walker, "Alice Walker."

4. Darwish, "Psalm 3."

Bibliography

Adeleke, Tunde. *Without Regard to Race: The Other Martin Robison Delany*. Jackson: University Press of Mississippi, 2004.

Adelman, Howard, and Elazar Barkan. *No Return, No Refuge: Rites and Rights in the Minority Repatriation*. New York: Columbia University Press, 2011.

Adorno, Theodor. *Minima Moralia: Reflections from Damaged Life*. London: Verso, 2006.

Agamben, Giorgio. *State of Exception*. Chicago: University of Chicago Press, 2005.

Akinsanya, Adeoye. "The Afro-Arab Alliance: Dream or Reality." *African Affairs* 75, no. 301 (October 1976): 511–29.

Alexander, Michelle. *The New Jim Crow*. New York: New Press, 2012.

Ali, Dusé Mohamed. *Ere Roosevelt Came: A Record of the Adventures of the Man in the Cloak*. Serialized in *The Comet*, Lagos, Nigeria, March 3–October 13, 1934.

———. "Forward." *African Times and Orient Review* 1, no. 1 (July 1912): 1.

———. *In the Land of the Pharaohs: A Short History of Egypt from the Fall of Ismail to the Assassination of Boutros Pasha*. London: Stanley Paul and Co., 1911.

———. *Leaves from an Active Life*. Serialized in *The Comet*, Lagos, Nigeria, June 12, 1937–March 5, 1938.

———. "Yesterday, To-Day, and To-Morrow." *African Times and Orient Review* 1, no. 5 (November 1912): 1.

Alim, H. Sami. *Roc the Mic Right: The Language of Hip Hop Culture*. London: Taylor and Francis, 2006.

Allouche, Jeremy. "The Oriental Communities in Israel, 1948–2003: The Social and Cultural Creation of an Ethnic Political Group." Etudes et travaux, Studies and Working Papers, Graduate Institute of International Studies, University of Geneva. http://www.scribd.com/doc/14710872/Jeremy-Allouche-The-Oriental-Communities-in-Israel-19482003. Accessed September 10, 2012.

al Madfai, Madiha Rashid. *Jordan, the United States, and the Middle East Peace Process, 1974–1991*. Cambridge: Cambridge Middle East Library, Cambridge University Press, 1993.

Aloni, Udi, Slavoj Žižek, and Alain Badiou. *What Does a Jew Want?: On Binationalism and Other Specters*. New York: Columbia University Press, 2011.

Alsultany, Evelyn. *Arabs and Muslims in the Media: Race and Representation after 9/11*. New York: New York University Press, 2012.

Ambrosius, Lloyd. *Wilsonianism: Woodrow Wilson and His Legacy in American Foreign Relations*. New York: Palgrave Macmillan, 2002.

Amnesty International. "Israel/Lebanon: Unlawful Killings during Operation 'Grapes of Wrath,'" July 23, 1996. http://www.amnesty.org/en/library/info/MDE15/042/1996. Accessed July 1, 2013.

Anderson, Betty. *The American University of Beirut: Arab Nationalism and Liberal Education.* Austin: University of Texas Press, 2011.

Anderson, Eric. "Black Émigrés: The Emergence of Nineteenth-Century United States Black Nationalism in Response to Haitian Emigration and Colonization, 1816–1840." *49th Parallel: An Interdisciplinary Journal of North American Studies* 1 (Winter 1999). http://artsweb.bham.ac.uk/49thparallel/backissues/issue1/emigres.htm.

Anderson, Jervis. *A. Philip Randolph: A Biographical Portrait.* Berkeley: University of California Press, 1985.

Anderson, Kevin. *Lenin, Hegel, and Western Marxism: A Critical Study.* Urbana: University of Illinois Press, 1995.

Anghie, Antony. "Colonialism and the Birth of International Institutions: Sovereignty, Economy, and the Mandate System of the League of Nations." *New York University Journal of International Law and Politics* 34, no. 3 (2002): 513.

Anglo-American Committee of Inquiry. "Report to the United States Government and His Majesty's Government in the United Kingdom." Lausanne, Switzerland, April 20, 1946. http://avalon.law.yale.edu/subject_menus/angtoc.asp. Accessed September 2, 2012.

Arendt, Hannah. "Can the Jewish–Arab Question Be Solved?" [1943]. In Arendt, *Jewish Writings*, 196–97.

———. "The Crisis of Zionism" [1943]. In Arendt, *Jewish Writings*, 334–36.

———. "Herzl and Lazare" [1942]. In Arendt, *Jewish Writings*, 338–42.

———. *The Jewish Writings.* New York: Schocken, 2008.

———. *The Origins of Totalitarianism.* New York: Harcourt, Brace, 1951.

———. "Zionism Reconsidered" [1944]. In Arendt, *Jewish Writings*, 343–45.

Ariel, Yaakov, and Ruth Kark. "Messianism, Holiness, Charisma, and Community: The American-Swedish Colony in Jerusalem." *Church History* 64, no. 4 (December 1996): 641–57.

Aronson, Shlomo. *David Ben-Gurion and the Jewish Renaissance.* Cambridge: Cambridge University Press, 2010.

Ashrawi, Hanan. "Racism, Racial Discrimination, Xenophobia, and Related Intolerances." *Islamic Studies* 41, no. 1 (2002): 97–104.

Bagley, Carolyn. *My Trip through Egypt and the Holy Land.* New York: Grafton Press, 1928.

Bailey, Sydney. *Four Arab-Israeli Wars and the Peace Process.* London: Macmillan, 1990.

Bain, David Haward. *Bitter Waters: America's Forgotten Naval Mission to the Dead Sea.* New York: Overlook Press, 2011.

Baker, Houston A. *Modernism and the Harlem Renaissance.* Chicago: University of Chicago Press, 1989.

Baker, Lee. *Anthropology and the Racial Politics of Culture.* Durham, N.C.: Duke University Press, 2010.

Banton, Michael. *The International Politics of Race.* Cambridge: Polity Press, 2002.

Barkan, Elazar. *The Retreat of Scientific Racism: Changing Concepts of Race in Britain and the United States between the World Wars.* Cambridge: Cambridge University Press, 1993.

Barkey, Karen. *Empire of Difference: The Ottomans in Comparative Perspective.* New York: Cambridge University Press, 2008.

Barnes, Kenneth C. *Journey of Hope: The Back-to-Africa Movement in Arkansas in the Late 1800s*. Chapel Hill: University of North Carolina Press, 2004.

Barr, James. *A Line in the Sand: The Anglo-French Struggle for the Middle East, 1914–1948*. New York: Norton, 2012.

Bayoumi, Moustafa. *How Does It Feel to Be a Problem?: Being Young and Arab in America*. New York: Penguin, 2008.

Begley, Louis. *Why the Dreyfus Affair Matters*. New Haven: Yale University Press, 2010.

Behbehani, Hashim. *The Soviet Union and Arab Nationalism, 1917–1966*. London: Routledge, 1986.

Beinin, Joel. "The Oslo Process and the Limits of a Pax Americana." In Beinin and Stein, *Struggle for Sovereignty*, 21–37.

———. "Palestine and Israel: Perils of a Neoliberal, Repressive 'Pax Americana.'" *Social Justice* 25, no. 4 (1998): 20–39.

———. *Was the Red Flag Flying There?: Marxist Politics and the Arab-Israeli Conflict in Egypt and Israel, 1948–1965*. Berkeley: University of California Press, 1990.

———. *Workers and Peasants in the Modern Middle East*. Cambridge: Cambridge University Press, 2001.

Beinin, Joel, and Rebecca L. Stein. *The Struggle for Sovereignty: Palestine and Israel, 1993–2005*. Palo Alto, Calif.: Stanford University Press, 2006.

Beitz, Charles R. *The Idea of Human Rights*. Oxford: Oxford University Press, 2009.

Bell, J. Bowyer. *Assassin: Theory and Practice of Political Violence*. New Brunswick, N.J.: Transaction, 1979.

Bell, Jonathan, and Timothy Stanley. *Making Sense of American Liberalism*. Champaign: University of Illinois Press, 2012.

Ben-Dror, Elad. "Ralph Bunche and the Establishment of Israel." *Israel Affairs* 14, no. 3 (July 2008): 519–37.

Benhabib, Seyla. *The Reluctant Modernism of Hannah Arendt*. Lanham, Md.: Rowman and Littlefield, 2003.

Bierman, David. "The Role of the United States as an Initiator and Intermediary in the Arab-Israeli-Palestinian Peace Process: Comparing the Approaches to the Bush and Clinton Administrations." In *Remaking the Middle East*, edited by Paul J. White and William S. Logan, 259–74. Oxford: Berg, 1997.

Biondi, Martha. "The Rise of the Reparations Movement." In *Redress for Historical Injustices in the United States: On Reparations for Slavery, Jim Crow, and Their Legacies*, edited by Michael T. Martin and Marilyn Yaquinto, 255–71. Durham, N.C.: Duke University Press, 2007.

———. "The Rise of the Reparations Movement." *Radical History Review* 87 (Fall 2003): 5–18.

———. *To Stand and Fight: The Struggle for Civil Rights in Postwar New York City*. Cambridge, Mass.: Harvard University Press, 2006.

Blackstock, Nelson. *Cointelpro: The FBI's Secret War on Political Freedom*. Atlanta: Pathfinder, 1988.

Bloom, Joshua, and Waldo E. Martin Jr. *Black against Empire: The History and Politics of the Black Panther Party*. Berkeley: University of California Press, 2013.

Blum, Edward, and Jason Young. *The Souls of W. E. B. Du Bois: New Essays and Reflections*. Macon, Ga.: Mercer University Press, 2009.

Blunt, Wilfrid Scawin. *Atrocities of Justice under British Rule in Egypt*. London: T. F. Unwin, 1907.

Blyden, Edward Wilmot. *From West Africa to Palestine*. London: T. J. Sawyer, 1873.

———. *The Jewish Question*. Liverpool: Lionel Hart & Co., 1898.

———. "Mohammedism and the Negro Race." *Methodist Quarterly Review*, January 1877.

Blyden, Nemata. "Edward Jones: An African American in Sierra Leone." In *Moving On: Black Loyalists in the Afro-Atlantic World*, edited by John W. Pulis. New York: Garland, 1999.

Boas, Franz. "The Instability of Human Types." In Spiller, *Papers on Interracial Problems*, 99–103.

Bowen, Jeremy. *Six Days: How the 1967 War Shaped the Middle East*. London: Simon and Schuster, 2003.

Brewer, William M. "Henry Highland Garnet." *Journal of Negro History* 13, no. 1 (January 1928): 36–52.

Brinner, William M. *Like All Nations?: The Life and Legacy of Judah L. Magnes*. New York: SUNY Press, 1987.

Brooks, William Sampson. *Footprints of a Black Man: The Holy Land*. St. Louis: Eden Publishing House, 1916.

Brotz, Howard, and B. William Austin, eds. *African American Social and Political Thought*. New Brunswick, N.J.: Transaction, 1991.

Brouwer, Steve, Paul Gifford, and Susan D. Rose. *Exporting the American Gospel: Global Christian Fundamentalism*. New York: Routledge, 1996.

Buber, Martin. "The Binational Approach to Zionism." In Buber, Magnes, and Simon, *Towards Union in Palestine*, 9–13.

———. "Hebrew Humanism." In Buber, *Israel and the World: Essays in a Time of Crisis*, 240–53. Syracuse, N.Y.: Syracuse University Press, 1997.

Buber, Martin, Judah Magnes, and Ernest Akiva Simon. eds. *Towards Union in Palestine: Essays on Zionism and Jewish-Arab Cooperation*. Westport, Conn: Greenwood, 1947.

Budeiri, Musa. *The Palestine Communist Party, 1919–1948: Arab and Jew in the Struggle for Internationalism*. Chicago: Haymarket Books, 2010.

Bunche, Ralph. "Critical Analysis of Tactics and Programs of Minority Groups." In Henry, *Ralph J. Bunche: Selected Speeches and Writings*, 49–62.

———. "Marxism and the Negro Question." In Henry, *Ralph J. Bunche: Selected Speeches and Writings*, 35–45.

———. "Review and Appraisal of Israeli-Arab Relations" (1951). In Henry, *Ralph J. Bunche: Selected Speeches and Writings*, 175–88.

———. *A World View of Race*. Port Washington, N.Y.: Kennikat Press, 1968.

Burke, Roland. *Decolonization and the Evolution of International Human Rights*. Philadelphia: University of Pennsylvania Press, 2010.

Burns, Michael. *France and the Dreyfus Affair: A Brief Documentary History*. New York: Bedford/St. Martin's, 1998.

Bush, Roderick. *We Are Not What We Seem: Black Nationalism and Class Struggle in the American Century*. New York: NYU Press, 2000.

Butler, Judith. "'I merely belong to them.'" *London Review of Books* 29, no. 9 (May 10, 2007): 26–28.

———. *Parting Ways: Jewishness and the Critique of Zionism*. New York: Columbia University Press, 2012.

Campos, Michelle U. *Ottoman Brothers: Muslims, Christians, and Jews in Early Twentieth-Century Palestine*. Palo Alto, Calif.: Stanford University Press, 2010.

Carapico, Sheila. "Foreign Aid for Promoting Democracy in the Arab World." *Middle East Journal* 56, no. 3 (Summer 2002): 379–95.

Carson, Clayborne. *In Struggle: SNCC and the Black Awakening of the 1960s*. Cambridge, Mass.: Harvard University Press, 1981.

Chamberlin, Paul. *The Global Offensive: The United States, the Palestine Liberation Organization, and the Making of the Post–Cold War Order*. Cambridge: Oxford University Press, 2012.

Chang, Jeff. *Can't Stop, Won't Stop: A History of the Hip-Hop Generation*. New York: Picador, 2005.

Chappell, Marisa. *The War on Welfare: Family, Poverty, and Politics in Modern America*. Philadelphia: University of Pennsylvania Press, 2010.

Chaterjee, Partha. *Nationalist Thought and the Colonial World: A Derivative Discourse*. Minneapolis: University of Minnesota Press. 1993.

———. *The Nation and Its Fragments: Colonial and Postcolonial Histories*. Princeton, N.J.: Princeton University Press. 1993.

Chetrit, Sami Shalom. *Intra-Jewish Ethnic Conflict in Israel: White Jews, Black Jews*. New York: Taylor and Francis, 2009.

Chireau, Yvonne, and Nathaniel Deutsch. *Black Zion: African American Religious Encounters with Judaism*. New York: Oxford University Press, 1999.

Choueiri, Youssef M. *Arab Nationalism: A History*. Hoboken, N.J.: John Wiley and Sons, 2001.

Chuck D. and Yusuf Jah. *Fight the Power*. Edinburgh: Canongate Books, 2010.

Churchill, Ward, and Jim Vader Wall. *Agents of Repression: The FBI's Secret War against the Black Panther Party and the American Indian Movement*. Boston: South End Press, 2001.

Cleaver, Eldridge. "Jails Are the First Black Concentration Camps." *Black Panther* 2, no. 3 (May 1968).

Clemens, Walter C. *Dynamics of International Relations: Conflict and Mutual Gain in an Era of Global Interdependence*. Lanham, Md.: Rowman and Littlefield, 2004.

Clifford, James. "Diasporas." *Cultural Anthropology* 9, no. 3, Further Inflections: Toward Ethnographies of the Future (August 1994): 302–38.

Cobban, Helena. *The Palestine Liberation Organization: People, Power, and Politics*. Cambridge: Cambridge University Press, 1985.

Connors, Edward, Barbara Webster, Neal Miller, Claire Johnson, Elizabeth Fraser, and Bill Falcon, eds. *Urban Street Gang Enforcement*. Collingdale, Pa.: DIANE Publishing, 1998.

Cooper, Frederick. *Africa since 1940: The Past and the Present*. Cambridge: Cambridge University Press, 2002.

Cooper, Frederick, and Ann Laura Stoler, eds. *Tensions of Empire: Colonial Cultures in a Bourgeois World*. Berkeley: University of California Press, 1997.

Cromer, Evelyn Baring, Earl of. *Modern Egypt, by the Earl of Cromer*. New York: Macmillan, 1908.

Cronon, David. *Black Moses: The Story of Marcus Garvey and the Universal Negro Improvement Association.* Madison: University of Wisconsin Press, 1960.

Crowder, Ralph L. *John Edward Bruce: Politician, Journalist, and Self-Trained Historian of the African Diaspora.* New York: New York University Press, 2004.

Curtis, Michael. *The Middle East Reader.* Piscataway, N.J.: Transaction, 1986.

Darwish, Mahmoud. "Psalm 3." In Darwish, *Psalms: Poems.* Translated by Ben Bennani. Pueblo, Colo.: Passeggiata Press, 1995.

Davis, Angela. *Are Prisons Obsolete?* New York: Seven Stories Press, 2003.

Davis, Mike. "The Pentagon as Global Slumlord." *TomDispatch.com*, April 19, 2004. http://www.commondreams.org/views04/0419-14.htm. Accessed January 31, 2013.

de Azcarate, Pablo. *League of Nations and National Minorities.* Washington, D.C.: Carnegie Endowment for International Peace, 1945.

Delany, Martin Robison. *The Condition, Elevation, Emigration, and Destiny of the Colored People of the United States.* Philadelphia, 1852. Reprint, New York: Arno Press, 1968.

DellaPergola, Sergio. "Demography in Israel/Palestine: Trends, Prospects, Policy Implications." Paper presented at IUSSP XXIV General Population Conference, Salvador de Bahia, August 2001. Available online at http://212.95.240.146/Brazil2001/s60/S64_02_dellapergola.pdf. Accessed September 1, 2012.

Denoeux, Guilain. "Promoting Democracy and Governance in Arab Countries: Strategic Choices for Donors." In *NGOs and Governance in the Arab World*, edited by Sarah Ben Nefissa, Nabil Abd al-Fattah, Sari Hanafi, and Carlos Milani, 69–100. Cairo: American University in Cairo Press, 2005.

Des Verney Sinnette, Elinor. *Arthur Alfonso Schomburg, Black Bibliophile and Collector: A Biography.* Detroit: Wayne State University Press, 1989.

Dixon, Chris. *African America and Haiti: Emigration and Black Nationalism in the Nineteenth Century.* Westport, Conn.: Greenwood, 2000.

Doran, Michael. *Pan-Arabism before Nasser: Egyptian Power Politics and the Palestine Question*, Oxford: Oxford University Press, 2002.

Dorman, Jacob. *Chosen People: The Rise of American Black Israelite Religions.* New York: Oxford University Press, 2012.

Dorr, David F. *A Colored Man Round the World.* 1858. Edited by Malini Johar Schueller. Ann Arbor: University of Michigan Press, 1999.

Drezon-Tepler, Marcia. *Interest Groups and Political Change in Israel.* New York: SUNY Press, 1990.

Duberman, Martin. *Paul Robeson: A Biography.* New York: New Press, 2005.

Du Bois, W. E. B. "As the Crow Flies." In *The Oxford W. E B. Du Bois Reader*, edited by Eric J. Sundquist, 639–40. New York: Oxford University Press, 1996.

———. *Black Reconstruction in America, 1860–1880.* New York: Free Press, 1999.

———. "The Case for the Jews." *Chicago Star*, May 8, 1948.

———. *Dark Princess: A Romance.* Jackson: University Press of Mississippi, 1928.

———. *Dusk of Dawn: An Essay Toward an Autobiography of a Race Concept.* Piscataway, N.J.: Transaction, 1984.

———. "A Hymn to the People." *Independent* 71 (1911): 400.

———. "The Negro Race in the United States of America." In Spiller, *Papers on Interracial Problems*, 348–64.

———. *Souls of Black Folk*. New York: Tribeca Books, 2011.

———. "The Talented Tenth." http://www.yale.edu/glc/archive/1148.htm. Accessed September 1, 2012.

Duffield, Ian. "Dusé Mohamed Ali and the Development of Pan-Africanism, 1866–1945." Ph.D. diss., Edinburgh University, October 1971.

Duggan, Lisa. *The Twilight of Equality?: Neoliberalism, Cultural Politics, and the Attack on Democracy*. Boston: Beacon, 2004.

Dyson, Michael Eric. *Come Hell or High Water: Hurricane Katrina and the Color of Disaster*. New York: Basic Civitas Books, 2007.

Edwards, Brent. *The Practice of Diaspora: Literature, Translation, and the Rise of Black Internationalism*. Cambridge, Mass.: Harvard University Press, 2003.

Edwards, Brian, and Dilip Parameshwar Gaonkar, eds. *Globalizing American Studies*. Chicago: University of Chicago Press, 2010.

Ellison, Ralph. *Shadow and Act*. New York: Vintage, 1995.

Erikson, Erik, and Huey P. Newton. *In Search of Common Ground*. New York: Norton, 1973.

Esherick, Joseph W., Hasan Kayali, and Eric Van Young, eds. *Empire to Nation: Historical Perspectives on the Making of the Modern World*. Lanham, Md.: Rowman and Littlefield, 2006.

Ewing, Katherine Pratt, ed. *Being and Belonging: Muslims in the United States Since 9/11*. New York: Russell Sage Foundation Press, 2011.

Eyal, Gil. *The Disenchantment of the Orient: Expertise in Arab Affairs and the Israeli State*. Palo Alto, Calif.: Stanford University Press, 2006.

Feldman, Keith. "Contrapuntalism and Rupture: Suheir Hammad's Breaking Poems and the Refugee as Relational Figure." In *Connections and Ruptures: America and the Middle East. Proceedings of the Third International Conference Sponsored by the Alwaleed Bin Talal Bin Abdulaziz Alsaud Center for American Studies and Research at American University of Beirut*, edited by Robert Myers, 159–74. Beirut: Center for American Studies and Research, 2011.

———. "Representing Permanent War: Black Panthers' Palestine and the End(s) of Civil Rights." *New Centennial Review* 8, no. 2 (2008): 193–231.

———. "Towards an Afro-Arab Diasporic Culture: The Translational Practice of David Graham Du Bois." *ALIF: Journal of Comparative Poetics* 31 (2011): 152–72.

Fieldhouse, D. K. *Western Imperialism in the Middle East, 1914–1958*. Oxford: Oxford University Press, 2006.

Fink, Carole. "The Paris Peace Conference and the Question of Minority Rights." *Peace and Change* 21, no. 3 (July 1996): 273–88.

Fisk, Robert. *Pity the Nation: Lebanon at War*. Oxford: Oxford University Press, 2001.

Fluck, Winfried, Donald E. Pease, and John Carlos Rowe, eds. *Re-Framing the Transnational Turn in American Studies*. Hanover, N.H.: Dartmouth College Press, 2011.

Foner, Philip S. "Black-Jewish Relations in the Opening Years of the Twentieth Century." *Phylon* 36, no. 4 (4th quarter 1975): 359–67.

Forman, Murray, and Mark Anthony Neal, eds. *The Hip-Hop Studies Reader*. New York: Routledge, 2004.

Fortier, P. A. "Gobineau and German Racism." *Comparative Literature* 19, no. 4 (1967): 341–50.

Frankel, Jonathan. "The Soviet Regime and Anti-Zionism: An Analysis." In *Jewish Culture and Identity in the Soviet Union*, edited by Yaacov Ro'i and Avi Beker, 310–54. New York: NYU Press, 1992.

Friedman, Maurice S. *Encounter on the Narrow Ridge: A Life of Martin Buber.* St. Paul: Paragon House, 1991.

Garrow, David J. *The Martin Luther King, Jr., FBI File.* Pt. 2, *The King-Levison File.* Frederick, Md.: University Publications of America, 1987.

Garvey, Marcus. "The British West Indies in the Mirror of Civilization: History Making by Colonial Negros." *African Times and Orient Review* 2, no. 15 (October 13, 1913): 160.

Geiss, Imanuel. *The Pan-African Movement: A History of Pan-Africanism in America.* New York: Holmes and Meier, 1974.

Gelber, Mark H. "The Concept of Diaspora and Exile in German-Jewish Literature and Art." In *Encyclopedia of the Jewish Diaspora: Origins, Experiences, and Culture*, vol. 1, edited by Mark Avrum Ehrlich, 42–48. Santa Barbara, Calif.: ABC-CLIO, 2009.

Gershenhorn, Jerry. *Melville J. Herskovits and the Racial Politics of Knowledge.* Lincoln: University of Nebraska Press, 2004.

Gerstle, Gary. *Working Class Americanism: The Politics of Labor in a Textile Industry, 1914–1960.* Princeton, N.J.: Princeton University Press, 2002.

GhaneaBassiri, Kambiz. *A History of Islam in America.* New York: Cambridge University Press, 2010.

Ghanim, Honaida. "Poetics of Disaster: Nationalism, Gender, and Social Change among Palestinian Poets in Israel after Nakba." *International Journal of Political and Cultural Science* 22 (2009): 33–39.

Gilbert, James. *Whose Fair?: Experience, Memory, and the History of the Great St. Louis Exposition.* Chicago: University of Chicago Press, 2009.

Gilmore, Ruth Wilson. *Golden Gulag: Prisons, Surplus, Crisis, and Opposition in Globalizing.* Berkeley: University of California Press, 2007.

Gilroy, Paul. *The Black Atlantic: Modernity and Double Consciousness.* Cambridge, Mass.: Harvard University Press. 1998.

Glendon, Mary Ann. *A World Made New: Eleanor Roosevelt and the Universal Declaration of Human Rights.* New York: Random House, 2001.

Go, Julian, and Anne L. Foster, eds. *The American Colonial State in the Philippines: Global Perspective.* Durham, N.C.: Duke University Press, 2003.

Gobineau, J. A. *Moral and Intellectual Diversity of Races.* Philadelphia: Lippincott, 1856.

Goldberg, David Theo. *The Threat of Race: Reflections on Racial Neoliberalism.* Malden, Mass.: John Wiley and Sons, 2011.

Goldstein, Alyosha. *Poverty in Common: The Politics of Community Action during the American Century.* Durham, N.C.: Duke University Press, 2012.

Goode, Judith G., and Jeff Maskovsky. *The New Poverty Studies.* New York: NYU Press, 2001.

Gooding-Williams, Robert, ed. *Reading Rodney King/Reading Urban Uprising.* New York: Routledge, 1993.

Graham Du Bois, David. . . . *And Bid Him Sing.* Palo Alto, Calif.: Ramparts Press, 1975.

Graham, Stephen. *Cities under Siege: The New Military Urbanism.* London: Verso, 2011.

Grant, Colin. *Negro with a Hat: The Rise and Fall of Marcus Garvey.* New York: Oxford University Press, 2008.

Greenfield, Bruce. *Narrating Discovery: The Romantic Explorer in American History, 1790–1855.* New York: Cambridge University Press, 1992.

Griffith, Cyril. *The African Dream: Martin R. Delany and the Emergence of Pan-African Thought.* College Station: Pennsylvania State University Press, 1975.

Gustafson, Kaaryn S. *Cheating Welfare: Public Assistance and the Criminalization of Poverty.* New York: NYU Press, 2011.

Gutiérrez, Ramón. "Internal Colonialism: An American Theory of Race." *Du Bois Review,* 1, no. 2 (September 2004): 281–95.

Hadad, William, and William Ochsenwald. *Nationalism in a Non-National State: The Dissolution of the Ottoman Empire.* Columbus: Ohio State University Press, 1977.

Hadawi, Sami. *Bitter Harvest: A Modern History of Palestine.* New York: Interlink Books, 1991.

Hall, Catherine, and Sonya O. Rose. *At Home with the Empire: Metropolitan Culture and the Imperial World.* Cambridge: Cambridge University Press, 2006.

Hammad, Suheir. *Born Palestinian, Born Black.* New York: UpSet Press, 2010.

———. *Breaking Poems.* New York: Cypher Books, 2008.

———. "On Refuge and Language." In James and the South End Press Collective, *What Lies Beneath,* 167–69.

Hancock, Ange-Marie. *The Politics of Disgust: The Public Identity of the Welfare Queen.* New York: NYU Press, 2004.

Hansen, Phillip. *Hannah Arendt: Politics, History, and Citizenship.* Palo Alto, Calif.: Stanford University Press, 1994.

Harris, Gordon. *The Organization of African Unity.* New Brunswick, N.J.: Transaction, 1994.

Harris, Joseph, ed. *Global Dimensions of the African Diaspora.* Washington, D.C.: Howard University Press, 1982.

Harvey, David. *A Brief History of Neoliberalism.* Oxford: Oxford University Press, 2007.

Haseeb, Khair El Din. *The Arabs and Africa.* New York: Taylor and Francis, 1985.

Hashav, Benjamin. *The Polyphony of Jewish Culture.* Palo Alto, Calif.: Stanford University Press, 2007.

Haskins, Henry S. "Problems of American Dependencies." *African Times and Orient Review* 1, no. 5 (November 1912): 159–60.

Hays, Sharon. *Flat Broke with Children: Women in the Age of Welfare Reform.* New York: Oxford University Press, 2004.

Heller, Joseph. *The Stern Gang: Ideology, Politics, and Terror, 1940–1949.* London: Routledge, 1995.

Henig, Ruth B., ed. *The League of Nations.* Edinburgh: Oliver and Boyd, 1973.

Henriksen, Thomas H. "Security Lessons from the Israeli Trenches." *Policy Review,* February and March 2007, 17–30.

Henry, Charles. *Long Overdue: The Politics of Racial Reparations.* New York: NYU Press, 2007.

———. *Ralph Bunche: Model Negro or American Others?* New York: NYU Press, 2005.

———, ed. *Ralph J. Bunche: Selected Speeches and Writings*. Ann Arbor: University of Michigan Press, 1996.

Herzl, Theodor. *Der Judenstaat*. 1896. Hamburg: Tredition Classics, 2012.

Higgins, John. *Raymond Williams: Literature, Marxism, and Cultural Materialism*. New York: Routledge, 1999.

Hilderbrand, Robert C. *Dumbarton Oaks: The Origins of the United Nations and the Search for Postwar Security*. Chapel Hill: University of North Carolina Press, 1990.

Hill, Lance. *The Deacons for Defense: Armed Resistance and the Civil Rights Movement*. Chapel Hill: University of North Carolina Press, 2004.

Hill, Robert, ed. *Marcus Garvey and the UNIA Papers*. Vol. 1. Berkeley: University of California Press, 1983.

———. *The Marcus Garvey and Universal Negro Improvement Association Papers*. Vol. 2, *August 1919–August 1920*. Berkeley: University of California Press, 1983.

Hodes, Aubrey. *Martin Buber: An Intimate Portrait*. New York: Viking, 1971.

Horne, Gerald. *Black Liberation/Red Scare: Ben Davis and the Communist Party*. Newark: University of Delaware Press, 1994.

Hourani, Albert. *Arabic Thought in the Liberal Age, 1798–1939*. Cambridge: Cambridge University Press, 1983.

Howe, Stephen. *Afrocentrism: Mythical Pasts and Imagined Homes*. London: Verso, 1998.

Human Rights Watch. "Operation Grapes of Wrath," vol. 9, no. 8 (September 1997). http://www.hrw.org/reports/1997/isrleb/Isrleb.htm. Accessed July 1, 2013.

Huggins, Nathan Irvin. *Harlem Renaissance*. New York: Oxford University Press, 2007.

Hurewitz, J. C. *The Struggle for Palestine*. Berlin: Schocken, 1976.

Hyden, Goran. *African Politics in Comparative Perspective*. Cambridge: Cambridge University Press, 2005.

Ismael, Tareq Y. *The Communist Movement in the Arab World*. London: Routledge Curzon, 2005.

———. *International Relations of the Contemporary Middle East: A Study in World Politics*. Syracuse, N.Y.: Syracuse University Press, 1986.

Jacobs, Ronald N. *Race, Media, and the Crisis of Civil Society: From Watts to Rodney King*. New York: Cambridge University Press, 2000.

Jamal, Amaney, and Nadine Naber, eds. *Race and Arab Americans before and after 9/11: From Invisible Citizens to Visible Subjects*. Syracuse, N.Y.: Syracuse University Press, 2008.

James, Joy, and the South End Press Collective, eds. *What Lies Beneath: Katrina, Race, and the State of the Nation*. Boston: South End Press, 2007.

Jameson, Frederic. *Postmodernism, or, the Cultural Logic of Late Capitalism*. Durham, N.C.: Duke University Press, 1990.

Jankowski, James P., and I. Gershoni, eds. *Rethinking Nationalism in the Arab Middle East*. New York: Columbia University Press, 1997.

Jenkins, David. *Black Zion: The Return of Afro-Americans and West Indians to Africa*. London: Wildwood House, 1975.

Jones, Deiniol Lloyd. *Cosmopolitan Mediation?: Conflict Resolution and the Oslo Accords*. Manchester: Manchester University Press, 1999.

Jones, Reverend W. L. *The Travel in Egypt and Scenes of Jerusalem*. Atlanta: Converse and Wing, 1908.

Jordan, June. "Eyewitness in Lebanon." *The Progressive* 60, no. 8 (August 1996): 13.

———. *Moving toward Home: Political Essays*. London: Virago, 1989.

Joseph, Peniel E. *Black Power Movement: Rethinking the Civil Rights–Black Power Era*. New York: Routledge, 2006.

Kamrava, Mehran. *The Modern Middle East: A Political History since the First World War*. Berkeley: University of California Press, 2005.

Kaplan, Amy. *The Anarchy of Empire in the Making of U.S. Culture*. Cambridge, Mass.: Harvard University Press, 2002.

———. "Homeland Insecurities: Some Reflections on Language and Space." *Radical History Review* 85 (2003): 82–93.

Kastan, David Scott. "Lawrence, T. E." In *The Oxford Encyclopedia of British Literature*, 249–52. Oxford: Oxford University Press, 2005.

Kaufman, Ilana. *Arab National Communism in the Jewish State*. Gainesville: University Press of Florida, 1997.

Kaufman, Jonathan. *Broken Alliance: The Turbulent Times between Blacks and Jews in America*. New York: Touchstone, 1995.

Kedourie, Elie. *In the Anglo-Arab Labyrinth: The McMahon-Husayn Correspondence and Its Interpretations, 1914–1939*. London: Routledge, 2000.

Kelley, Robin D. G. *Freedom Dreams: The Black Radical Imagination*. Boston: Beacon, 2003.

———. *Hammer and Hoe: Alabama Communists during the Great Depression*. Chapel Hill: University of North Carolina Press, 1990.

———. "Polycultural Me." *ColorLines*, September–October 1999. Republished in *Utne Reader* online: http://www.utne.com/1999-09-01/the-people-in-me.aspx. Accessed January 25, 2013.

———. *Race Rebels: Culture, Politics, and the Black Working Class*. New York: Free Press, 1996.

Kelley, Robin D. G., and Elizabeth Esch. "Black Like Mao: Red China and Black Revolution." *Souls* 1, no. 4 (1999): 6–41.

Kesteloot, Lilyan. *Black Writers in French*. Translated by Ellen Conroy Kennedy. Washington, D.C.: Howard University Press, 1991.

Khalaf, Samir. *Protestant Missionaries in the Levant: Ungodly Puritans, 1820–1860*. New York: Routledge, 2012.

Khalidi, Rashid. *The Iron Cage: The Story of the Palestinian Struggle for Palestinian Statehood*. Boston: Beacon, 2006.

———. "The Palestinians and 1948: The Underlying Causes of Failure." In Rogan and Shlaim, *War for Palestine*, 12–36.

Khalidi, Walid. *From Haven to Conquest: Readings in Zionism and the Palestine Problem until 1948*. Beirut: Institute for Palestine Studies, 1987.

Khalili, Laleh. "The Location of Palestine in Global Counterinsurgencies." *International Journal of Middle East Studies* 42, no. 3 (2010): 413–33.

Khoury, Philip S. "Factionalism among Syrian Nationalists during the French Mandate." *International Journal of Middle East Studies* 13, no. 4 (1981): 441–69.

Kirby, John B. *Black Americans in the Roosevelt Era: Liberalism and Race*. Knoxville: University of Tennessee Press, 1982.

———. "Race, Class, and Politics: Ralph Bunche and Black Protest." In *Ralph Bunche: The Man and His Times*, edited by Benjamin Rivlin, 28–49. New York: Holmes and Meier, 1990.

Klein, Naomi. *The Shock Doctrine: The Rise of Disaster Capitalism*. New York: Picador, 2008.

Klinker, Phillip A., and Roger M. Smith. *The Unsteady March: The Rise and Decline of Racial Equality in America*. Chicago: University of Chicago Press, 1999.

Knock, Thomas J. *To End All Wars: Woodrow Wilson and the Quest for a New World Order*. Princeton, N.J.: Princeton University Press, 1995.

Kolsky, Thomas. *Jews against Zionism: The American Council for Judaism, 1942–1948*. Philadelphia: Temple University Press, 1992.

Kotzin, Daniel. *Judah L. Magnes: An American Jewish Nonconformist*. Syracuse, N.Y.: Syracuse University Press, 2010.

Kramer, Paul. "Empires, Exceptions, and Anglo-Saxons: Race and Rule between the British and United States Empires, 1880–1919." *Journal of American History* 88 (2002): 1315–53.

Kristeva, Julia. *Hannah Arendt*. New York: Columbia University Press, 2001.

Lake, Marilyn, and Henry Reynolds. *Drawing the Global Colour Line: White Men's Countries and the International Challenge of Racial Equality*. Cambridge: Cambridge University Press, 2008.

Lapsansky-Werner, Emma J., and Margaret Hope Bacon, eds. *Back to Africa: Benjamin Coates and the Colonization Movement in America, 1848–1880*. College Station: Pennsylvania State University Press, 2005.

Laquer, Walter. *A History of Zionism: From the French Revolution to the Establishment of the State of Israeli*. Berlin: Schocken, 2003.

Lefkowitz, Daniel. *Words and Stones: The Politics of Language and Identity in Israel*. New York: Oxford University Press, 2004.

Lenin, Vladimir. *Imperialism: The Highest Stage of Capitalism*. London: Penguin Classics, 2010.

Lerner, Michael, and Cornel West. *Jews and Blacks: A Dialogue on Race, Religion, and Culture*. New York: Plume, 1996.

Levine, Daniel. *Bayard Rustin and the Civil Rights Movement*. New Brunswick, N.J.: Rutgers University Press, 1999.

Levine, Robert S. *Martin Delany, Frederick Douglass, and the Politics of Representative Identity*. Chapel Hill: University of North Carolina Press, 1997.

Lewis, David Levering. *When Harlem Was in Vogue*. New York: Penguin, 1997.

———. "Parallels and Divergences: Assimilationist Strategies of Afro-American and Jewish Elites from 1910 to the Early 1930s." *Journal of American History* 71 (1984): 543–64.

Lewis, Earl. "To Turn as on a Pivot: Writing African Americans into a History of Overlapping Diasporas." *American Historical Review* 100, no. 3 (1995): 765–87.

Lipshutz, Ronnie D. "Beyond the Neoliberal Peace: From Conflict Resolution to Social Reconciliation." *Social Justice* 25, no. 4 (1998): 5–19.

Lipsitz, George. *American Studies in a Moment of Danger*. Minneapolis: University of Minnesota Press, 2001.

Little, Douglas. *American Orientalism: The United States and the Middle East since 1945*. Chapel Hill: University of North Carolina Press, 2004.

Lockman, Zachary. *Contending Visions of the Middle East: The History and Politics of Orientalism*. Cambridge: Cambridge University Press, 2004.

Lubin, Alex. "We Are All Israeli: The Politics of Colonial Comparisons." *South Atlantic Quarterly* 107, no. 4 (Fall 2008): 671–90.

Lulat, Y. G. M. *United States Relations with South Africa: A Critical Overview from the Colonial Period to the Present*. New York: Peter Lang, 2008.

Lynch, Hollis. *Edward Wilmot Blyden: Pan-Negro Patriot, 1832–1912*. Oxford: Oxford University Press, 1970.

Lynch, William Francis. *Narrative of the United States' Expedition to the River Jordan and the Dead Sea*. New and condensed ed. Philadelphia: Lea and Blanchard, 1850.

Mahmood, Saba. "Religious Freedom, the Minority Question, and Geopolitics in the Middle East." *Comparative Studies in Society and History* 54, no. 2 (2012): 418–46.

Maira, Sunaina. "'We Ain't Missing': Palestinian Hip Hop—A Transnational Youth Movement." *New Centennial Review* 8, no. 2 (2008): 161–92.

Makdisi, Ussama. *The Artillery of Heaven: American Missionaries and the Failed Conversion of the Middle East*. Ithaca, N.Y.: Cornell University Press, 2009.

———. *Faith Misplaced: The Broken Promise of U.S.-Arab Relations, 1820–2001*. New York: Public Affairs, 2010.

Mamigonian, Beatriz Galloti, and Karen Racine. *The Human Tradition in the Black Atlantic, 1500–2000*. Lanham, Md.: Rowman and Littlefield, 2010.

Manela, Terez. *The Wilsonian Moment: Self-Determination and the International Origins of Anticolonial Nationalism*. New York: Oxford University Press, 2007.

Marable, Manning. *How Capitalism Underdeveloped Black America: Problems in Race, Political Economy, and Society*. New York: South End Press, 1999.

Marable, Manning. *Malcolm X: A Life of Reinvention*. New York: Viking, 2011.

Marable, Manning, and Hisham Aidi, eds. *Black Routes to Islam*. New York: Palgrave, 2009.

Marable, Manning, and Leith Mullings. *Let Nobody Turn Us Around: Voices of Resistance, Reform, and Renewal: An African American Anthology*. Lanham, Md.: Rowman and Littlefield, 2009.

Marx, Karl, and Frederick Engels. *Collected Works*. Vol. 39. New York: International Publishers, 1983.

Masrui, Ali. "Black Orientalism?: Further Reflections on 'Wonders of the African World.'" *Black Scholar* 30, no. 1 (Spring 2000): 10–14.

Massad, Joseph. "Zionism's Internal Others: Israel and the Oriental Jews." *Journal of Palestine Studies* 25, no. 4 (Summer 1996): 53–68.

Mathieu, Sarah-Jane. *North of the Color Line: Migration and Black Resistance in Canada, 1870–1955*. Chapel Hill: University of North Carolina Press, 2010.

McAlister, Melani. *Epic Encounters: Culture, Media, and U.S. Interests in the Middle East since 1945*. Berkeley: University of California Press, 2005.

McGreal, Chris. "Brothers in Arms—Israel's Secret Pact with Pretoria." *Guardian* (London). February 7, 2006. http://www.guardian.co.uk/world/2006/feb/07/southafrica.israel. Accessed July 1, 2013.

McVey, Aaron David. *The 1989 NCCD Prison Population Forecast: The Impact of the War on Drugs*. San Francisco: National Council on Crime and Delinquency, 1989.

Melamed, Jodi. "The Spirit of Neoliberalism: From Racial Liberalism to Neoliberal Multiculturalism." *Social Text* 89 (Winter 2006): 1–24.

Mendes-Flohr, Paul R. *Divided Passions: Jewish Intellectuals and the Experience of Modernity*. Detroit: Wayne State University Press, 1991.

Mignolo, Walter D. *Local Histories/Global Designs: Coloniality, Subaltern Knowledges, and Border Thinking*. Princeton, N.J.: Princeton University Press, 2000.

Miller, Joyce L. "The Syrian Revolt of 1925." *International Journal of Middle East Studies* 8, no. 4 (1977): 545–63.

Mitchell, Timothy. *Colonising Egypt*. Berkeley: University of California Press, 1991.

Moore, Donald. *Martin Buber: Prophet of Religious Secularism*. New York: Fordham University Press, 1996.

Morris, Benny. *Righteous Victims: A History of the Zionist-Arab Conflict, 1881–2001*. New York: Vintage. 2001.

Moses, Wilson Jeremiah. *Creative Conflict in African American Thought*. Cambridge: Cambridge University Press, 2004.

Moten, Fred. *In the Break: The Aesthetics of the Black Radical Tradition*. Minneapolis: Minnesota University Press, 2003.

Moyn, Samuel. *The Last Utopia: Human Rights in History*. Cambridge, Mass.: Belknap Press of Harvard University Press, 2010.

Mullen, Bill. "Global Intifada: The Case for Boycott, Divestment, and Sanctions against Israel." *Counterpunch*, November 27, 2012. http://www.counterpunch.org/2012/11/27/global-intifada/. Accessed February 2, 2013.

———. *Popular Fronts: Chicago and African American Cultural Politics, 1935–1946*. Champaign: University of Illinois Press, 1999.

Mullen, Bill, and Fred Ho, eds. *Afro Asia: Revolutionary Political and Cultural Connections between African Americans and Asian Americans*. Durham, N.C.: Duke University Press, 2008.

Muravchik, Joshua. "Exporting Democracy to the Arab World." In *Democracy in the Middle East: Defining the Challenge*, edited by Yehudah Mirsky and Matt Ahrens, 1–10. Washington, D.C.: Washington Institute for Near East Policy, 1993.

Murphy, Emma C. "Buying Poverty: International Aid and the Peace Process." In Beinin and Stein, *Struggle for Sovereignty*, 54–61.

Nachmani, Amikam. *Great Power Discord in Palestine: The Anglo-American Committee of Inquiry into the Problems of European Jewry and Palestine, 1945–46*. London: Taylor and Francis, 1987.

Naison, Mark. *Communists in Harlem during the Depression*. Champaign: University of Illinois Press, 2004.

Newton, Huey P. "Let Us Hold High the Banner of Intercommunalism and the Invincible Thoughts of Huey P. Newton, Minister of Defense and Supreme Commander of the Black Panther Party." *Black Panther* 5, no. 30 (January 23, 1971).

———. "On the Middle East: September 5, 1970." In *To Die for the People: The Writings of Huey P. Newton*, edited by Toni Morrison, 194–99. San Francisco City Lights, 1990.

———. "Position Paper on the Middle East." *Black Panther* 11, no. 19 (May 25, 1974).

———. "We Are Nationalists and Internationalists." In *The Coming of the New International: A Revolutionary Anthology*, edited by John Gerassi, 593–95. New York: World Pub. Co., 1971.

Niva, Steve. "Walling Off Iraq: Israel's Imprint on U.S. Counterinsurgency Doctrine." *Middle East Policy* 15, no. 3 (Fall 2008): 67–79.

Nkrumah, Gamal. "Through African Eyes." *Al Ahram Weekly*, March 30–April 5, 2000. http://weekly.ahram.org.eg/2000/475/spec2.htm. Accessed August 12, 2012.

Nofal, Mamdough. "Yasir Arafat, the Political Player: A Mixed Legacy." *Journal of Palestine Studies* 35, no. 2 (Winter 2006): 23–37.

Obama, Barack. "A More Perfect Union." *Politico*, March 18, 2008. http://www.politico.com/news/stories/0308/9100.html. Accessed August 23, 2012.

———. "Remarks by the President on a New Beginning." Cairo University, Cairo, June 4, 2009. Transcript of speech can be found at http://www.whitehouse.gov/the-press-office/remarks-president-cairo-university-6-04-09. Accessed August 21, 2012.

Obenzinger, Hilton. *American Palestine: Melville, Twain, and the Holy Land Mania*. Princeton, N.J.: Princeton University Press, 1999.

———. "Naturalizing Cultural Pluralism, Americanizing Zionism: The Settler Colonial Basis to Early-Twentieth-Century Progressive Thought." *South Atlantic Quarterly*, 107, no. 4 (Fall 2008): 651–69.

Ogletree, Charles J., Jr. "Litigating the Legacy of Slavery." *New York Times*, March 31, 2002.

Orage, A. R. *Orage as Critic*. Edited by Wallace Martin. New York: Routledge, 1975.

Paled, Yoav. "From Zionism to Capitalism: The Political Economy of the Neoliberal Warfare State in Israel." In Beinin and Stein, *Struggle for Sovereignty*, 38–53.

Palmowski, Jan. "Arab Revolt." In *A Dictionary of Contemporary World History*. New York: Oxford University Press, 2003.

Pappé, Ilan. *The Ethnic Cleansing of Palestine*. Oxford: One World, 2007.

———. *A History of Modern Palestine: One Land, Two Peoples*. New York: Cambridge University Press, 2006.

———. *The Making of the Arab Israeli Conflict, 1947–1951*. London: I. B. Tauris, 1994.

———. *The Modern Middle East*. London: Routledge, 2005.

Paul, Catherine. *The Discourse of Palestinian-Israeli Relations*. Oxford: Taylor and Francis, 2009.

Pease, Donald. *The New American Exceptionalism*. Minneapolis: University of Minnesota Press, 2009.

Peck, Jamie. *Constructions of Neoliberalism*. New York: Oxford University Press, 2010.

Peer, Tajuddin. "Muslim Unity." *African Times and Orient Review* 2, no. 17 (November–December 1913): 193.

Peery, Nelson. *The Negro National Colonial Question*. 2nd ed. Chicago: Workers Press, 1972.

Peretz, Don. "U.S. Middle East Policy in the 1990s." In *The Middle East and the Peace Process: The Impact of the Oslo Accords*, edited by Robert O. Freedman, 347–64. Gainesville: University Press of Florida, 1998.

Pianko, Naomi. *Zionism and the Roads Not Taken: Rawidowicz, Kaplan, Kohn.* Bloomington: Indiana University Press, 2010.

Piterberg, Gabriel. "Zion's Rebel Daughter." *New Left Review* 48 (November–December 2007).

Plummer, Brenda Gayle. *Rising Wind: Black Americans and U.S. Foreign Affairs, 1935–1960.* Chapel Hill: University of North Carolina Press, 1996.

Podeh, Elie. *The Decline of Arab Unity: The Rise and Fall of the United Arab Republic.* Brighton, U.K.: Sussex Academic Press, 1999.

Polakow-Suransky, Sasha. *The Unspoken Alliance: Israel's Secret Relationship with Apartheid South Africa.* Johannesburg: Jacana Media, 2010.

Posnock, Ross. *Color and Culture: Black Writers and the Making of the Modern Intellectual.* Cambridge, Mass.: Harvard University Press, 2000.

Powell, Adam Clayton. *Palestine and Saints in Caesar's Household.* New York: R. R. Smith, 1939.

Powell, Eve Troutt. *Egypt, Great Britain, and the Mastery of the Sudan.* Berkeley: University of California Press, 2003.

Prashad, Vijay. *The Darker Nations: A People's History of the Third World.* New York: New Press, 2007.

———. *The Poorer Nations: A Possible History of the Gobal South.* New Delhi, India: Left Word Press, 2013.

Pratt, Mary Louis. *Imperial Eyes: Travel Writing and Transculturation.* New York: Routledge. 1992.

Pulido, Laura, and David Lloyd. "From La Frontera to Gaza: Chicano-Palestinian Connections." *American Quarterly* 62, no. 4 (December 2010): 791–94.

Quijano, Anibal. "Coloniality of Power, Eurocentrism, and Latin America." *Nepantla: Views from South* 1, no. 3 (2000).

Ra'ad, Bassem. *Hidden Histories: Palestine and the Eastern Mediterranean.* London: Pluto Press, 2010.

Rabbani, Mouin. "Palestinian Authority, Israeli Rule." In Beinin and Stein, *Struggle for Sovereignty*, 75–83.

Rabinow, Paul. *French Modern: Norms and Forms of the Social Environment.* Cambridge, Mass.: MIT Press, 1989.

Raja, Sundara. "The Real Situation in India." *African Times and Orient Review* 2, no. 14 (mid-August 1913): 62.

Read, Piers Paul. *The Dreyfus Affair: The Scandal That Tore France in Two.* London: Bloomsbury Press, 2012.

Redkey, Edwin. *Black Exodus: Black Nationalist and Back-to-Africa Movements, 1890–1910.* New Haven: Yale University Press, 1970.

Rejwan, Nissim. *Nasserist Ideology: Its Exponents and Critics.* Piscataway, N.J.: Transaction, 1974.

Rhodes, Evan. "Beyond the Exceptionalist Thesis, a Global American Studies 2.0." *American Quarterly* 64, no. 4 (December 2012): 899–912.

Robinson, Cedric J. *Black Marxism: The Making of the Black Radical Tradition.* Chapel Hill: University of North Carolina Press, 2000.

———. "Du Bois and Black Sovereignty: The Case of Liberia." *Race and Class* 32, no. 2 (1990): 39-50.

Robinson, Glenn E. *Building a Palestinian State: The Incomplete Revolution.* Bloomington: Indiana University Press, 1997.

Roediger, David. *Working toward Whiteness: How America's Immigrants Became White.* New York: Basic Books, 2006.

Rogan, Eugene, and Avi Shlaim, eds. *The War for Palestine: Rewriting the History of 1948.* Cambridge: Cambridge University Press, 2001.

Rogers, Stephanie Stidham. *Inventing the Holy Land: American Protestant Pilgrimage to Palestine, 1865-1941.* New York: Lexington Books, 2011.

Rose, Tricia. *Black Noise: Rap Music and Black Culture in Contemporary America.* Middletown, Conn.: Wesleyan University Press, 1994.

———. "A Style Nobody Can Deal With: Politics, Style, and the Post-Industrial City in Hip Hop." In *Popular Music: Music and Identity*, vol. 4, edited by Simon Frith, 341-59. New York: Routledge, 2004.

Rowe, John Carlos. *Afterlives of Modernism: Liberalism, Transnationalism, and Political Critique.* Hanover, N.H.: Dartmouth College Press, 2011.

Rubin, Rehav. "When Jerusalem Was Built in St. Louis: A Large Scale Model of Jerusalem in the Louisiana Purchase Exposition, 1907." *Palestine Exploration Quarterly* 132 (2000): 59-70.

Rudra, Nita. "Globalization and the Decline of the Welfare State in Less-Developed Countries." *International Organization* 56, no. 2 (Spring 2002): 411-45.

Rydell, Robert. *All the World's a Fair: Visions of Empire at American International Expositions, 1876-1919.* Chicago: University of Chicago Press, 1987.

Sabry, Tarik. *Arab Cultural Studies: Mapping the Field.* London: I. B. Tauris, 2012.

Safran, William. "Diasporas in Modern Societies: Myths of Homeland and Return." *Diaspora* 1, no. 1 (1991): 83-99.

Said, Edward. "America's Last Taboo." *New Left Review* 6 (November–December 2000): 45-53.

———. *Culture and Imperialism.* New York: Vintage, 1994.

———. *Orientalism.* New York: Vintage, 1979.

———. "Reflections on Exile." In Said, *Reflections on Exile and Other Essays*, 137-49.

———. *Reflections on Exile and Other Essays.* Cambridge, Mass.: Harvard University Press, 2000.

Saldivar, Ramon. *The Borderlands of Culture: Americo Peredes and the Transnational Imaginary.* Durham, N.C.: Duke University Press, 2006.

Sales, William, Jr. *From Civil Rights to Black Liberation: Malcolm X and the Organization of Afro-American Unity.* Boston: South End Press, 1999.

Salibi, Kamal. *A House of Many Mansions: The History of Lebanon Reconsidered.* London: I. B. Tauris, 2003.

Sayigh, Yezid. "Struggle Within, Struggle Without: The Transformation of PLO Politics since 1982." *International Affairs* 65, no. 2 (Spring 1989): 247-71.

Schaeder, Grete. *The Hebrew Humanism of Martin Buber.* Detroit: Wayne State University Press, 1973.

Schaeffer, Robert K. *Severed States: Dilemmas of Democracy in a Divided World.* Lanham, Md.: Rowman and Littlefield, 1999.

Schechter, Micha. *United Nations Global Conferences.* New York: Routledge, 2005.

Schmidt Camacho, Alicia. *Migrant Imaginaries: Latino Cultural Politics in the U.S.-Mexico Borderlands.* New York: New York University Press. 2008.

Schneer, Jonathan. *The Balfour Declaration: The Origins of the Arab-Israeli Conflict.* New York: Random House, 2010.

Schneier, Marc. *Martin Luther King Jr. and the Jewish Community.* Woodstock, Vt.: Jewish Lights Publishing, 2009.

Schueller, Malini Johar. *U.S. Orientalisms: Race, Nation, and Gender in Literature, 1790–1890.* Ann Arbor: University of Michigan Press, 2001.

Schulz, Helena Lindholm, with Juliane Hammer. *The Palestinian Diaspora: Formation of Identities and Politics of Homeland.* London: Routledge, 2003.

Schulze, Kirsten E. *Jews of Lebanon: Between Coexistence and Conflict.* Brighton, U.K.: Sussex Academic Press, 2009.

Scram, Sanford F. *Welfare Discipline: Discourse, Governance, and Globalization.* Philadelphia: Temple University Press, 2007.

Seaton, Daniel P. *The Land of Promise; or, the Bible Land and Its Revelation.* Nashville: Publishing House of the A.M.E. Church, 1895.

Shama, Avraham, and Mark Iris. *Immigration without Integration: Third World Jews in Israel.* Cambridge, Mass.: Schenkman Pub. Co., 1977.

Shamir, Milette. "'Our Jerusalem': Americans in the Holy Land and Protestant Narratives of National Entitlement." *American Quarterly* 55, no. 1 (March 2003): 29–60.

Shapiro, Michael. "Moral Geographies and the Ethnics of Post-Sovereignty." *Public Culture* 6 (1994): 479–502.

Sharp, Alan. "Britain and the Protection of Minorities at the Paris Peace Conference, 1919." In *Minorities and History*, edited by A. C. Hepburn, 170–88. Oxford: Berg, 1993.

Sharpley-Whiting, T. Denean. *Negritude Women.* Minneapolis: University of Minnesota Press, 2002.

Shaw, Stanford Jay. *The Jews of the Ottoman Empire and the Turkish Republic.* New York: Macmillan, 1991.

Sheehi, Stephen. *Islamophobia: The Ideological Campaign against Muslims.* Atlanta: Clarity Press, 2001.

Shlaim, Avi. *The Iron Wall: Israel and the Arab World.* New York: Norton, 2000.

Shohat, Ella. "Sephardim in Israel: Zionism from the Standpoint of Its Jewish Victims." *Social Text*, no. 19/20 (Autumn 1988): 1–35.

———. *Taboo Memories: Diasporic Voices.* Durham, N.C.: Duke University Press, 2006.

Shore, Mari. *Caviar and Ashes: A Warsaw Generation's Life and Death in Marxism, 1918–1968.* New Haven: Yale University Press, 2009.

Shyrock, Andrew, ed. *Islamophobia/Islamophilia: Beyond the Politics of Enemy and Friend.* Bloomington: Indiana University Press, 2010.

Simon, Reeva Spector, and Eleanor H. Tejirian. *The Creation of Iraq, 1914–1921.* New York: Columbia University Press, 2004.

Simon, Reeva Spector, Michael M. Laskier, and Sara Reguer. *The Jews of the Middle East and North Africa in Modern Times.* New York: Columbia University Press, 2003.

Singh, Nikihl. *Black Is a Country: Race and the Unfinished Struggle for Democracy.* Cambridge, Mass.: Harvard University Press, 2005.

———. "The Black Panthers and the 'Undeveloped Country' of the Left." In *The Black Panther Party Reconsidered,* edited by Charles E. Jones, 57-108. Baltimore: Black Classic Press, 1998.

Sitkoff, Harvard. *A New Deal for Blacks: The Emergence of Civil Rights as a National Issue.* New York: Oxford University Press, 2008.

Smethurst, James. *The New Red Negro: The Literary Left and African America Poetry, 1930-1946.* New York: Oxford University Press, 1999.

Smith, Anna Marie. *Welfare Reform and Sexual Regulation.* Cambridge: Cambridge University Press, 2007.

Smith, Charles D. *Palestine and the Arab-Israeli Conflict.* 4th ed. New York: St. Martin's Press, 2001.

Solomon, Mark. *The Cry Was Unity: Communists and African Americans, 1917-1936.* Jackson: University Press of Mississippi, 1998.

Spiller, Gustav. "First Universal Races Congress, London University, July 26-29, 1911. Questionnaire." *Mind* 20, no. 77 (January 1911): 159-60.

———, ed. *Papers on Interracial Problems Communicated to the First Universal Races Congress Held at the University of London, July 26-29, 1911.* Boston: Ginn and Co., 1912.

Spur, David. *The Rhetoric of Empire: Colonial Discourse in Journalism, Travel Writing, and Imperial Administration.* Durham, N.C.: Duke University Press, 1993.

Squires, Gregory, and Chester Hartman, eds. *There Is No Such Thing as a Natural Disaster: Race, Class, and Hurricane Katrina.* New York: Routledge, 2013.

Stanislawski, Michael. *Zionism and the Fin de Siècle: Cosmopolitanism and Nationalism from Nordau to Jabotinsky.* Berkeley: University of California Press, 2001.

Stecopolis, Harry. *Reconstructing the World: Southern Fictions and U.S. Imperialisms, 1898-1976.* Ithaca, N.Y.: Cornell University Press, 2008.

Stein, Rebecca L., and Ted Swedenburg, eds. *Palestine, Israel, and the Politics of Popular Culture.* Durham, N.C.: Duke University Press, 2005.

Stevens, Richard Drent, and Abdelwahab M. Elmessiri. *Israel and South Africa: The Progression of a Relationship.* Philadelphia: North American Publisher, 1977.

Stoval, Tyler. *Paris Noir: African Americans in the City of Light.* Boston: Houghton Mifflin, 1996.

———, ed. *Black France/France Noire: The History and Politics of Blackness.* Durham, N.C.: Duke University Press, 2012.

Stuckey, Sterling. *Slave Culture: Nationalist Theory and the Foundations of Black America.* New York: Oxford University Press, 1988.

Sundiata, Ibrihim. *Brothers and Strangers: Black Zion, Black Slavery, 1914-1940.* Durham, N.C.: Duke University Press, 2004.

Sundquist, Eric J. *Strangers in the Land: Blacks, Jews, Post-Holocaust America.* Cambridge, Mass.: Harvard University Press, 2005.

Tamari, Shai M. "Conflict over Palestine: Zionism and the Anglo-American Committee of Inquiry, 1945-1947." M.A. thesis, University of North Carolina, Chapel Hill, 2008.

Taylor, Gary. *Orage and the New Age*. Sheffield, U.K.: Sheffield Hallam University Press, 2004.

Tomeh, George Joseph. *Israel and South Africa: The Unholy Alliance*. New York: New World Press, 1973.

Traboulsi, Fawwaz. *A History of Modern Lebanon*. 2nd ed. London: Pluto Press, 2012.

Trafton, Scott. *Egyptland: Race and Nineteenth-Century American Egyptomania*. Durham, N.C.: Duke University Press, 2004.

Tripp, Charles. *A History of Iraq*. Cambridge: Cambridge University Press, 2007.

Turner, Richard Brent. *Islam in the African American Experience*. 2nd ed. Bloomington: Indiana University Press, 2003.

Twain, Mark. *The Innocents Abroad; or, the New Pilgrim's Progress*. 1869. West Jordan, Utah: Velvet Elements Books, 2008.

Tyson, Timothy B. *Radio Free Dixie: Robert F. Williams and the Roots of Black Power*. Chapel Hill: University of North Carolina Press, 2001.

United Nations Special Committee on Palestine. "Official Records of the Second Session of the General Assembly, Supplement No. 11, UNSCOP." Vol. 3, "Oral Evidence Presented at Public Meeting." Lake Success, N.Y., July 14, 1947. A/364/Add.2 PV.30. See http://unispal.org/unispal.nsf. Accessed June 14, 2012.

———. "Report of the General Assembly." Vol. 3, "Oral Evidence Presented at Public Meeting." Lake Success, N.Y., July 15, 1947. A/364/Add.2 PV.32. See http://unispal.org/unispal.nsf. Accessed June 14, 2012.

———. "Verbatim Record of the Twenty-Ninth Meeting (Public), Held at the Y.M.C.A. Building." Jerusalem Palestine, Saturday, 13 July 1937. A/AC.13/PV.29. See http://unispal.org/unispal.nsf. Accessed June 14, 2012.

Urquhart, Brian. *Ralph Bunche: An American Odyssey*. New York: Norton, 1998.

Usher, Graham. *Palestine in Crisis: The Struggle for Peace and Political Independence*. London: Pluto Press, 1995.

Vogel, Lester. *To See a Promised Land: Americans and the Holy Land in the Nineteenth Century*. College Station: Pennsylvania State University Press, 1993.

Von Eschen, Penny. *Race against Empire: Black Americans and Anticolonialism, 1937–1957*. Ithaca, N.Y.: Cornell University Press, 1997.

Vreeland, James Raymond. *The International Monetary Fund: Politics of Conditional Lending*. New York: Taylor and Francis, 2006.

Wacquant, Loic. *Prisons of Poverty*. Minneapolis: University of Minnesota Press, 2009.

———. *Punishing the Poor: The Neoliberal Government of Social Insecurity*. Durham, N.C.: Duke University Press. 2009.

Walker, Alice. "Alice Walker: Why I'm Joining the Freedom Flotilla to Gaza." *The Guardian*, June 25, 2011. http://www.guardian.co.uk/world/2011/jun/25/alice-walker-gaza-freedom-flotilla. Accessed February 3, 2013.

Walt, Stephen M. *The Origins of Alliances*. Ithaca, N.Y.: Cornell University Press, 1987.

Walter, Alexander. *My Life and Work*. New York: Fleming H. Revell Co., 1917.

Walters, F. P. *A History of the League of Nations*. Oxford: Oxford University Press, 1952.

Weisbord, Robert G., and Richard Kazarian Jr. *Israel in the Black American Perspective*. Santa Barbara, Calif.: Praeger, 1985.

Wilkins, Roy. "Israel's Time of Trial Also America's." *Philadelphia Afro-American*, June 24, 1967.

Williams, Raymond. *The Long Revolution*. Reprint, Swansea, U.K.: Parthian Books, 2012.

Williams, Robert F. *Negroes with Guns*. New York: Marzani and Munsell, 1962. Reprint, Detroit: Wayne State University Press, 1998.

Winant, Howard. *The New Politics of Race: Globalism, Difference, Justice*. Minneapolis: University of Minnesota Press, 2004.

Winthrop, John. "A Model of Christian Charity." Delivered on board the Arbella, 1630. Full text available at http://religiousfreedom.lib.virginia.edu/sacred/charity.html. Accessed September 1, 2012.

Wittner, Lawrence S. "The National Negro Congress: A Reassessment." *American Quarterly* 22 (Winter 1970): 883–901.

Wolfe, Patrick. *Settler Colonialism and the Transformation of Anthropology: The Politics and Poetics of an Ethnographic Event*. New York: Continuum, 1998.

Wolters, Raymond. *Negroes and the Great Depression: The Problem of Economic Recovery*. Westport, Conn.: Greenwood, 1970.

Wood, Gordon S. *Empire of Liberty: A History of the Early Republic, 1789–1815*. New York: Oxford University Press, 2009.

Woodward, C. Vann. *The Strange Career of Jim Crow*. New York: Oxford University Press, 2001.

Yacobi, Haim, ed. *Constructing a Sense of Place: Architecture and the Zionist Discourse*. Aldershot, U.K: Ashgate Publishing, 2004.

Yapp, M. E. *The Making of the Modern Near East, 1792–1923*. Harlow, U.K.: Longman, 1987.

Yothers, Brian. *The Romance of the Holy Land in American Travel Writing*. Aldershot, U.K.: Scholar Press, 2007.

Young, Cynthia. *Soul Power: Culture, Radicalism, and the Making of a U.S. Third World Left*. Durham, N.C.: Duke University Press, 2006.

Young, Lewis. "American Blacks and the Arab-Israeli Conflict." *Journal of Palestine Studies* 2, no. 1 (Autumn 1972): 70–85.

Zinn, Howard. *A People's History of the United States, 1492 to Present*. London: Harper Perennial Modern Classics, 2005.

———. *SNCC: The New Abolitionists*. Boston: South End Press, 2002.

Index

Arab Americans, as new blacks, 160, 200 (n. 58)
Arab High Commission, 101
Arabian Outlaw, 162
Arab-Israeli War (1947–48), 11, 81; and de-population/ethic cleansing, 192 (n. 89)
Arab Jews, 12, 14, 16, 113, 124, 130–32, 136, 139, 174, 190 (n. 34), 192 (n. 8)
Arab revolt of 1916–18, 68–69; of 1920, 69; of 1936–39, 76
Arab Spring, 175
Arafat, Yasser, 115, 122, 126–27, 130, 137, 139–40, 194 (n. 19); and the Oslo Peace Accords, 147–48
Aram, Morris, 118
Arendt, Hannah, 7, 78, 97, 181 (n. 33); and antinationalism, 97–100
Ashkenazi Jews, 131; attitudes of about Arab Jews, 132–33
Ashrawi, Hannan, 142, 151
Austerity protests, 175

Bagley, Carolyn, 32
Balfour, Arthur James, 69; Balfour declaration, 69
Bandung conference, 110, 111
Black Americans in Support of Israel Committee (BASIC), 5–6, 118
Beinin, Joel, 92, 108
Ben Gurion, David, 132
Bernadotte, Count Folke, 87, 102–3
Bey, Mohamed Farid, 57
Biden, Joe, 177 (n. 1)
BIG, The Notorious, 166
Binationalism, 10, 15,16, 77, 80, 100, 172; Palestine Communist Party and, 81, 87, 90–94; and colonialism, 81, 95, 106; Ralph Bunche and, 85, 104, 106, 108, 173; Jewish antinationalists and, 87, 94, 173; Anglo American Committee of Inquiry and, 87–88; U.S. State Department and, 89; and Ihud, 94–97; Judah Magnes and, 95–96, 102; Hannah Arendt and, 97–100; Count Folke Bernadotte and, 103; Soviet Union and, 108
Biton, Charlie, 136
Black Americans in Support of Israel Committee (BASIC), 5, 118
Black Belt thesis, of the Communist Party USA, 72, 86
Black/Jewish relations, 6, 130, 174, 179 (n. 19), 194 (n. 21)
Black Jews, 130
Black Loyalists, 36
Black Muslims, 73, 111
Black orientalism, 26–28
Black Panther Intercommunal News Agency, 112, 121–22; and Zionism, 123
Black Panther Party, 6, 8, 10, 16, 110, 131, 140, 143, 157, 173; David Graham Du Bois and, 112; and intercommunalism, 112–13, 119–21; and the PLO, 114, 126–27; and revolutionary nationalism, 119–20; and the question of Palestine, 121–22; and apartheid, 125–26; and the PFLP, 126; relationship of with Israeli Black Panthers, 135, 137–39
Black radical tradition, 8, 17, 26, 78, 113, 114, 123, 141, 170, 174
Black September, 115
Bliss, Howard, 55
Blunt, Wilfred Sacwan, 52
Blyden, Edward Wilmot, 18, 40, 44, 57, 185 (n. 72); and Liberia, 37; and Zionism, 39, 42–43; *From West Africa to Palestine*, 40–42; *The Jewish Question*, 42–43; "Mohammedism and the Negro Race," 43–44; and Islam, 44; Marcus Garvey and, 60
Boas, Franz, 45, 54–55
Boggs, Grace Lee, 119
Boggs, James, 119
Boycott, divestment, and sanctions movement, 175
Break dancing, 163
Briggs, Cyril, 72
British Empire, 49, 59, 71
British mandatory government, 32, 68–70; and Iraq, 69; and Arthur James Balfour, 69, 109; and Jewish immigrants to Palestine, 131
Brooks, William Sampson, 31
Brown, Sterling, 82
Bruce, John Edward, 59

CPSIA information can be obtained
at www.ICGtesting.com
Printed in the USA
LVHW08s0955160718
583898LV00002B/58/P